Buddhist Fundamentalism and Minority Identities in Sri Lanka

Tessa J. Bartholomeusz and Chandra R. de Silva, Editors

State University of New York Press

Published by
State University of New York Press, Albany

Printed in the United States of America

For information, address State University of New York
Press, State University Plaza, Albany, N.Y., 12246

Production by E. Moore
Marketing by Anne Valentine

Library of Congress Cataloging-in-Publication Data

Buddhist fundamentalism and minority identities in Sri Lanka / Tessa J.
Bartholomeusz and Chandra R. de Silva, editors.
p. cm.
Includes bibliographical references and index.
ISBN 0-7914-3833-3 (hc : alk. paper). — ISBN 0-7914-3834-1 (pb :
alk. paper)
1. Buddhist fundamentalism—Sri Lanka. 2. Ethnicity—Religious
aspects. 3. Buddhism—Relations. 4. Buddhism—Social aspects—Sri
Lanka. 5. Ethnicity—Sri Lanka. 6. Sri Lanka—Religion.
I. Bartholomeusz, Tessa J. II. De Silva, Chandra Richard, 1940–
BQ359.B83 1998
294.3′095493—dc21 97-35501
CIP

10 9 8 7 6 5 4 3 2 1

Buddhist Fundamentalism and Minority Identities in Sri Lanka

Contents

Preface

The idea for this book came to us the day we learned that President Premadasa of Sri Lanka had been assassinated, May 1, 1993. Sitting in Terre Haute, Indiana, pondering the future of Sri Lanka in the wake of another violent episode in Colombo, we wondered if and when there again would be peace in the tiny island nation that in the past few decades has been ravaged by ethnic violence. We wondered who killed Premadasa. Was it a Tamil separatist? Was it a disillusioned Sinhala? These questions about the ethnicity of the killer(s) spawned a lively debate over what it meant to be a Sri Lankan in the present context of violence.

We agreed that, in the present and despite one's ethnicity or religion, being Sri Lankan is inextricably bound to ideas about Sri Lanka's relationship to Buddhism, whether one repudiates those ideas or not. In other words, we isolated a hegemonic idea about the island and its destiny as guardian of Buddhism, something several scholars before us had done, albeit with different emphasis. That hegemonic force we refer to as Sinhala-Buddhist fundamentalism.

In the pages that follow, Sinhala-Buddhist fundamentalism will be nuanced and explored fully. Here, what must be kept in mind is that the arguments that we make in this volume about Buddhist fundamentalism are meant to be confined to the study of Sri Lanka. In other words, we are not making general claims about Buddhism; any inferences based on this study that can be drawn about Buddhism in other parts of the world are purely accidental.

Many people made this study possible. We would like to pay special thanks to the Department of Religion, Florida State University, for helping to offset the cost of the Index. Regarding the Index, Scott MacLagan's work is much appreciated, especially his careful attention to detail. We would like to thank Zina Lawrence and Elizabeth Moore of the State University of New York Press (SUNY) for their valuable suggestions. We would also like to thank SUNY's anonymous readers of previous drafts of this study for their extremely helpful recommendations. Finally, we are deeply grateful to Jeff Tatum and Daya de Silva for their abiding interest in this project. Any mistakes, however, we claim solely as our own.

TESSA BARTHOLOMEUSZ
CHANDRA R. DE SILVA

Chapter 1

Buddhist Fundamentalism and Identity in Sri Lanka[1]

Tessa J. Bartholomeusz and Chandra R. de Silva

Why We Speak of Sinhala-Buddhist Fundamentalism

In the pages that follow, several scholars investigate Sinhala-Buddhist fundamentalism in regard to Sri Lanka's ethnic and religious minorities—namely, Tamils, Muslims,[2] Burghers and other Christians, and how it shapes the identities of these non-Buddhist peoples. In other words, we examine Sinhala-Buddhist fundamentalism from the vantage of minorities who are affected by it in a variety of ways.

But before we turn to those minority views, we need to discuss why, among the various designations for the phenomenon under discussion here, we choose "Sinhala-Buddhist fundamentalism." We do so, partly following the practice of writers who have isolated phenomena elsewhere in the world similar to the phenomenon explored in this volume. Thus, to speak of certain trends within Sinhala Buddhism as "fundamentalist" helps to place those trends on a larger map of movements analyzed by scholars of religion and politics. In particular, this designation enables comparisons with the wide-ranging set of phenomena analyzed by Martin E. Marty, R. Scott Appleby, and others, under the umbrella of the Fundamentalism Project. In turn, such comparisons help to draw out certain features of Sinhala Buddhism that we consider important.

In their Fundamentalism Project, Marty, Appleby, and a host of scholars explore the phenomenon of religious fundamentalism from North America to Iran to Japan. As they point out, it is difficult to find an essence of the phenomenon, especially given its manifestations worldwide. After all, it seems unlikely that religious fundamentalism among Sikhs in India and among Roman Catholics in the United States would have much in common. Yet similarities exist between movements that do not share a common history, culture, language, or worldview. In fact, Marty and Appleby describe a variety of "family resemblances" of religious fundamentalism that appear in widely divergent cultures.[3] They include, in particular, a reliance on religion as a source for identity; boundary setting that determines who belongs and who does not; dramatic eschatologies; and the dramatization and mythologization of enemies.[4]

Sinhala-Buddhist fundamentalism shares many of these characteristics to one degree or another. Like most fundamentalist movements, Sinhala-Buddhist fundamentalism relies on religion—namely, Buddhism—as a foundation for identity. In their reading of Buddhism, Sinhala-Buddhist fundamentalists identify Buddhist Sinhalas as the people who have been charged by the Buddha himself to maintain and protect Buddhism. In addition, they identify the island of Sri Lanka as *dhammadipa*, the island (*dipa*) of the *dhamma,* the Buddhist teachings. The identity between the Sinhala people and the *dhamma*, based on a reading of the fifth century Sri Lankan "mythohistory,"[5] the *Mahavamsa*, has contributed to the notion that Sri Lanka, destined to be the island of the *dhamma*, should be dominated by Buddhists.

Variations of this view occupy one end of the spectrum of Sinhala-Buddhist fundamentalism and exert considerable pressure in contemporary politics. In his essay on Sarvodaya, George Bond, following S.J. Tambiah, refers to political interpretations of the *Mahavamsa* as "political Buddhism," which he considers a manifestation of Buddhist fundamentalism. In its most strident form, political Buddhism has been deadly. As E. Valentine Daniel has noted, "Sinhalas do die and do kill because of and for their history, and especially when such a history contradicts the lived experience of myth."[6] The middle of the spectrum has been occupied by a variety of people whose relationship to Sri Lanka has been shaped by mythohistory, especially by readings of their own role in Sri Lanka's destiny. Among them are former President J.R. Jayewardene, who drew inspiration from the *Mahavamsa* as he enacted his own heroic career.[7] The other end of the spectrum of Buddhist fundamentalism, the more moderate view, is instantiated by the Mahanayakas' (leading monks') decision early in 1997 to withdraw from the Supreme Advisory Council to the president because, as they argued, President Kumaranatunga's plan for devolution of power compromised the integrity of the Buddhist island.[8]

Like the other types of fundamentalism Marty and Appleby have explored, Sinhala-Buddhist fundamentalism is concerned with boundaries, in this case, with who is a rightful heir to the island (*dhammadipa*) and who should dominate it. There is a variety of opinions on this issue. A fundamentalist minority opinion argues that only Sinhala Buddhists are the true inheritors of the island. Though this view, especially appealing in the immediate postindependence period, has never been attractive to more than a minority, it drones in the background like the *tambura*, threatening to elongate Sri Lanka's already protracted Sinhala-Tamil ethnic crisis.

The majority among fundamentalists argues that anyone can live in Sri Lanka as long as Sinhala Buddhists can enjoy cultural, religious, economic, and linguistic hegemony. Sinhala-Buddhist fundamentalism is thus inextricably linked to ethnic chauvinism, which privileges the Sinhala people above all others of the island. Like other fundamentalists, and like their counterparts in late nineteenth-century Sri Lanka—the period which gives rise to Buddhist fundamentalism[9]—Sinhala-Buddhist fundamentalists "retrieve, privilege, and sanction" fundamentals "as a means of protecting or forging anew an ethnic or national identity seeking validation in the postcolonial era."[10]

This boundary setting (fueled by ethnic chauvinism) over who is rightful heir to *dhammadipa* is tied to ideas about purity, another facet of cross-cultural fundamentalism to which Marty and Appleby have called our attention. For Sinhala-Buddhist fundamentalists, their religion, and hence their island, are vulnerable to corruption by impure forces deemed hostile to Buddhism, whether internal or external. The protection of the *dhamma* thus means a focus upon purity, on only the righteous having sovereignty over *dhammadipa*. The unrighteous, whether other Sinhalas, or non-Sinhala peoples, are cast as the enemy of the island and of Buddhism. In their dependence upon religion and ethnicity as their basis for identity (for "Self" and "Other"), which includes awesome roles as defenders of Buddhism, Sinhala-Buddhist fundamentalists share many of the "family resemblances" of cross-cultural fundamentalism that Marty and Appleby have isolated.

While there are resemblances, however, there are also important differences. For instance, many of the world's fundamentalist movements share a missionary zeal that is, for the most part, absent in Sinhala-Buddhist fundamentalism.[11] Moreover, unlike Christian or Muslim fundamentalism, for instance, there is no insistence on strict behavioral standards in Sinhala-Buddhist fundamentalism, though there have been moments in history when such standards have been imposed.[12]

More important, however, unlike many of the fundamentalist movements that Marty and Appleby have explored, Sinhala-Buddhist fundamentalists do not form a coherent, readily identifiable group. Indeed, the term "fundamentalist" is not used by Sinhala-Buddhists in contemporary Sri Lanka as a self-designation, nor has it ever been.[13] Rather, there are a variety of interpretations of the destiny of Sri Lanka, and the role of the Sinhala-Buddhist people in that destiny (which we consider fundamentalist in nature), that drive some Buddhist groups and individuals to respond in specific ways to events in Sri Lanka, most of which are political in nature. While many Sinhala-Buddhist leaders condemn extreme fundamentalist views, and indeed are criticized for being "disloyal" to Buddhism, they nevertheless share the idea that Sri Lanka has been, and should be, a predominately Sinhala-Buddhist country.

Finally, among the major differences, we must note that there is no "sacred" text or scripture for Sinhala-Buddhist fundamentalists that serves as a blueprint for society as is often the case in fundamentalist movements. Yet there is a mythohistorical text—namely, the *Mahavamsa*—which, we argue, carries similar weight. Indeed, while the *Mahavamsa* is not a canonical text, it nonetheless has canonical authority. From a reading of it, Sinhala-Buddhist fundamentalists construe standards for an orthodox ideology about the nature and destiny of the Sinhala people and Sri Lanka. From a reading of it fundamentalists hone a dramatic eschatology about the destiny of the Sinhala people and their enemies that informs action in the present. Moreover, Sinhala-Buddhist fundamentalists find enshrined in the *Mahavamsa* a symbol system that they decode as having sacrosanct and authoritative status.

In her provocative comparative analysis of the Veda and the Torah, Barbara A. Holdrege contends that the category of "sacred text" needs to be reexamined. Though Holdrege focuses on the limiting nature of a definition of text that precludes text as a cosmological principle, ideas irrelevant to this study, her study of the relationship between texts and society is of import here. Like William A. Graham, Holdrege argues that scripture, broadly defined, is a "relational category, which refers not simply to a text but to a text in its relationship to a religious community for whom it is sacred and authoritative."[14] Citing Graham's work on scripture, Holdrege further contends that the study of scripture is concerned with:

> The "history of effects," which encompasses the ongoing roles that a sacred text has assumed in the cumulative tradition of a religious community both as a normative source of authority and as a prodigious living force.[15]

While the *Mahavamsa* is not a "sacred" scripture in the narrowest sense of the term inasmuch as it is not an embodiment of the Word (as in Hinduism or Judaism),[16] it nonetheless serves as a cloak of authority to wrap around contemporary views in Buddhist Sri Lanka. In regard to the meaning of scripture, then, we agree with Graham, who argues that:

> No text, written or oral or both is sacred or authoritative in isolation from a community . . . A book is only "scripture" insofar as a group of persons perceive it to be sacred or holy, powerful and portentous, possessed of an exalted authority.[17]

Liberalizing the definition of "sacred" to mean "authoritative" (and following Graham) we maintain that sacred texts remain symbols of authoritative power only because believers position themselves in relation to them. In Buddhist Sri Lanka, the most authoritative text for the formulation of religious and political attitudes is not a canonical Pali *sutta*, but rather the *Mahavamsa*, the meaning of which may be contested by an array of Buddhist fundamentalists, but which is "powerful and portentous" for all of them. Most Sinhala-Buddhist fundamentalists agree that it contains fundamentals for a righteous society and world order. Along these lines, though Gananath Obeyesekere may be correct when he states that the *soteriology* of Buddhism (embodied by the Pali canon) does not possess a conception of a world order that the believer must live by,[18] he is also correct in asserting that Buddhist history, or, more precisely, the *Mahavamsa*, does.

Indeed, the *Mahavamsa*, functioning as a sacred text, authorizes Sinhala-Buddhist fundamentalism. From readings of it, Sinhala Buddhists can boast an illustrious pedigree with a prestigious history and a portentous future. Thus, while there may not be a sacred text that serves as a license for Buddhist fundamentalism in Sri Lanka, there is nonetheless a text—namely, the *Mahavamsa*—that is deemed "sacred" by those who are embraced by its living authority.

That the *Mahavamsa* redounds with political significance in contemporary Sri Lanka has not been lost on contemporary scholars of Sri Lanka. Steven Kemper's work on the *Mahavamsa* reminds us that the past encoded in the *Mahavamsa* is a political resource in the present and that, like the authors of the *Mahavamsa*, contemporary Sinhala people "have every reason to look for continuity in the past."[19] For the monk-authors of the *Mahavamsa*, drawing a connection between their school of Buddhism and the Buddha's alleged visits to the island of Sri Lanka legitimated a particular type of orthodoxy. In the present, connection with the past authorizes a connection between religion and state. But, as Kemper has remarked, the monk-authors' "compilation of traditions imposes on the Sri Lankan past a single and continuous point of view that is Sinhala and Theravada Buddhist, however much more complicated that past may have been in actuality."[20] Locating the presence of the past in contemporary political discourse, Kemper reminds us that "the *Mahavamsa* has become the warrant for the interlocked beliefs that the island and its government have traditionally been Sinhala and Buddhist."[21]

The Buddhist history contained within the *Mahavamsa* is certainly complex. Though it alleges that Tamils, along with Sinhalas, are co-founders of the island,[22] some modern readings of the *Mahavamsa* construe Tamils, the large majority of whom are Hindu, as the enemy. They allege Tamils are nothing but interlopers on a sacred Buddhist island. The complexity of the *Mahavamsa* is now commonplace in contemporary scholarship on Sri Lanka, due to the work of Jonathan Spencer, R.A.L.H. Gunawardena, and others.[23] As they remind us, despite distortions in the fundamentalist construction of the *Mahavamsa*, the fusion of the past with the present stimulates and reinforces Sinhala-Buddhist feelings about non-Buddhist peoples.

The ramifications of these sentiments are far reaching: "this Sinhala historical consciousness that equate[s] the mythical Demale [Tamil] enemies with the Tamils in the North [has] seemed to squeeze out and deny the Tamils their right to the country."[24] Despite centuries of mixing between the predominantly Buddhist majority—the Sinhalas—and the largest minority—the Tamils[25]—Buddhists with fundamentalist ideas about history have constructed Tamils as the "Other," as threatening and dangerous to the prosperity of Buddhism and Sri Lanka. In their competition for the most glorious history, Sinhalas and Tamils compete for political status and privilege.[26] In Sri Lanka, ideas about the past thus shape ideas about the present, and Sinhala-Buddhist fundamentalists set the tone.

Though E. Valentine Daniel has argued persuasively that *history* constitutes a *Sinhala* disposition toward the past and *heritage* a *Tamil* disposition toward the past,[27] both Sinhalas and Tamils are guided by a past that is at once transformed and determined by the present. In his study of violence in Sri Lanka, Daniel notes that in one instance Tamil "militants claimed that the TULF [Tamil United Liberation Front] and its ilk only recently found it expedient to recall the existence of a Jaffna kingdom merely in reaction to Sinhala hyperbole about the ancient kingdoms."[28] In short, echoing Tamils before them and thus seeing the power of the Sinhala past to consolidate identity in the present, some Tamils in the present continue to respond to marginalization by finding and making their own glorious history. It is not at all coincidental that Tamil "histories" have developed in the same period that has witnessed the rise of Sinhala-Buddhist fundamentalism—namely, the period spanning the late nineteenth century to the present.

Here, it is worth remembering that in the latter decades of the nineteenth century—when, as Gananath Obeyesekere has argued, contemporary Sinhala-Buddhist identity was forged,[29] the very foundation of Sinhala-Buddhist fundamentalism—we find the first attempts to write a history of the Jaffna kingdom (considered by Tamils to be the highpoint of Tamil culture in Sri Lanka).[30] Moreover, it is not a coincidence that "the 50 years between roughly 1880–1930 . . . the critical period when Tamil ethnic consciousness was shaped and the need for history was becoming virulent,"[31] that a Sinhala-Buddhist identity was fashioned. Dagmar-Hellmann Rajanayagam, in a study of the meaning of history for Tamils in Sri Lanka, argues that late nineteenth-century Tamils used history, such as the history of the Jaffna kingdom, to prove that they, like the Sinhala people, had "a right to be" in Sri Lanka.[32] Until that time, Tamils confirmed their identity not by means of history, but by other means, "namely religion, cultural, literary, and social."[33] That is, to use Daniel's terms, by means of "heritage." Indeed, as late nineteenth-century Tamils in Sri Lanka responded to the force of Sinhala-Buddhist identity, they also constructed the idea of a Sri Lankan Tamil community, distinct from the Tamil community in India.

To be sure, until the late nineteenth century, Tamils did not feel the need to compile a history perhaps "because . . . they felt a common bond with Tamils in the southern Indian state, Tamil Nadu. Yet, the late nineteenth-century belief that India and Jaffna belonged together vanished with the emergence of the rediscovery of the kingdom of Jaffna."[34] Tamils had to prove, in the face of burgeoning Sinhala-Buddhist fundamentalism, that they had a right to be in Ceylon, that they were not Indian, and that they had a right to exist as Tamils. These forces, while enraging Sinhala-Buddhist fundamentalists who claimed that they are the only group with an inherent birthright to the island, doubtless have fueled Tamil chauvinism in contemporary Sri Lanka.[35] In the case of the Tamils of Sri Lanka, we thus have a clear example of the ways in which identity and "history" can be formed in relation to people construed as a closely related Other (the Indian Tamil) and a less proximate Other (the Sinhala Buddhist), an often repeated theme in this volume. The Sinhala people, on the other hand, have used history to claim that they—rather than Tamils—are the rightful heirs to the island. For the Sinhala-Buddhist fundamentalist, the Tamil is cast as an enemy in the island's dramatic history and destiny.

To a lesser degree, Sinhala-Buddhist fundamentalists perceive the other minorities, including Muslims, and Burghers (descendants of European colonists and hence largely Christian), as alien and thus threatening. George Bond, in his essay in this volume, explores the ways in which the mythohistory of *dhammadipa* is used differently by majority Buddhist fundamentalists, on the one hand, and "engaged Buddhists," on the other, as he narrates the history of the Sarvodaya movement in Sri Lanka. As Bond points out, Sarvodaya's view of Sri Lanka's history, unlike the majority Buddhist fundamentalist view, easily embraces the Tamil. Bond's analysis provides an interesting lens through which to view contemporary historiography in Sri Lanka, and the way in which Buddhists compete for valid interpretations of "history."

The fundamentalist interpretation of the *Mahavamsa*, a volume penned by a Buddhist monk or monks, is the history of the island that the *sangha*, the order of Buddhist monks, usually considers normative. In other words, the *sangha* is the repository of the history, although the laity, as much as the *sangha*, keeps this version of the *Mahavamsa's* history alive. In fact, the ideology of Sinhala-Buddhist fundamentalist factions in the *sangha* is shaped by this view of history because such a history is expedient for the laity. This is most striking in political circumstances. Bond's essay reminds us that, just as in other areas of the world, in Buddhist Sri Lanka fundamentalists "arise and come to prominence in times of crisis, actual or perceived."[36] These crises are usually fueled by politics and center on the relationship of the Sinhala polity to the island of Sri Lanka (*dhammadipa*), as Bond's look at Sarvodaya suggests.

Bond's essay brings into focus another feature of Sinhala-Buddhist fundamentalism: it is determined not only by historical tradition and ideology, but by politics as well. In other words, Sinhala-Buddhist fundamentalism has political overtones, not unlike, for instance, Christian fundamentalism in the United States, though the content of the politics is different. As R.L. Stirrat has argued, the distinction between "religion" and "politics" in most contexts is "scarcely tenable,"[37] and such is the case with Sri Lanka generally. Stirrat points out that the distinction is "fragile," mainly because "both religion and politics are centrally concerned with the nature and practice of power and authority despite all attempts to limit the religious to matters of spirituality, theology, soteriology or whatever."[38]

As our essayists argue, Sinhala-Buddhist fundamentalism, used as a platform for politicians and patriots since the late nineteenth century, is concerned directly with power and dominance, especially dominance by the ethnic majority, the Sinhalas. Along these lines, Donald Swearer has argued that Sinhala ethnic chauvinism, or Sinhala dominance, is wedded to an ideology of a politicized Buddhism and a dangerously simplified racism, which foreshadows "fundamentalistic Sinhalese Buddhism."[39] The relationship between ethnicity, religion, and politics that Swearer charts was so striking in the 1980s and early 1990s that today it makes more sense to talk about "Sinhala-Buddhist fundamentalism" than to talk about "fundamentalistic Sinhalese Buddhism."

While characterizing fundamentalism in South Asia by focusing upon the relationship between ethnicity and religion, George Matthew argues that all types of fundamentalism—Christian, Muslim, Hindu, and Buddhist—"mixing with political power, veers around homogenisation, and racial superiority."[40] As we shall see in the essays here, Matthew's ideas are illustrated by ethnic chauvinism in Sri Lanka, especially the brand that views "Sinhala" and "Tamil" as monolithic categories, and connects them to a variety of fundamental political and economic "rights."

This homogenizing tendency has helped to guide Sri Lanka's most recent history, especially as it manifests itself in discourses on Sinhala unity and Tamil unity. Regarding the former, as Stanley J. Tambiah rightly has pointed out, in Sri Lanka "the need for and benefits of Sinhala national unity has been an ever recurring theme in Sinhala political discourse for over a century."[41] Many of the essays here suggest that the goal of this unity has been the "protection of Buddhism and the recovery of the entire island" for the Sinhala people.[42] As Oddvar Hollup argues, Sinhala-Buddhist fundamentalists, shaped by the mythic traditions of the *Mahavamsa*, see themselves in opposition to a monolithic Tamil community, bound together in a cosmic drama that essentializes both "Sinhala" and "Tamil" identity.

Rajan Hoole has noted that, even though there is diversity among Tamils in Sri Lanka, some Tamils, especially the separatist LTTE (Liberation Tigers of Tamil Eelam), perceive a uniform Tamil identity. We find this tendency among mainstream Tamils, as well, especially in the political views of such great Tamil leaders of the past like Ponnambalam Ramanathan, and also G.G. Ponnambalam, who helped to foster a Tamil nationalism.[43] According to Hoole, such a view "may be safe and politically correct, but utterly sterile. To maintain this position, diversity has to be ignored, and the South [or the Sinhala government] characterized as essentially and permanently demonic."[44] In other words, Hoole warns against essentializing Tamil, and, for that matter, Sinhala, identity. Hollup makes a similar point. He argues that Sinhala Buddhists, who tend to lump Tamils into one group—the enemy—are undermining the separate identity of the Plantation or Estate Tamil. Echoing Hoole's warnings, Hollup's research suggests that Sri Lankan Tamil extremists, like Buddhist fundamentalists, tend to deny the plurality of the Tamils of Sri Lanka. Instead, they are inclined to speak for all Tamils, despite the fact that Plantation (Estate) Tamils do not identify themselves with the larger Tamil community, and have remained geographically distinct from it. As E. Valentine Daniel has argued, "Estate Tamils think of themselves as an ancient people belonging to an ancient civilization, with an ancient heritage. However, these Tamils see their claim to this great heritage as being openly monopolized by Jaffna [Sri Lankan; Ceylon] Tamils."[45]

In other words, as Hollup's essay alleges, many Plantation Tamils are comfortable remaining at the margins of the Tamil community, especially if it would ensure preserving their cultural, linguistic, and social distinctiveness. Thus, some Sinhala-Buddhist fundamentalist ideas about Sri Lanka's largest ethnic minority ironically are shared by Sri Lankan Tamils, who, as Hollup suggests, have political and economic reasons for creating a monolithic Tamil identity and pushing for unity. In its insistence upon a unified identity, much like fundamentalist movements elsewhere, Sinhala-Buddhist fundamentalism (and Tamil ethnic chauvinism, for that matter) "manifests itself as a strategy, or set of strategies, by which the beleaguered believers attempt to preserve their distinctive identity as a people or group."[46]

Completing his definition, Matthew adds that "fundamentalism of the majority breeds fundamentalism of the minority and vice versa." Victor de Munck dilates on this theme as he recounts the development of Muslim fundamentalism in Sri Lanka. As de Munck argues, some Muslims have responded to Muslim assimilation of Buddhist practices—itself a reaction to

Sinhala-Buddhist fundamentalism—by forging a larger, transnational identity that has fundamentalist overtones. And as the history of the past few decades in Sri Lanka suggests, such competing fundamentalisms often result "in strife between communities and even civil war."[47] Indeed, since 1983, Sri Lanka has experienced civil unrest that is unparalleled in its recent history. Pradeep Jeganathan's essay plays on these themes while exploring an alternative Tamil response to Sinhala-Buddhist fundamentalism—namely, assimilation.

Thus, while some Tamils in contemporary Sri Lanka, in response to Sinhala "claims," have constructed a political discourse based on "rights," and some have actually fought and died for those rights, others have found optional ways of coping with marginalization. Jeganathan's poignant essay on violence suggests that the 1983 riots in Sri Lanka against Tamils have forced some Tamils to assimilate Buddhist sociocultural practices, practices linked to the idea of *dhammadipa*. Not all Tamils have responded to violence in this way. Yet, Jeganathan's essay reminds us of the power of Sinhala political discourse, linked as it has been with Buddhist fundamentalism, especially in the 1980s and early 1990s. The variety of Tamil responses to Sinhala claims warns us that today in Sri Lanka there is no such thing as a singular, monolithic Tamil identity, nor does history suggest that there ever has been.

Sinhala-Buddhist fundamentalism (though not always identified as such) has captured the attention of many scholars in Sri Lanka and elsewhere in recent years.[48] Sinhala-Buddhist fundamentalism has yet to be explored, however, from the vantage of the Buddhist fundamentalist's Other—that is, the minority communities of Sri Lanka—and a number of nonfundamentalist, or traditional, Buddhists. In this volume, an ensemble of scholars from a variety of disciplines addresses what it means to be (1) a non-Buddhist, and a nonfundamentalist Buddhist, in contemporary Sri Lanka, and (2) the ways and extent to which minority identities are fashioned by Sinhala-Buddhist fundamentalism.

Sinhala-Buddhist Fundamentalism and Alterity

Though all minority religious and ethnic communities are the Other for the Sinhala-Buddhist fundamentalist, they are not all the same in regard to their Otherness. Some of them, including a large population of Buddhists, and Tamils who are predominantly Hindu, are what we call the "near Other—" that is, people who Buddhist fundamentalists would agree share a common origin—both groups hail from India—yet nonetheless pose a threat to purity and order. In these cases, as well as in others, we shall see that circumstances tend to determine who is a near Other, and who is less proximate.

Some Sri Lankan minorities, such as the Muslims, are, for Buddhist fundamentalists, the "far Other—" that is, people who are perceived, and who perceive themselves, as being from a totally different cultural tradition. Some, such as Buddhist Burghers, are the "Other's Other," or people alienated from their own community, which itself has been a constant far Other for Buddhists since the inception of the nearly exclusively Christian Burgher, or Eurasian, community in the early 1500s. Moreover, in the same way that Sinhala-Buddhist fundamentalists perceive minority groups as alien and threatening, each minority group likewise sees Sinhala-Buddhist fundamentalists as the Other. To illustrate, Stirrat here calls our attention to the ways in which global and local forces in the late nineteenth century created a significant Other for Sri Lankan Catholics: the Sinhala-Buddhist fundamentalist. In addition, Sri Lanka's minorities note gradations of Otherness among themselves: for instance, Plantation Tamils regard Sri Lankan Tamils as their near Other, similar in some ways, yet distinctive enough to warrant boundaries, as Hollup argues in his essay.

Jonathan Z. Smith has remarked recently that issues of Otherness, and similarity,[49] for that matter, "are particularly prevalent in religious discourse and imagination."[50] His observations provide a useful starting point for our study of Sinhala-Buddhist fundamentalism in Sri Lanka. Like the essayists in this volume, Smith locates in religious conflicts the language of similarity and alienation and, more importantly, "moments when proximity becomes more a matter of territoriality than of thought."[51] One does not have to search too far into Sri Lanka's Buddhist history to find this notion exemplified—namely, in some ideas about the Sri Lankan Tamil, a relatively near Other of the Buddhist fundamentalist. As some Sinhala people "recover" the entire island for their own, and Tamil separatists fight in the north for their homeland, Eelam, both spurred on by (quasi-religious) texts, blood is spilled and territories are claimed.

As Chandra R. de Silva points out, however, some Buddhists—even fundamentalists—feel solidarity with Sri Lankan Hindus, whose religion they construe, like their own, as having been disenfranchised during the colonial era. The Hindus' Tamil ethnicity, however, evoked quite a different response from de Silva's informants. In this case, religion is one thing and ethnicity quite another. In de Silva's study we are reminded once again of the tension between religion and ethnicity in Sri Lanka, especially its perilous results.

Smith might refer to the Tamil as the Buddhist fundamentalist's "proximate," rather than near, Other.[52] The implication, however, is the same: people who are thought of as being "near neighbors or descendants,"[53] or near, even in terms of power relationships, are more troublesome than a far Other.[54] In the case of the Sinhala-Buddhist fundamentalist, Tamils, who, like themselves, are cultural heirs of India, are more troublesome than a far Other, such as a Burgher or a Muslim. In other words, people who are entirely different pose a lesser threat than people who are similar. Put differently, theories of difference are really theories of Self, and the less different a people are—the more recognizable they are—the more easily they can be "projected internally."[55] This projection then becomes a critique of the Self, and ultimately locates Otherness within. Along these lines, as Smith argues, "The deepest intellectual issues are not based upon perceptions of alterity, but, rather, of similarity, at times, even, of identity."[56] As de Silva suggests in his essay on monks, Buddhist fundamentalists in Sri Lanka often construe themselves in terms of their most proximate Other—the traditional Buddhist of the golden age of the *Mahavamsa*'s past—exposing their deepest vulnerabilities.

In regard to the idea of the near Other, the relationship between Tamils and Muslims in Sri Lanka warrants further investigation. As K.M. de Silva reminds us,[57] most Muslims and Tamils have much more in common than Tamil, the language they share. For example, the 1920s and 1930s witnessed an alliance between the Muslims and Tamils "based . . . on Muslim fears of Sinhala domination."[58] One spokesperson (among many) in those decades was not a Muslim, but rather a Tamil, Ponnambalam Ramanathan. Indeed, "Ramanathan as representative of the Tamil community was often inclined to talk expansively on behalf of the Tamil speaking peoples of Sri Lanka, a categorization which enabled him to place Muslims within the scope of his tutelage as legislator."[59] Yet, Ramanathan held views about Muslims in Sri Lanka that many Sri Lankan Muslims considered unorthodox. He argued that the Moors of Ceylon were Tamils in "nationality" and "Mohammedans" in religion, which offended Muslims and resulted in a refusal of his leadership,[60] especially because, as Victor de Munck argues here, Muslims have usually invoked religion as the primary identity referent.

At other times, Muslims have pitted themselves against Tamils in no uncertain terms. Perhaps the most notable incident revolved around the language debate of the 1940s, when A.R.A. Razik, a Muslim legislator, voted with Sinhala legislators to make Sinhala the sole national language.[61] No longer could the Tamils take Muslim support for granted in their political campaigns. This cycle of rejection and affirmation of Tamil leadership created a pattern that continues to the present. Remarks made (prior to the 1994 presidential election) by Mr. A.H.M. Ashraff, leader of the Sri Lanka Muslim Congress, suggest as much.

In a letter to V. Prabakaran, head of the Liberation Tigers of Tamil Eelam (LTTE), Ashraff suggested that "If the Tamils and the Muslims could work some sort of an agreement at a time when the presidential and general elections are around the corner, it would . . . definitely create a headache for majority community chauvinism."[62] In short, Ashraff urged Prabakaran to unite with Muslims to create a minority identity powerful enough to battle Sinhala-Buddhist fundamentalism, echoing S.J.V. Chelvanayakam's Tamil Federal Party's platform in the 1940s and 1950s to "promote the unity of the Tamil speaking peoples regardless of region."[63] In urging for unity, Ashraff clearly identified with Tamils—whom he perceives as his most proximate Other in terms of identity—rather than one of the other minority communities.

Though similarities between Self and Other can be disastrous, just as ethnic strife between Tamils and Sinhalas indicates, Ashraff's agenda suggests that they can also be used to unite rather than to divide. In fact, the idea of uniting the non-Sinhala minorities and using such a union as a counterpoise to Sinhala Buddhism has had a continuous history since the late nineteenth century. This is clearly seen in G.G. Ponnambalam's 1938 "50–50" campaign which, in many ways, was a reaction to universal suffrage, that guaranteed "the permanent Sinhalese domination in politics."[64] In his "50–50" campaign, Ponnambalam argued that half of the legislature should be represented by Sinhalas, while the remaining half should be comprised of the other communities of the island.[65] Making himself spokesperson for all minority interests, Ponnambalam sought solidarity in Otherness, among communities that traditionally maintained separate identities.

Victor de Munck explores further Ponnambalam's attitudes about minority identity and the way that it has affected Muslim self-perception. De Munck uses Ponnambalam's ideas as a springboard for understanding contemporary Sri Lankan Muslim attitudes on what constitutes a "true" Muslim. On the one hand, as de Munck suggests, some Muslims, in response to Buddhist fundamentalism and Sinhala claims, have assimilated obvious Sinhala-Buddhist sociocultural practices as a strategy for survival in a Sinhala-Buddhist "nation." Using "Tactics of anticipation [of violence]," or Jeganathan's description of a similar phenomenon among Tamils, some in the Muslim minority community of Sri Lanka assimilate to survive. Others, however, have responded by purging their religion of alien accretions and identifying with a pan-Arabic Islamic fundamentalism, unsullied by Buddhism and even "unorthodox" Muslim traditions, including Sufism.

De Munck's essay, much like Jeganathan's, points out that there has been a variety of responses to being considered the Other: some hinge on assimilation; others, on alienation. Yet, as both de Munck and Jeganathan suggest, while the responses differ, the origin is the same: Sinhala-Buddhist fundamentalism and its power to shape minority identities in Sri Lanka. In de Munck's essay, the local and global forces that shape identity in Sri Lanka come to the fore in a narrative that focuses on an often overlooked group of Sri Lankans—namely, Sinhala-speaking Muslims. Due in part to the exclusive image of a Sinhala-Buddhist nation that has been forged by Buddhist fundamentalists, some Muslims in Sri Lanka have developed a pan-Arabic identity, while others have done the opposite: they have forged an identity that has accommodated obvious Sinhala-Buddhist features. Despite these differences, both types of Muslims have internalized the status of Other that Sinhala-Buddhist fundamentalists have deemed for them.

In his survey of the way in which the Other is used as an intellectual tool in shaping identity, Smith finds three distinct models. They are: 1) the metonymical model; 2) the model of center and periphery; and 3) the model of unintelligibility.[66] The first two models have special relevance for our study. According to Smith, the metonymical model critiques the Self via the "naming" of differences, and, thus, similarities, between Self and Other. In this model, then, the group makes statements about itself while naming and discerning alterity. In short, it claims: "I am [or have; or can do] what you are not [or do not have; or cannot do]." De Silva's essay on monks' ideas about Buddhism exemplifies the metonymical model of alterity; de Silva explores the ways in which monks with fundamentalist concerns discern who is a good Buddhist (monk) and who is not. Implicit in their often conflicting attitudes about who is an authentic Buddhist, and thus an authentic Sri Lankan, is a concern for naming—that is, for identifying what is distinctive about Self and Other, and what might be similar. In other words, in analyzing the Other—that is, monks and Buddhist laypersons they deem unrighteous—these monks say much about themselves.

We see this same tendency also among the contemporary Sinhala-Anglican community, which continues the process of indigenization that it began in the late 1800s. As Tessa Bartholomeusz argues, Sinhala Anglicans today, more so than their counterparts at the turn of the twentieth century, find more that is similar in the wider Sinhala, and thus Buddhist, community than they see that is different. This self-critique is shared by some Catholics of Sri Lanka, who also have been indigenizing for several decades.

Much like Sinhala Anglicans, Sinhala Catholics (often consciously so) conflate religious and ethnic identity in their search for indigenous idioms to represent their faith. To illustrate, in an address at the 1994 Seminar of Inculturation organized by the Catholic National Commission for Liturgy and Culture, a Sinhala priest linked Catholicism to "Sinhala culture" via Theravada Buddhism. Referring to a historian who addressed the seminar earlier on, the Catholic priest praised the historian and reiterated the latter's claims:

> He [the historian] vividly presented the simple and serene features of the Sinhala Culture (sic) that has been guided and molded by the Theravada Buddhism. Religion is a powerful force in the formation and development of culture. We see that Christian culture is very close to our Sinhala culture.[67]

In other words, the Catholic speaker argued that there are striking similarities between Catholicism (a religion) and the Sinhala people (a linguistic/ethnic group), who have been guided by Buddhism. He continued by linking Buddhism to nationalism and, finally, to Catholicism. In the process, he praised the most famous Buddhist revivalists in Sri Lanka's modern history:

> At the beginning of the 20th century patriots like Anagarika Dharmapala, Valisinghe Harischandra and Piyadasa Sirisena brought about a national renaissance. This national awakening [had] its effect on the Catholic Church as well.[68]

Indeed, as Bartholomeusz argues, the "national" and Buddhist awakening has stimulated Christians to rethink their position in Sri Lanka. Stirrat explores this theme further as he addresses, among other things, the controversy over the "Voice of America" in Sri Lanka. As Stirrat makes clear, Catholics in Sri Lanka, like other religious minorities on the island, constantly negotiate their identity depending on the context. In the present context, where being Sinhala means being empowered, Sinhala Catholics have responded to Sinhala nationalism and Buddhist fundamentalism by asking what it means to be an "authentic" Sri Lankan and an "authentic" Catholic.

In the process of their naming, moreover, contemporary Sinhala Catholics, and Anglicans, for that matter, assess their own values while they assess the values of Buddhists; in other words, their naming, or discovering who is Other, is in fact a reflexive process. In these specific cases of Catholic and Anglican indigenization, the similarities are not perceived of as threatening, even though, as Stirrat has pointed out elsewhere, there are notable exceptions.[69] Rather, for the indigenizing Sinhala Anglican and Catholic, both of whom have construed a shared cultural heritage between Christians and Buddhists, the similarities often can be empowering. Regarding the former, it is ironic that indigenizing Sinhala Anglicans allege that they, rather than a Sinhala-Buddhist fundamentalist group, first used the phrase "Jathika Chinthanaya" to describe the process of preserving Sinhala culture.[70] This recalls Tamil-Christian attempts to define and preserve Tamil culture long before Tamil Hindus took the initiative.

As Rajanayagam points out, nineteenth-century Tamil Christians could not rely for their identity on their religion or on a sacred text.[71] Like Sinhala Anglicans, Tamil Christians have had to rely on secular or cultural institutions for their identity, no matter how much those institutions have been linked to another religion. For the Sinhala Anglican, the preservation of Sinhala culture includes the incarnation of Christ among the Sinhalas, while for the Buddhist fundamentalist group, the Jathika Chinthanaya, it means the opposite. In fact chances are that fundamentalist Buddhists such as the Jathika Chinthanaya will continue to consider Anglicans, and Catholics, for that matter, peripheral Sri Lankans, at best.

In the most usual manifestation of the model of center and periphery, inhabitants of cities are contrasted with the hinterlands.[72] The center/periphery model can be viewed more generally to include contrasts between "a thickness of cultural similarity in the center, relative to the observer, [and] a thinness, an alienation, at the margins."[73] This observation can be meaningfully expanded to include the Eurasians, or Burghers, of Sri Lanka. Buddhist Burghers and Christian Burghers illustrate the duality of center/periphery inasmuch as the latter have placed their renegade relatives at the margins of their community. From the point of view of the Christian Burgher, the margins of the Burgher community, where Sinhala and Burgher meet, are chaotic, weak, and have the possibility of corrupting bloodlines, of polluting.

Yet, while Sinhala Buddhists normally view the Burgher community, on the whole, as being peripheral to Sri Lankan culture, they have accommodated Buddhist Burghers, who have moved to the center of Sinhala-Buddhist life. In fact, the margin that the Christian Burgher fears is projected positively by the Sinhala-Buddhist fundamentalist. There, the Burgher convert to Buddhism represents all the positive features of his or her new religion. Because converts have been culturally separated from popular Buddhism, they have the ability to represent true Buddhism, unaffected by the corruptions of rituals and other accretions deemed unauthentic. The battle over what constitutes authentic Buddhism continues to the present day.

Buddhists themselves have been aware that critics of Buddhism might be suspicious of converts and of the authenticity of their faith. In the late nineteenth century, one writer addressed this problem and advised his readers that Buddhists should "not be misled by the enemies of Buddhism who wished to sow disunion (sic) by spreading about the false statement that European [and, by extension, Burgher] Buddhism was distinct and opposed to Ceylon Buddhism."[74] Rather, according to him, the religion of the convert, created at the margins, was the most unadulterated form of Buddhism. The margin between Sinhalas and Burghers indeed has been viewed differently by Buddhist Sinhalas and Christian Burghers: while it is a powerful place for both, for the former it has the potential to be positive and strong, while for the latter, it can be negative, weak, dangerous, and chaotic. Christian Burghers' notions about the periphery of their community recalls Harjot Oberoi's ideas about the construction of religious boundaries. Reflecting on religious identity in India, Oberoi reminds us that while groups negotiate identities, "a norm is constructed, and the world outside the norm is viewed as deviant, marginal, threatening or unimportant."[75] Bartholomeusz ferrets out these themes as she explores what it means for Burghers to live on the margins of Sinhala-Buddhist society.

Recalling Mary Douglas's insights about the agents of pollution,[76] the margin is safe for the Buddhist fundamentalist only if it can be contained.

Generally, what Buddhism in Sri Lanka has been able to integrate, domesticate, and thus contain and make its own, it does not distinguish as polluting. In other words, Sinhala Buddhism defends against disorder through containment.[77] Gananath Obeyesekere and Richard Gombrich, in their 1988 study of Buddhism in Sri Lanka,[78] provide numerous examples of the ways in which Sinhala Buddhism has integrated, or "contained," elements of Tamil-Hindu culture, normally considered dangerous. Among these is the domestication of Hindu devotionalism or, more specifically, *bhakti*. In its assimilation (and eventual transformation) of *bhakti*, Buddhism has contained, tamed, and purified it; it has removed its threat of danger, of pollution. Of course, pollution—ritual, cultural, or otherwise—is relative. Regardless of the type of pollution, however, its transformation (or avoidance) "is a creative moment, an attempt to relate form to function, to make unity of experience."[79]

Sinhala Buddhism creates and re-creates itself each time it integrates aspects of the Other, which, left uncontained, would pollute. As the 1994 ordination of a Tamil as a Buddhist monk indicates,[80] Sinhala Buddhism can contain Tamils themselves. Once domesticated, even the Tamil loses his or her impurity. Sinhala Buddhism thus creates order out of disorder and, as the essays in this study suggest, is richly organized by "purity and contagion."[81] In regard to this, Sinhala-Buddhist fundamentalism, then, is the dimension of Sinhala Buddhism that locates disorder, impurity, and contagion, and attempts to remedy it.

Though Sinhala-Buddhist fundamentalism has clear ideas about who belongs, and who does not, and thus is heavily safeguarded, these ideas are not rigid. In short, Sinhala-Buddhist fundamentalism provides a scope for change in its process of containing, or avoiding, the Other. Its ideas about pollution thus say something about social life in Sri Lanka. Indeed, its reflections upon danger and purity are also reflections upon the Other, and thus what is Other within. Sinhala-Buddhist fundamentalists are not unique in their polarization of the world as pure/dangerous and Self/Other, or even center/periphery. As the essays in this study indicate, Tamils, Muslims, Burghers, and the other minorities of Sri Lanka too employ these dualisms to assess themselves and those around them. Sinhala-Buddhist fundamentalists, however, set the tone, which began to resonate loud and clear in the late nineteenth century under the British.

Sinhala-Buddhist Fundamentalism: History and Destiny

As John D. Rogers in a recent study cautions, we should be wary of interpretations of ethnic studies that place great importance on the role of the

British in the construction of new identities in South Asia.[82] Indeed, colonial identities and boundaries between a variety of groups in Sri Lanka began to form long before the advent of the British.[83] Doubtless, this process continued well into the British period. Yet it nevertheless is the case that in the late nineteenth century (the zenith of the British colonial period), Sinhala-Buddhist fundamentalist ideology, which perhaps had been brimming in the pre-British period, sharpened the process of identity formation.

Living, as many fundamentalists do, in an "increasingly alien world,"[84] a number of Sri Lankans in the late nineteenth-century empowered themselves to fight against what they perceived to be the dissolution of traditions and orthodoxies. As Bartholomeusz has argued,[85] however, those Sri Lankans who challenged disruption were not limited to Sinhalas who were Buddhist. Rather, the sources reveal that Tamil Hindus and even Burghers, as well as a few Sinhala Christians,[86] mobilized their support with Buddhists. In other words, the late nineteenth century exemplifies the fluid nature of Sinhala-Buddhism's politics. At that time, Buddhists actively united with non-Buddhist Sri Lankans in their struggles against Christian proselytization. In short, in the late nineteenth century, though there are clear exceptions, there was at least some interpenetration and overlapping of religious identities. Put differently, under the British, Buddhists, Hindus, and Muslims shared a similar identity: they were all non-Christians. A Buddhist Burgher, whom we shall meet again later in this volume, provides in his writings a description of this late nineteenth-century religious solidarity:

> Buddhist, Hindu and Mohammedan have united in one common purpose, and soon the missionaries will have to pack up their trunks, and go for converts to the slums of London and Liverpool, or to the desert of Africa.[87]

Such rhetoric suggests that in the latter decades of the nineteenth century, Otherness was determined by religion. At the same time, the polarities of colonial/colonizer and native/alien—or, center (colonial; native)/periphery (colonizer; alien)—determined Buddhist revivalists' sympathies. In this way, colonialism generated religious solidarity. For instance, in commenting upon the control of a large number of English schools by Christian missions, one Buddhist writer identified with his Hindu neighbor: "By this act the Christian clergy received a tremendous accession of power, and the national freedom of the Buddhists and Hindus has since been threatened to be destroyed."[88] In short, Buddhists perceived that non-Christians shared their grievances. But, as our discussion on alterity thus far suggests, identity can have perilous results. Indeed, in the twentieth century, it has. While colonization generated solidarity in Sri Lanka, it nevertheless sharpened divisions.

In resisting Christian conversion, late nineteenth-century Buddhists, Hindus, and Muslims began to articulate religious identities that would soon be conflated with national, or ethnic, identities and nationalisms. In an extremely complex process, religion—as a mode of identity—became linked to "being Sinhala," "being Tamil," "being Moor," and "being Burgher." The newspaper and magazine articles of the period abound with examples of this conflation. For instance, in an article that praised Tamils for their work in the Buddhist education program, a Buddhist writer nonetheless highlighted the Otherness of the Tamil, especially his or her "nationality":

> While thanking those two gentlemen above-mentioned, who, though of quite distinct faith and nationality, have come to the assistance of the school, I hope Mr. Tudor Rajepakse, of *our faith and nationality*, will also cheerfully come forward.[89]

In this way, Buddhists consciously began to push for a distinct and separate religious and cultural identity. And it was in their schools that Buddhists with fundamentalist ideas, like religious fundamentalists elsewhere, propagated their fundamentalist faith and worldview.[90] In the wedding of religious and cultural identity, ethnicity and its relationship to the nation were brought to the fore. To illustrate, in a description of an English-medium journal of Buddhism launched in 1889, the journal's editor linked ideas concerning the territoriality of religion to ethnicity and the island. He explained that the journal's purpose was "to be the exponent of the views of the Sinhalese people with regard to matters which concern their national religion."[91] The Buddhist revival that these ideas helped spawn has been documented amply.[92] Here, it is worth remembering that in the late nineteenth century the *Mahavamsa*—the charter for Buddhist fundamentalists—(once again) entered Sri Lankan consciousness, helping to shape views about Buddhism, the Sinhala people, and their link to Sri Lanka.

Tourner's 1837 translation of the Pali *Mahavamsa* into English, republished in 1889, supplied Sinhala Buddhists with what they needed to argue that, like the British, they too were Aryan, and like the British, they could vaunt an incredibly sophisticated history.[93] Moreover, if the publications of the period are any indication, some Buddhists perceived Christians to be a most pernicious enemy. Buddhists argued that Christianity was responsible for corrupting the Buddhist culture of the island. One writer summed up the problem thus:

> Many Buddhists in this Island, especially in our towns, have fallen victims to the demon of intemperance—the most terrible of the curses for which we have to thank our European conquerors.[94]

Yet, as Buddhists began to boast against Europeans a superior cultural and religious heritage, non-Buddhists—even if they had worked for the elevation of Buddhism—moved from the center, to the periphery, of who was "alien" and who was not. Though a few Tamils, such as the Honorable P. Ramanathan, a Tamil judge who extolled the work of Buddhists, were extolled by Buddhists,[95] ideas that non-Buddhists threatened the Buddhist order were beginning to be honed.[96] Non-Buddhist Sinhala people were not exempted from this critique. In fact, one 1889 writer, scandalized that a Christian Sinhala represented the Sinhala people in the Legislative Council, voiced his criticism of Christian Sinhalas in no uncertain terms:

> At present two-thirds of the inhabitants are *entirely unrepresented*; for the so-called representative of the Sinhalese "community" is a member of a hostile faith, and by that very fact . . . is unfitted to act for the Buddhists.[97]

For the 1889 Buddhist, "Christian Sinhala" was an oxymoron. In his worldview, Buddhism and Sinhala were inextricably linked; even a Christian who claimed to be Sinhala was regarded as alien, as Other.

The 1889 correspondent's ideas were based loosely on an interpretation of the *Mahavamsa* as a record of the exploits of Buddhist kings, who in a glorious age had protected the island from alien forces, including Tamils, which contributed to fundamentalism. So did visions of Sri Lanka as a sacred isle. Tamil "historians" at the same time argued that the "Sinhalese are a mixture of indigenous tribes, Aryans and Dravidians, more Tamil than anything else." In fact, "[one work] openly suggest[ed] that Sinhalese and Tamil are in reality one, viz. Dravidian."[98] Thus, much like other religious fundamentalist movements, in Sri Lanka they began as an ideological battle for control over the way Sri Lankans would view not only their past, but their future, as well.[99] As de Silva's contribution to this volume suggests, the past that fundamentalist Buddhist monks "imagine," doubtless based on readings of the *Mahavamsa*, reminds us once again how this process has continued to the present.

Unlike other religious fundamentalisms, however, Sinhala-Buddhist fundamentalism in Sri Lanka did not begin as a reaction to the challenges of modern science, or modernity, per se.[100] In fact, in the late nineteenth century, those who planted the seeds for contemporary Sinhala-Buddhist fundamentalism argued that Buddhism, unlike Christianity, for instance, is congruent with science.[101] In her discussion of Christian fundamentalism in America, Nancy Ammerman points out that one of the greatest challenges nineteenth-century Christians faced was science.[102] How to reconcile the "word of God" and the findings of science became a preeminent concern of laity and clergy, alike. On the other hand, Sri Lankan Buddhists boasted that Buddhism had no such problem, and that Buddhism, among all the religions, was the most scientific. Doubtless defending Buddhism against Christian missionary attacks, Buddhists argued for its supremacy based on its affinities with science and thus its usefulness in the modern world. Yet, Buddhism was not to be *adapted to* the burgeoning modern Sri Lankan world; rather, it was to *guide it.* It is here that Sinhala-Buddhist fundamentalism again converges with other religious fundamentalisms, including North American Christian movements.

Like North American Christian fundamentalism,[103] the fledgling Buddhist fundamentalist movement in late nineteenth-century Sri Lanka began in part as a campaign to educate its youth in schools deemed appropriate for providing a proper religious education. The campaign was a huge success, crystalizing in the foundation of several schools in a few short years.[104] Many of the schools that Sri Lankans established in the late nineteenth century continue to function to the present. Ananda College, perhaps the most well-known, was one of the first. It remains one of the most well-respected schools in the island.

Ananda College, and Buddhist education in general, was much more than a local concern. In fact, so was the Sri Lankan Buddhist revival. Even Europeans, Australians, and North Americans involved themselves in the elevation of Buddhism in Sri Lanka. In a manner very reminiscent of church revivals in the United States, international contingents of Buddhists made their way to the most remote parts of the island, preaching the Buddhist "gospel" under large circus tents.[105]

Perhaps the most notable international Buddhist of the period was the Theosophical Society's co-founder, Colonel Henry S. Olcott, about whom much has been written.[106] He and his Buddhist Theosophical Society attracted the attention of many Sri Lankans. Within days of Olcott's arrival in Sri Lanka in 1880, concerned Buddhists and others committed themselves to the American's campaign to resuscitate Buddhism. Olcott established in Sri Lanka a branch of his Theosophical Society and, soon after, he and his supporters began organizing and establishing Buddhist schools throughout the country. In those schools, Buddhist teachers taught the Buddhist scriptures and imparted a traditional secular education, as well.

At the establishment of one such institution, a Buddhist school for boys in Galle, a Buddhist monk argued that education was the fundamental means of reestablishing Sri Lanka as a Buddhist isle:

> The Reverend Siri Sumanatissa, Principal of Vijayananda Pali College, in a very eloquent speech, deplored the present condition of education in Lanka. During the time of the early Buddhist kings thriving schools

> existed in great numbers and the education of the people reached a high level. Owing to foreign conquests and the presence of invaders hostile to the ancient religion, such institutions were abolished.[107]

In other words, for Reverend Sumanatissa, restoration of Buddhist education was the first step in creating a righteous order. His ideas, based loosely on the *Mahavamsa* and widespread as they were, suggest that Sinhala-Buddhist fundamentalism clearly had taken shape in the latter decades of the nineteenth century. Privileging the past, as fundamentalists often do, the monk-principal defined Buddhist "history" as the remedy "for the challenges of the present and the opportunities of the future."[108] To promote the righteous order that Sumanatissa and others described, in addition to establishing schools, Buddhists founded a Buddhist Defense Committee, and created also printing presses to disseminate news of the progress of their work.[109] Their agenda—ethnic unity—indeed demanded grand organizational schemes.

The education campaign in many ways continued the process of separating the pure from the impure, which, as we have seen, is a hallmark of religious fundamentalism. As the schools mushroomed, enthusiasm waxed for the elevation of Buddhism to its former glory alleged in the *Mahavamsa.* Like North American Christian fundamentalists,[110] Buddhists made a large step in the direction of a separate identity by establishing schools, the preeminent concern of which was the protection of Buddhist values and institutions. Indeed, according to late nineteenth-century Buddhists, "the movement for [Buddhist] education [was] a national movement,"[111] and Buddhist schools were considered "the life of the nation."[112] It was a small leap to connect these fundamentalist ideas about Buddhist education and the nation to the welfare of the Sinhala people.

Some Sri Lankan Buddhists have kept alive the nineteenth-century construction of Buddhism and its rightful position in Sri Lanka. In contemporary Sri Lanka, critics draw parallels between these claims and ideology centered around the "Promised Land." According to a Sri Lankan commentator writing between the 1994 parliamentary elections and the 1994 presidential election:

> The Sinhalese are suffering from the "Mahavamsa complex," something similar to the "chosen people complex" of the Jews. It is this complex that has made the Sinhala people so chauvinistic.[113]

As recent scholarship on Sinhala-Buddhist hegemony suggests, this parallel concerning a homeland may not be overstated. One of the problems that has evolved from the idea of the Sinhala homeland, or *dhammadipa*, is the problem of language—the vehicle of culture, literature, and administration.

While late nineteenth-century Buddhists (invented and) revived religious institutions,[114] they turned their attention also to Sinhala literary endeavors, yet another form of cultural resistance against the British. At a time in which the language of administration was English, as was instruction in the best schools, Buddhists began to advocate the use of the vernacular: they praised their Hindu neighbors for reviving use of Tamil,[115] and rallied for their own Sinhala-medium schools. As is well known, many of the architects of the Buddhist revival were the island's deracinated, such as Anagarika Dharmapala, who grew up in English-speaking homes, and who wrote and thought in English.[116] It is not surprising that it is they who focused upon language as part of the renaissance that they had helped to craft.

The journals and other writings of these late nineteenth-century Buddhist revivalists contain the seeds for the language debate that were sown in the 1940s and 1950s. As we mentioned above, these revivalists did not claim that Sinhala should be the sole language of administration and education. Rather, they urged that Tamil, too, be privileged above English. Within the next fifty years, as has been well documented,[117] the issue of language—one among many foci of the revival—gained primacy. Unlike late nineteenth-century discourse about language, however, the debates in the 1950s were unambiguously linked to the rights of the Sinhala people, and clearly had become interwoven with politics.

In postindependence politics, which, like the Buddhist renaissance similarly involved the deracinated, the language issue determined the status of the peoples of Sri Lanka. Emerging from the British period, many with Buddhist fundamentalist leanings argued that the Sinhala people and their Buddhist culture were in peril. Focusing on the politics of language as a remedy, Buddhist politicians and others in the 1950s pushed for a "Sinhala-only" policy, which has helped to divide the country and fuel ethnic strife. Tamils countered that their language, too, should be given constitutional protection, only to be protested against by Buddhist monks and laity, thus stoking the fires of ethnic hostility. The outcome has been well documented,[118] and need not be rehearsed here. What must be kept in mind, however, is that in the mid-twentieth century, latent and ill-defined feelings of ethnic, religious, and cultural superiority across the board in Sri Lanka shaped and honed identities that emerged in the late 1800s. In the pages that follow, we further nuance these themes and link them to the fundamentalism of the majority and minority communities of Sri Lanka.

Before turning to the essays, however, we must pause to consider what impact current politics will make on Sinhala-Buddhist fundamentalism in Sri Lanka and vice versa. Though it is necessary to bring this study as close to the present situation as possible, even as we write that situation, like everything else, is in flux. Writing in mid-1997, a period in which the predominantly Sinhala government's negotiations with the LTTE seem doomed, it is difficult to predict when there will be peace in Sri Lanka again.

In the 1980s and early 1990s, Sinhala-Buddhist fundamentalism set the tone of Sri Lankan political discourse, as de Munck's essay on Muslims in this study indicates. In his study, de Munck explores the ways in which political discourse, informed by Sinhala-Buddhist fundamentalism, has shaped the ideas of Muslims living in a predominately Sinhala area. As he argues, contemporary Muslims in Sri Lanka have responded to Sinhala-Buddhist fundamentalism by rethinking their own identity: religious, political, and social. Though, Muslims—most of whom speak Tamil—have been lumped with Tamils, a conflation that at times they have encouraged, in the present situation some Muslims move for a discrete identity. Whether time will reverse this situation remains to be seen. Moreover, the impact that such a conflation will have on *Sinhala* speaking Muslims, the group that de Munck has studied, remains an open question.

In addition to shaping the politics of both the minority and majority communities of the island, Sinhala-Buddhist fundamentalism also has affected views about foreign elements in Sri Lanka, which created in the 1980s a rather insular way of looking at the world. Regarding this, Bond's essay chronicles the affect that Sinhala-Buddhist fundamentalism has had on Sarvodaya Shramadana, which began as a movement of social change and development based on Buddhist thought. In the course of time, and in large part due to the contribution of foreign powers, Sarvodaya was seen by former President Premadasa as a font of Western, Christian, and thus corrupting, influences in Sri Lanka. In a smear campaign that continues to the present, Premadasa, and those who carried on his ideas after his death, have labeled Sarvodaya as an anti-Sri Lankan, and thus anti-Buddhist, agency. Bond's study offers an interesting instance of the way in which Buddhists compete with one another for legitimacy, or the ways in which a near Other can be one's worst enemy. Along these lines, Stirrat's study explores the degree to which some Sinhala-Buddhists have remained suspicious of their far Other, the Christian, whom they consider to be the vehicle of the corrupting influence of the West.

Despite the loathing of some concerning Sarvodaya, and of Catholicism and other Christian traditions today in Sri Lanka, there are as many, if not more, voices that warn against all types of chauvinism. What impact they will have on the peace process is an open question. Yet, if the 1994 and 1997 election results are any indication, Sinhala chauvinism, linked as it is with Sinhala-Buddhist fundamentalism, now only drones softly in the background.

Notwithstanding the current situation, prior to the November 1994 presidential elections, early postindependence ideas about the dangers that faced the Sinhala people were voiced by a few in Sri Lanka. According to Gamini Jayasuriya,[119] who "shudder[s] to imagine the plight of the Sinhalese race by the turn of this century,"[120] the Sinhala people are doomed to extinction if they concede to Tamil demands. Like other fundamentalists elsewhere, Jayasuriya "perceives a crisis of identity" and fears "extinction as a people or absorption into an overarching syncretistic culture."[121] This much is clear in one of his speeches, in which he summed up his and his supporters' work and a warning to his brethren:

> The Sinhala people woke up from their slumber and as a result the non-political movement—the Sinhala Arakshaka Sanvidhanaya [or, the Society for Sinhala Preservation] was born in January 1991. From then onwards to the present day I have visited villages and hamlets throughout the country to explain to them to the best of my ability the grave threat we are facing.[122]

Despite Jayasuriya's warning of the imminent destruction of the Sinhala-Buddhist people, the polls suggest that most Sinhala-Buddhists are willing to allow the new government to work with Prabakaran to settle the problem in the north. According to Amaradasa Fernando, a Sinhala critic of Jayasuriya's type of rhetoric:

> The parties which took an ultra racist line in the recently concluded election were the UNP [United National Party],[123] MEP [Mahajana Eksath Peramuna],[124] and the Sinhalaye Mahasammatha Bhumiputhra [the Party of the Sinhala Sons of the Soil].[125] . . . They followed their usual racist line wooing the Sinhala-Buddhist voter. . . . The Sinhala-Buddhist voter meted out poetic justice to this *fide defensor* of Buddhism [Dinesh Gunawardena, leader of the MEP], by helping to give him a crushing defeat." [126]

Fernando continued by explaining the relationship of the MEP to politics, ethnic chauvinism, and the Jathika Chinthanaya, the latter of which we explored earlier:

> It was not good enough for the MEP just to be shouting empty shibboleths. It was necessary to base the party on an ideology. Therefore, Dinesh Gunawarena and Dr. Gunadasa Amarasekera, of "Jathika Chinthanaya" fame formed a symbiotic relationship. The MEP had a ready-made small, mass base to propagate the Jathika Chinthanaya ideal.[127]

In other words, as is the case in other fundamentalist movements elsewhere, the MEP's 1994 politics fused with religious and ethnic ideology to create a platform of ethnic and religious nationalism. The agenda, like that of many fundamentalist movements (as we have seen), was unity:

> They [the MEP] pleaded for the unity of the Sinhalese on the basis of their ethnic identity and saw differentiation along political party lines as the main obstacle to unity. Their argument was that, if the Sinhalese remained fragmented, the minorities would exploit these differences and achieve their objectives. The Sinhala-Buddhist nature of Sri Lankan society would then be irreparably damaged.[128]

In their demand for ethnic unity, they indeed echoed the concerns of fundamentalist movements worldwide and of many in Sri Lanka since independence: loss of Sinhala identity in a fractured sea of enemies.

In the 1994 parliamentary elections, and again in the 1997 local government elections, however, the MEP's platform failed, despite its ideology that elevated the concerns of the Sinhala people above all others, and its focus upon re-creating Sri Lanka as a Buddhist nation. According to one interpreter of the 1994 elections, even though the MEP "ha[d] taken an unequivocal stand for the interests of the Sinhala people, for the dominance of Sinhala-Buddhists in culture, society, and polity of [Sri Lanka],"[129] it nonetheless was squashed, especially in predominantly Sinhala areas.[130] The majority of the Sinhala people rejected also the Sinhalaye Mahasammatha Bhumiputhra, which also espoused a type of Sinhala nationalism that similarly was fused with Sinhala-Buddhist fundamentalism.

As a corrective to what they perceive as Sinhala-Buddhist chauvinism and fundamentalism, some Sri Lankans—liberal Sinhalas, Tamils, and Muslims—have argued recently for a common Sri Lankan identity that transcends ethnicity and religion.[131] Paradoxically, the liberals and the fundamentalists have one goal in common: both in the end hope to homogenize Sri Lanka. Doubtless responding in part to a "totalitarian impulse,"[132] a family characteristic of fundamentalism, liberals, and others, too, push for a unity that can compete with Buddhist fundamentalism.

To illustrate: according to Bond in this volume, Sarvodaya's leader argued early on for a common Sri Lankan identity as a corrective to Sri Lankan civil strife, which has bifurcated the "races" and "nations" of the island. What do such ideas bode for the future? Given its bad showing at recent polls, what role will Buddhist fundamentalist politics play in Sri Lanka's future? Those questions shall remain unanswered for the moment, but will be addressed by John Holt in the concluding chapter of this volume. We now shall turn our attention toward the way Sinhala-Buddhist fundamentalism, often directly and sometimes indirectly, has helped to shape minority identities in Sri Lanka. Those identities, after all, give rise to new ones that, despite their constant state of flux, help us to understand further the consequences of fundamentalist ideology.

Notes

1. We would like to thank SUNY Press's three anonymous readers, and John Holt and John Kelsay, for their careful readings of an earlier version of this chapter. For the sake of uniformity and owing to inconsistent practice in our sources, diacritics will be eschewed in this book.

2. In scholarship on Sri Lanka, it is generally held that "Sri Lankan Muslims consist of several distinct groups between whom the common link [is] their religion." In fact, controversy over the use of the terms Moor and Muslim has been ongoing. According to K.M. de Silva, "'Moor' [has] emphasized their Arabic heritage and the historical origins of the community, and its strong indigenous roots in Sri Lanka," . . . while "the term Muslim . . . bring[s] in a number of other Islamic groups in the island and who had come there in Dutch and British times." In other words, "Muslim" can denote an ethnic category in Sri Lanka. For more, see K.M. de Silva, *Managing Ethnic Tensions in Multi-Ethnic Societies: Sri Lanka, 1880–1985* (Lanham, MD: University Press of America, 1986). For a discussion of the politicization of the term "Muslim" among the English speakers of Sri Lanka, see Michael Roberts, "Filial devotion in Tamil culture and the Tiger cult of Martyrdom," *Contributions to Indian Sociology* (n.s.) 30, 2 (1996): 246–47.

3. Martin E. Marty and R. Scott Appleby, *Fundamentalisms Observed* (Chicago: University of Chicago Press, 1991), p. ix. For a provocative critique of the Fundamentalism Project, see Peter Berger, "Secularism in Retreat," *The National Interest* 46 (Winter): 3–12.

4. Ibid., summarized from pp. 819–21.

5. S. J. Tambiah, *Sri Lanka: Ethnic Fratricide and the Dismantling of Democracy* (Chicago: University of Chicago Press, 1986), p. 70.

6. E. Valentine Daniel, *Charred Lullabies: Chapters in an Anthropography of Violence* (Princeton: Princeton University Press, 1996), p. 54.

7. Josine van der Horst, *Who is He, What is He Doing? Religious Rhetoric and Performances in Sri Lanka during R. Premadasa's Presidency (1989–1993)* (Amsterdam: VU University Press, 1995), p. 26.

8. "Editorial: Politics in Buddhism," *Sri Lanka Net*, Thursday, 30 January 1997.

9. See below.

10. Martin E. Marty and R. Scott Appleby, *Fundamentalisms Observed*, p. 816.

11. Ibid., p. 822.

12. Anagarika Dharmapala tried to impose a standard of behavior in the late 1890s that he thought accorded with proper Buddhist etiquette. For more on this, see

Gananath Obeyesekere, "Personal Identity and Cultural Crisis, The Case of Anagarika Dharmapala of Sri Lanka," in *The Biographical Process: Studies in the History and Psychology of Religion*, Frank E. Reynolds and Donald Capps, eds. (The Hague: Mouton, 1976).

13. See Nancy Ammerman's essay, "North American Protestant Fundamentalism," in *Fundamentalisms Observed*, for the ways in which the term was used as a self-referent by North American fundamentalists. Though Buddhists in Sri Lanka have never used the term to refer to themselves, they have been self-conscious of their mobilization. For instance, in a representative article from the 1890s, they refer to their activities as a "Buddhist movement" (*The Buddhist*, 9 September 1892, vol. 4, no. 36).

14. Barbara A. Holdrege, *Veda and Torah* (Albany: State University of New York Press, 1996), p. 4.

15. Ibid.

16. Ibid., p. 407.

17. Quoted in ibid., p. 4.

18. Gananath Obeyesekere, "Buddhism, Nationhood and Cultural Identity: A Question of Fundamentals," in *Fundamentalisms Comprehended*, Martin E. Marty and R. Scott Appleby, eds. (Chicago: University of Chicago Press, 1995), p. 32.

19. Steven Kemper, *The Presence of the Past* (Ithaca: Cornell University Press, 1991), p. 2.

20. Ibid.

21. Ibid., p. 3.

22. Gananath Obeyesekere, "Buddhism, Nationhood and Cultural Identity," p. 14.

23. Jonathan Spencer, ed., *Sri Lanka: History and the Roots of Conflict* (London: Routledge, 1990). See within Gunawardena's "The People of the Lion: The Sinhala Identity and Ideology in History and Historiography," pp. 45–86.

24. Dagmar-Hellmann Rajanayagam, "Tamils and the Meaning of History," in *The Sri Lankan Tamils: Ethnicity and Identity*, Chelvadurai Manogaran and Bryan Pfaffenberger, eds. (Boulder: Westview Press, 1994), p. 76.

25. This mixing has resulted in, among other things, caste groups that now identify themselves as Sinhala. For more, see John D. Rogers, "Post Orientalism and the Interpretation of Premodern and Modern Political Identities: The Case of Sri Lanka," the *Journal of Asian Studies*, vol. 53, no. 1 (February 1994): 17. As Rogers points out, "the ease with which South Indian emigrants became Sinhalese points to the notion of Sinhalese identity as cultural and political rather than ethnic or racial."

26. Dagmar-Hellmann Rajanayagam, "Tamils and the Meaning of History," p. 76.

27. E. Valentine Daniel, *Charred Lullabies*, p. 28 (italics ours).

28. Ibid., p. 27.

29. According to Gananath Obeyesekere, Buddhist missionary activity, as well as the bringing of Indian (Tamil) plantation workers to Sinhala speaking areas, contributed to the development of this identity. For more on Buddhist missionary activity, see Gananath Obeyesekere, "The Vicissitudes of the Sinhala-Buddhist Identity through Time and Change," in *Collective Identities, Nationalisms and Protest in Modern Sri Lanka*, Michael Roberts, ed. (Colombo: Marga Institute, 1979), pp. 279–313. We would like to thank Gananath Obeyesekere for calling our attention in personal communications to the ways in which the presence of Tamil plantation workers among the Sinhalas helped to forge Sinhala-Buddhist identity.

30. In mind are the *Yalpana Carittiram* of S. John (1879) and the *Yalpana Vaipavam* of V. Catacivapillai (1884). For a discussion of these works, see Dagmar-Hellmann Rajanayagam, "Tamils and the Meaning of History," pp. 54–83.

31. Ibid., p. 62.

32. Ibid., p. 54.

33. Ibid., p. 58.

34. Ibid., p. 77.

35. Paraphrased from ibid., pp. 62–70.

36. Martin E. Marty and R. Scott Appleby, *Fundamentalisms Observed*, p. 822.

37. R.L. Stirrat, *Power and Religiosity in a Post-Colonial Setting* (New York: Cambridge University Press, 1992), p. 9.

38. Ibid.

39. Donald K. Swearer, "Fundamentalistic Movements in Theravada Buddhism," in *Fundamentalisms Observed*, p. 642.

40. "The Menace of Fundamentalism," *The Island* (Colombo), 13 August 1994.

41. Stanley Jeyaraja Tambiah, *Buddhism Betrayed?: Religion, Politics, and Violence in Sri Lanka* (Chicago: University of Chicago Press, 1992), p. 105.

42. Ibid.

43. K.M. de Silva, *Managing Ethnic Tension*, p. 58.

44. Rajan Hoole, "Wake Up, Tamils!," *The Sunday Times*, 6 November 1994.

45. E. Valentine Daniel, *Charred Lullabies*, p. 29.

46. Martin E. Marty and R. Scott Appleby, *Fundamentalisms Observed*, p. 835.

47. "The Menace of Fundamentalism," *The Island*, 13 August 1994.

48. See especially Stanley Tambiah, *Buddhism Betrayed?*, and Jonathan Spencer, ed., *Sri Lanka: History and the Roots of Conflict.* For a valuable reading of Sinhala-Buddhist fundamentalism, see Donald Swearer, "Fundamentalist Movements in Theravada Buddhism."

49. Jonathan Z. Smith, "Differential Equations: On Constructing the 'Other,'" Thirteenth Annual University Lecture in Religion, ASU, March 5, 1992, p. 1.

50. Ibid., p. 13.

51. Ibid., p. 14.

52. Ibid., pp. 13–14.

53. Ibid.

54. For more on Otherness and power, see the discussion of the relationship of Buddhists and Christians (and Europeans) below.

55. Jonathan Z. Smith, "Differential Equations," p. 14.

56. Ibid., p. 13.

57. K.M. de Silva, *Managing Ethnic Tensions.*

58. Ibid., p. 117.

59. Ibid.

60. Ibid. See also *Unmooring Identity*, Pradeep Jeganathan and Qadri Ismail, eds. (Colombo: SSA, 1995), 68–71.

61. K.M. de Silva, *Managing Ethnic Tensions*, p. 122.

62. "Veerakesari on Ashraff's letter to Prabakaran," *Daily News* (Colombo), 12 August 1994.

63. A. Jeyaratnam Wilson, "The Colombo Man, the Jaffna Man, and the Batticaloa Man: Regional Identities and the Rise of the Federal Party," in *The Sri Lankan Tamils: Ethnicity and Identity*, p. 135.

64. K.M. de Silva, *Managing Ethnic Tensions*, p. 98.

65. See Chandra Richard de Silva, *Sri Lanka: A History* (Delhi: Vikas Publishing House; reprinted 1992), p. 197. See also K.M. de Silva, *Managing Ethnic Tensions*, pp. 103–5.

66. The following discussion is based on Jonathan Z. Smith, "Differential Equations," pp. 3–9.

67. "Let Us Identify Christian Culture in Terms of Indigenous Culture," *The Island*, 3 September 1994.

68. Ibid.

69. As R.L. Stirrat has pointed out in his book, *Power and Religiosity in a Post-Colonial Setting*, especially pp. 9–11 and 198–203, Catholic identity is constantly negotiated in Sri Lanka.

70. Interview conducted by Bartholomeusz with Father Yohan Devananda in Navala, June 1992.

71. Dagmar-Hellmann Rajanayagam, "Tamils and the Meaning of History," p. 60.

72. Jonathan Z. Smith, "Differential Equations," p. 4.

73. Ibid., p. 6.

74. "Lectures at Battaramulle," *The Buddhist*, 16 January 1891, vol. 3, no. 4, 31.

75. Harjot Oberoi, *The Construction of Religious Identity Boundaries* (Chicago: University of Chicago Press, 1994), p. 34.

76. For more, see Mary Douglas, *Purity and Danger: An Analysis of Concepts of Pollution and Taboo* (London: Ark Paperbacks, 1966). Jonathan Z. Smith makes a similar point in "Differential Equations," p. 1.

77. See Mary Douglas, *Purity and Danger*, pp. 1–6.

78. Gananath Obeyesekere and Richard Gombrich, *Buddhism Transformed* (Princeton: Princeton University Press, 1988).

79. Mary Douglas, *Purity and Danger*, p. 2.

80. "Krishna: Convert of the Highest Order," *The Sunday Times* (Colombo), 6 November 1994. The Tamil's conversion and ordination as a Buddhist monk were also reported in a Sinhala paper: "Nissanka Uyanee Dravida Hamuduruvoo," *Lankadipa* (Colombo), 17 November 1994.

81. Mary Douglas, *Purity and Danger*, p. 5.

82. John D. Rogers, "Post-Orientalism," 10.

83. For more see Chandra R. de Silva, *Sri Lanka: A History*, especially pp. 11–13.

84. Martin E. Marty and R. Scott Appleby, *Fundamentalisms Observed*, p. 14.

85. See, Tessa Bartholomeusz, "Buddhist Woman as Self and Other," in *Daughters of the Soil*, Kumari Jayawardena, ed. (Colombo: Social Scientists' Association, forthcoming).

86. In the opening of a Buddhist school in southern Sri Lanka in 1892, "Mr. F. Perera, made a very impressive speech in the course of which he remarked that though

a Christian by profession, he could safely cooperate with Buddhists in the matter of education, and therefore he wished all success to the Mahinda College" ("Mahinda College, Galle," *The Buddhist*, 11 March 1892, vol. 4, no. 11, 85).

87. "Missionary Methods of Conversion," *The Buddhist*, 15 July 1892, vol. 4, no. 28, 219.

88. "The Ceylon Government and the Buddhists," *The Buddhist*, 9 September 1892, vol. 4, no. 36, 284.

89. "Correspondence," *The Buddhist*, 1889, vol. 1, no. 23, 183. Italics are in the original.

90. Martin E. Marty and R. Scott Appleby, *Fundamentalisms Observed*, p. 831.

91. "The Buddhist," *The Buddhist*, 18 December 1891, vol. 3, no. 52, 412.

92. Among others, see George Bond, *The Buddhist Revival in Sri Lanka: Religious Tradition, Reinterpretation and Response* (Columbia: University of South Carolina Press, 1988) and Tessa Bartholomeusz, *Women under the Bo Tree: Buddhist Nuns in Sri Lanka* (Cambridge: Cambridge University Press, 1994; reprinted 1996).

93. In a representative article from *The Buddhist*, an English language weekly, one writer, a Buddhist Burgher, alleges a history of Buddhism based on the *Mahavamsa* (*The Buddhist*, 19 June 1891, vol 3, no. 26, 206).

94. "Are We Worse Than the Heathen?," *The Buddhist*, 1889, vol. 1, no. 6, 46.

95. "Hon. P. Ramanathan, in his speech, expresses his profound admiration of the good work being carried on by his countrywomen for elevating their sisters. They were doing their work without any help from the Government. . . . The honorable gentleman sat down amidst applause" (*The Buddhist*, 2 February 1894, vol. 6, no. 4, 26). A separate article praises Ramanathan and mentions another Tamil: "and the presence of such gentlemen as Mr. Ramanathan and Mr. Coomaraswamy on that occasion and the promises of donations or prizes held out by them to the school, shows that the working of the school has been heartily appreciated by them" ("Correspondence," *The Buddhist*, 1889, vol. 1, no. 23, 184).

96. In a representative article of the period, one writer urged readers that "We Buddhists should not buy any flowers from Roman Catholics and others, idolaters (sic), who are our sworn enemies, and fill their coffers with our money" (*The Buddhist*, 10 April 1891, vol. 3, no. 16, 128).

97. "Correspondence: To the Editor of The Buddhist," *The Buddhist*, 1889, vol. 1, no. 6, 47. Italics are in the original.

98. Dagmar-Hellmann Rajanayagam, "Tamils and the Meaning of History," p. 71.

99. For more on this idea in Christian fundamentalism, see Nancy Ammerman, "North American Protestant Fundamentalism," p. 47.

100. See Martin E. Marty and R. Scott Appleby, "Introduction," *Fundamentalisms Observed.*

101. See Dharmapala's essay on science in Ananda Guruge, ed., *Anagarika Dharmapala: Return to Righteousness* (Colombo: Department of Cultural Affairs, 1967); also Gananath Obeyesekere, "Buddhism, Nationhood and Cultural Identity," p. 43.

102. Nancy Ammerman, "North American Protestant Fundamentalism," p. 13.

103. Ibid., pp. 32–33.

104. By 1892, Buddhists had established 43 schools in the island within a period of ten years ("Proposed New Building for the Colombo Buddhist School," *The Buddhist*, 15 July 1892, vol. 4, no. 28, 221). For more on the establishment of Buddhist schools in Sri Lanka, see Tessa Bartholomeusz, *Women under the Bo Tree*, pp. 44–67.

105. In the late 1890s, Anagarika Dharmapala and his American coreligionists journeyed around the island in rickshaws drawing large crowds under their tents. According to one account, at one "revival," the tent actually fell, sending scores of people running (*Sarasavisandaresa*, 7 July 1897).

106. See, among other works, S. Karunaratne, *Olcott's Contribution to the Buddhist Renaissance* (abridged version of Olcott's diary, *Old Diary Leaves*) (Colombo: Ministry of Cultural Affairs, N.D.); Gananath Obeyesekere, "Sinhalese-Buddhist Identity in Ceylon," in *Ethnic Identity: Cultural Continuities and Change*, George de Vos and Lola Romanucci-Ross, eds. (Palo Alto: Mayfield Publishing Company, 1975); and Stephen Prothero, *The White Buddhist* (Bloomington: Indiana University Press, 1996).

107. "Mahinda College, Galle," *The Buddhist*, 11 March 1892, vol. 4, no. 11, 84.

108. Martin E. Marty and R. Scott Appleby, *Fundamentalisms Observed*, p. 825.

109. The Buddhist Defense Committee was established in the late 1880s after the Kotahena riots; Buddhist printing presses continued to be established well into the twentieth century. Among them, one of the largest, the Kandy Buddhist Press, was established in 1892 ("Kandy T.S.," *The Buddhist*, 9 December 1892, vol. 4, no. 49, 387).

110. See Nancy Ammerman, "North American Protestant Fundamentalism," pp. 32–33, 41, 42–43, 50.

111. "The Quarter-Mile Clause," *The Buddhist*, 9 December 1892, vol. 4, no. 49, 387.

112. Ibid.

113. Quoted in "Buddhist-Christian Relations," *The Island*, 20 August 1994.

114. For more on the invention of tradition, see Michael Carrithers, *The Forest Monks of Sri Lanka: An Anthropological and Historical Study* (Delhi: Oxford University Press, 1983).

115. In "The Hindu Organ," the editor of *The Buddhist* lauds Tamils for their new publication: "We rejoice to welcome a new contemporary in *The Hindu Organ* of Jaffna. It is a bi-weekly paper, published partly in English and partly in Tamil, and, as its name denotes, it is established to give a channel for the expression of the opinion and feelings of the Hindu natives of this Island, which have hitherto been quite unrepresented in the English papers of Ceylon" (11 October 1889, vol. 1, no. 43, 343).

116. Dharmapala even wrote his diaries in English. They are housed in the Maha Bodhi Society, Maligakanda Road, Maradana, Colombo.

117. See, among other writings, Stanley J. Tambiah, *Buddhism Betrayed?*; K.M. de Silva and Howard Wriggins, *J.R. Jayewardene of Sri Lanka: A Political Biography* (Honolulu: University of Hawaii Press, 1994); David Little, *Sri Lanka: The Invention of Enmity* (Washington, D.C.: The United States Institute of Peace Press, 1994); and K.M. de Silva, "Coming Full Circle: The Politics of Language in Sri Lanka, 1943–1996," *Ethnic Studies Report*, vol. xiv, no. 1 (January 1996): 11–49.

118. Ibid., for a variety of points of view.

119. Gamini Jayasuriya recently left the UNP of which he had served previously as General Secretary and Cabinet Member.

120. Gamini Jayasuriya, "The North-East Question and the Sinhala Race," *The Sunday Times* (Colombo), 7 August 1994.

121. Martin E. Marty and R. Scott Appleby, *Fundamentalisms Observed*, p. 823.

122. "Gamini Jayasuriya Appeals to Maha Sangha," *Sunday Observer*, 7 August 1994.

123. The United National Party, which assumed power in 1977, was defeated in the 1994 elections.

124. The MEP has moved progressively toward Sinhala-Buddhist nationalism since its inception.

125. This new party was headed by Dr. Harishchandra Wijetunga and suffered a smashing defeat in the 1994 elections.

126. Amaradasa Fernando, "Last Chance for Peace," *Sunday Observer* 11 September 1994.

127. Ibid.

128. "Sinhala Nationalism in Decline," *Pravada*, July/August 1994, vol. 3, no. 5, 3.

129. Ibid.

130. "Chauvinism and the General Election," *The Island*, 21 September 1994.

131. For example, the theme of the first Open Forum of the Lalith Athulathmudali Foundation was "Toward a Common Sri Lankan Identity" (*Daily News*, 7 October 1994). Common identity is the subject also of "The Disunity in This Land" (*The Island*, 20 October 1994).

132. Martin E. Marty and R. Scott Appleby, *Fundamentalisms Observed*, p. 824.

Chapter 2

Conflicts of Identity and Interpretation in Buddhism: The Clash between the Sarvodaya Shramadana Movement and the Government of President Premadasa

George D. Bond

Introduction

Although the Buddhist revival is often discussed as if it were a single, monolithic movement, this period of ferment in Sri Lankan Buddhism actually produced a spectrum of reinterpretations of Buddhism. These reinterpretations had in common that they all sought to represent Buddhism for the modern age, but they differed in their perceptions of both the challenges of the modern age and the ways that Buddhism should be reinterpreted to meet them.[1]

Over time, however, and with the intensification of the ethnic conflict—which certain reinterpretations of Buddhism helped to foster—the one interpretation that became dominant was the conservative and nationalist viewpoint. This chauvinist, Buddhist fundamentalism is now frequently regarded as the stereotypical viewpoint of the Buddhist revival. This conservative interpretation has driven all the other, more liberal interpretations, to the margins. Thus, observers such as S.J. Tambiah can say that in Sri Lanka today, Buddhism has betrayed its heritage by assuming a "militant, populist, fetishized form . . . emptied of much of its normative and humane ethic" and functioning primarily as a part of a "homogenizing national identity" which sanctions and instigates "spurts of violence."[2]

Some of the other reinterpretations that arose during the Buddhist revival, however, still exist in Sri Lanka as minority voices seeking to proclaim that Buddhism has not betrayed its heritage. The clash that occurred between the government of Sri Lanka led by President Premadasa and the Sarvodaya Shramadana Movement from 1989 to 1993 dramatized the difference between the dominant Sinhala-Buddhist fundamentalism and one of these minority voices. The reasons behind the clash were doubtless complex and included factors such as Premadasa's personal anger at A.T. Ariyaratne, the leader of the Sarvodaya movement, for not supporting his campaign for president as well as Premadasa'a political fears about Ariyaratne's popularity among the rural masses.

What was significant about the clash, however, for our purposes, is that the debate between the two sides was argued on Buddhist grounds and demonstrated the differences between these two reinterpretations of Buddhism: the political Buddhist fundamentalism of the government and the socially engaged Buddhism of Sarvodaya. In opposing Ariyaratne, President Premadasa argued from his fundamentalist Buddhist stance, challenging Ariyaratne's authenticity as a Buddhist leader and charging that he constituted a threat to the purity and the stability of the Buddhist nation. Premadasa's government and the government media portrayed the Sarvodaya movement as a dangerous Other that had links with both the Tamils and the Christians. Ariyaratne and Sarvodaya responded to these attacks by calling the government's own interpretation of Buddhism into question. During this clash, each side charged the other with being anti-Buddhist and *adharmic*. Thus, the rhetoric of the exchanges and the actions that each side took during the clash brought their two contrasting interpretations of Buddhism clearly into focus. In this chapter, I examine these two reinterpretations of Buddhism and Buddhist identity that clashed in the confrontation between President Premadasa and the Sarvodaya movement.

The Sarvodaya Movement

The Sarvodaya Shramadana Movement began in the late 1950s as a lay Buddhist association that worked to alleviate poverty in the rural villages of Sri Lanka. It had its genesis in a series of work camps organized by the faculty and students of Nalanda College, Colombo. A.T. Ariyaratne, then a teacher at Nalanda College, led these work camps as a way for the urban youth to come in contact with and help their village countrymen. Thus, in its origins Sarvodaya is related to Sinhala-Buddhist fundamentalism because Sarvodaya began as a movement within a key Buddhist college. As Bartholomeusz and de Silva have discussed in the Introduction to this volume,

Buddhist schools played a crucial role in establishing a Buddhist identity during the revival. Sarvodaya's interest, however, came to be not Buddhist identity, but Buddhist values and their application to society in the development process.

Another key point of contrast between Sarvodaya and the dominant form of Sinhala-Buddhist fundamentalism has to do with their perceptions of the Other that their interpretations of Buddhism were intended to oppose. The Sinhala-Buddhist fundamentalist reinterpretation was employed to oppose Western domination from without and the domination of other ethnic groups from within. In this case, as in others, "politics fused with religion and ethnic ideology to create a platform of ethnic and religious nationalism."[3] Sarvodaya's reinterpretation of Buddhism, however, opposed not an ethnic or national Other but an economic and cultural Other—the materialist system of the West that threatened to destroy Sri Lankan village society and values. Sarvodaya's leaders drew upon Buddhist philosophy and Sri Lankan culture to frame an alternative development strategy. Ariyaratne has said that the "village awakening programme of Sarvodaya" represents an effort "to transform the Buddhist doctrines into a developmental process."[4] Drawing on Buddhist thought as well as Gandhian ideas, Sarvodaya emphasized values such as truth, nonviolence and self-denial.

At the beginning and for about a decade, Sarvodaya developed as a work camp movement, reviving what it regarded as an ancient practice called *shramadana* or the "giving of labor to assist others." The idea of *shramadana* attracted many people to the movement; work camps to assist the poorest of the poor were held in all parts of the island. The early motto of Sarvodaya was "Let us go from village to village to do service." While performing this social service, Ariyaratne and the other leaders of this early phase of Sarvodaya came to believe that development had to occur at the grassroots level and could not be imposed from the top by government dictate. By describing the central thrust of the kind of development that Sarvodaya sought as "awakening," the leaders clarified the connections between their approach and Buddhism. Sarvodaya's aim, however, was not to promote institutional Buddhism but to bring about a process that it described as "the awakening of all." One of Sarvodaya's earliest and most consistently held teachings declares that awakening is an integrated process involving six intertwined elements: the spiritual, the moral, the cultural, the social, the political, and the economic. This process begins with the individual and radiates outward through the village, the nation and the world. This conception of development reveals the way that Sarvodaya's approach explicitly relies on *dharmic* notions such as *paticca samuppada* or the interrelatedness and interconnectedness of all things.

Sarvodaya's understanding of an integrated development process entailed a critique of Western, materialistic development theories. According to Ariyaratne, true wealth is spiritual and existential. Development should not be measured by affluence and production, but by whether it creates a way of life that allows people to fulfil their spiritual, intellectual, and social potentials. From this early period, Ariyaratne opposed the kind of materialistic development schemes that the government and international agencies had attempted in Sri Lanka. He said, "In production-centered societies the total perspective of human personality and sustainable relationships between humans and nature is lost sight of. . . . The higher ideals of human personality and social values are disregarded."[5] What Sarvodaya sought to facilitate was an idealistic vision of a "no affluence, no poverty" society, where the human and spiritual virtues were allowed to flourish. Pursuing this vision of development and Buddhist values, Sarvodaya grew from a small work camp movement to become a large nongovernmental organization with volunteers and centers in the rural areas all over the island.

Occasionally, in arguing for social change and development, Ariyaratne has referred to ancient Sri Lanka as a place where "in the time of the Sinhalese kings, the people were able to realise the goal of an Island of Righteousness (*dhammadipa*) and a granary, following the path of the Buddha and Asoka. Within that Island of Righteousness and that granary every person had the privilege of living as equals, protecting their language, religion and culture."[6] The language that he uses here causes one to ask whether Sarvodaya is advocating the idea of a Sinhala-Buddhist identity since its statements reflect strongly the rhetoric of identity from the earlier phases of the Buddhist revival when Dharmapala and others used images drawn from the *Mahavamsa* to build up a sense of Sinhala-Buddhist identity.

Has Sarvodaya sought to create a similar sense of Buddhist identity? The short answer is no. Sarvodaya has never been interested in creating or strengthening a Buddhist identity. Sarvodaya employs these phrases for a quite different purpose. The goal of the Buddhist revivalists, such as Dharmapala, was to establish a Buddhist and Sinhala identity, which meant distinguishing the Sinhala Buddhists from the Other. Sarvodaya's goal in using these references to ancient Sri Lanka and the *dhammadipa* is not to define an identity that stands over against an Other, but rather to emphasize the former existence and future possibility of a civilization based on Buddhist values.

That Sarvodaya is emphasizing values over identity in their use of this language, can be seen by noting the way that it employs the three key terms from the Buddhist revival: the land, the race, and the religion. Sarvodaya's references to the land are intended to lift up an image of the ancient, ideal civilization. Ariyaratne writes that people should not forget that "a system capable of organizing human society free from the exploitation of man by man had been discovered and implemented by our forefathers."[7] Ariyaratne employs this *Mahavamsa* image of the ancient civilization as a model to give meaning and legitimacy to his vision of a Sarvodaya society based on Buddhist values. He says that the colonial and even the postcolonial experiences have ingrained in the people's minds the idea that Western civilization with its capitalist economy represents the only model of success. By referring to the glories of Sri Lanka's ancient civilizations, whose magnificent ruins can still be seen today, Ariyaratne hopes to persuade the people that there are other, more indigenous models of a successful civilization. Sarvodaya is not interested in identity building, but in consciousness raising, a kind of postcolonial liberation that requires opposing materialism in favor of a system based on spiritual and populist values.

When asked if he thinks that the Tamils might be put off by these references to the ancient cities and this use of apparently Sinhala-Buddhist language such as "*dhammadipa,*" Ariyaratne replies that he hopes that they see not the rhetorical language but the meaning behind it. He translates the term *dhammadipa* to stand for three of the goals of a Sarvodaya society: spiritual, cultural, and moral development. He says that the term "Granary of the East" signifies the other three goals of Sarvodaya: social, economic, and political development.[8] This hope that the Tamils will understand his construction of the meaning of *dhammadipa* may be somewhat naive on Ariyaratne's part, yet his movement has worked extensively with the Tamils and other ethnic groups.[9]

Sarvodaya teaches that this ideal civilization can be attained by all people, it in no way restricts the vision to the Sinhala race. Sarvodaya universalizes both the image of the people who created the original civilization in ancient Sri Lanka and the vision of the people who can create and enjoy the Sarvodaya society. The ancient civilization symbolizes for Ariyaratne the possibility of a Sarvodaya society "in which a person is not regarded as high or low on account of his birth and which accepts the humanity of all."[10]

Ariyaratne has written that the ethnic problems in the country began when people started viewing the Sinhalas and the Tamils as separate "races" and "nations" rather than simply communities with different languages. Sarvodaya is not interested in a Sinhala-Buddhist identity, but in a Sri Lankan identity, or even a global identity.

Sarvodaya also universalizes the idea behind the term "religion" in this triad. Sarvodaya has refused to label itself as a Buddhist movement and points proudly to its Gandhian roots. Although Ariyaratne acknowledges that much of Sarvodaya's philosophy derives from Buddhism, he regards these truths of the *dharma* to be spiritual truths that are common to all religions. Spiritual qualities such as truth, nonviolence, and compassion, he says, do not require labels such as Buddhist or Christian. Ariyaratne observes that, "truth cannot be institutionalised."[11] This viewpoint again reflects a kind of idealistic naivety on the part of Ariyaratne and the other leaders of Sarvodaya. It might also be seen as the revival, or survival, of a Victorian notion of a universal spirituality underlying all the great religions.

This notion has largely been rejected by more recent religious studies but can be seen to live on in Sri Lanka and other parts of South Asia. The practical effect of these ideas was that the Sarvodaya movement sought to work in all areas of the country and accepted members from any and all religions.

Sarvodaya and the Government of Sri Lanka

Since the election of SWRD Bandaranaike in 1956, the governments of Sri Lanka have regarded themselves as the protectors of Buddhism. They have risen to power by appealing to the Buddhist majority in the country, and have pledged to support the interests of both the Buddhist religion and the Sinhala Buddhist people. Sarvodaya coexisted with these governments because, first, it assumed that since it derived its own philosophy of development from Buddhism it should have something in common with them, and, second, it hoped that it could influence the government to follow some of the Sarvodaya development goals. That these assumptions entailed risks became increasingly apparent during the reign of the UNP (United National Party) government which began with President J.R. Jayewardene and continued under President R. Premadasa. As time went on it became clear that the government's priorities and its understanding of Buddhism ran counter to Sarvodaya's interpretation and use of Buddhist values.

J.R. Jayewardene and the UNP came to power in 1977 promising to establish a *dharmistha* society, a society based on the principles of the Buddha's *dhamma.* Jayewardene said, "The U.N.P. government aims at building a new society on the foundation of the principles of Buddha *dhamma.* We have a duty to protect the Buddha Sasana [religion] and to pledge that every possible action will be taken to develop it."[12] The emphasis in his government, however, was more on identity than values, more on protecting the current institution of Buddhism than on enacting the principles of its *dhamma.* He believed that the Buddhist heritage provided a mandate for the government to rule and protect the land, the race and the Buddhist establishment.

Although he frequently invoked the ideal of the Emperor Asoka, Jayewardene seldom acknowledged that the *dhamma* had implications for the social and economic policy-making of his government. Both the UNP and Jayewardene were committed to fostering a capitalist, free market economy that would produce prosperity for the country. Jayewardene saw no conflict between these goals and Buddhism because he understood Buddhism to be primarily a religion of personal morality and individual responsibility.[13] Jayewardene followed this path and the Sinhala Buddhists who elected him were impressed with his elaborate displays of merit-making such as sponsoring the lighting of 84,000 oil lamps at the Buddhist shrines.[14] Although Jayewardene participated in these public affirmations of Buddhism, he refused to enact policies and laws that would enforce Buddhist morality. Even when Buddhists appealed to the government to ban the slaughter of animals or the production and sale of liquor, Jayewardene refused to support such legislation. To him, Buddhism was a personal matter and should be kept separate from government policy formation, even in a *dharmistha* state.

One factor that probably helped determine Jayewardene's views on these matters stemmed from his background as a member of the English-educated elite that inherited power from the British. His generation of leaders had been trained to believe that the achievement of modernization and progress in both society and government required one to devalue the role of religion. Traditional societies were characterized, so this theory held, by religion's having an integral role. Therefore, to build a modern society, political leaders had to diminish the pervasive influence of religion and move toward secularization. Applying this kind of modernization theory while maintaining that one was establishing a *dharmistha* state might seem difficult, but Jayewardene's view that religion was only a matter of personal responsibility enabled him to keep the political and religious realms separate in much the same way that conservative politicians have in the West.

Jayewardene's successor, R. Premadasa, also came to power as a strong supporter of Buddhism and even had worked closely with Sarvodaya and Ariyaratne on several major projects. In many ways Premadasa's interpretation of Buddhism was much more dangerous—for the country and for Sarvodaya—than that of Jayewardene. A primary reason for this danger was that Premadasa did not share the commitment that Jayewardene and the previous leaders since independence had had to maintaining the government's secular status. Premadasa explicitly said that he did not "believe in the policy that the administration of the government and the religious or the spiritual well-being of the people are separate things and should be divorced from one another. If King Dharmasoka was able to infuse Dhamma and spiritualism into the administrative set up, why cannot we achieve it? We can certainly pursue such a policy."[15]

Premadasa's reference to King Asoka in this statement provides a key insight into the way that he seems to have understood his role as president and his relation to Buddhism. Much more explicitly than his predecessors, Premadasa sought to link his role as head of state with that of the ancient and ideal Buddhist kings such as Asoka. According to the chronicles of Sri Lanka, these ideal kings exercised two important and related functions: they were the supreme devotees and patrons of Buddhism, and they were the active defenders of Buddhism, even using violence when necessary to protect the *dhamma*.

That Premadasa aspired to be regarded after the image of this kind of ideal Buddhist king can be seen by his personally holding the portfolios of both the Ministry of Buddha Sasana and the Ministry of Defense. He identified himself as both the spiritual and the military leader of the people; and he understood both of these roles to be involved with the government's duty to support Buddhism.[16]

To fulfill the role of the spiritual leader of the nation, Premadasa established a separate government agency for the support and promotion of Buddhism, the Ministry of Buddha Sasana. When he inaugurated this ministry in 1990, the president convened a conference of the *sangha* and Buddhist leaders. On that occasion, Premadasa explicitly compared the conference and the establishment of the Ministry of Buddha Sasana to the actions of ancient Buddhist kings such as Asoka who convened Buddhist councils to purify and support Buddhism. The inaugural address for the Ministry of Buddha Sasana also served as the occasion for Premadasa to declare that he would follow Asoka in carrying out a campaign of *dharmavijaya*, or conquest by *dharma* (*dhamma*).

Throughout Premadasa's time in office, the country was barraged with examples of the president's patronage of Buddhism. The government controlled press and media daily carried stories about the president's appearances at various Buddhist ceremonies and his gifts to large and small Buddhist temples. He sponsored and participated in countless Bodhi pujas and almsgivings. He presented temples with golden Buddha statues and renovated ancient Buddhist shrines. To be sure, the president also supported the other religions of the country, but this too helped him to play the role of a modern day Asoka, who, according to the chronicles, patronized all the religions in his realm.

Although Premadasa was considerably more energetic than Jayewardene in his participation in and support of Buddhism, the nature of his participation reveals that he understood Buddhism in much the same way as his predecessor had. For both, Buddhism was a religion of individual morality and merit-making. By sponsoring enormous alms-giving ceremonies such as one held in Kandy for three thousand handicapped persons, Premadasa demonstrated to the public how great was the merit that he was accumulating. To show his adherence to Buddhist morality, he proudly declared that he followed a strict Buddhist lifestyle that prohibited excesses such as the use of tobacco or alcohol.

Premadasa's zealous support of the rituals and institutions of Buddhism related directly to the other aspect of the royal identity that he desired: the protection and defense of Buddhism. He seems to have been drawn to the image of Asoka as a righteous king who had been involved with violence and continued to exercise force to protect the *dharma*. This image of Asoka seems to have become especially attractive to Premadasa after the bloody battles with the JVP (Janatha Vimukti Peramuna) during and after 1989. As van der Horst observed, "Premadasa's Asokan ideology with its particular interpretation of Cakkavatti kingship following the procedure of peace after conquest provides a new framework which—being well-embedded in the cultural habitus—Premadasa hopes will render the past acceptable."[17] However, the violent force with which Premadasa's army and secret police smashed this insurgency movement caused many people to regard Premadasa as a tyrant rather than as the ideal Buddhist that his ritual performances proclaimed him to be.

A third factor that figured in Premadasa's Buddhist identity, was his portraying himself as a Buddhist leader who helped the poor—who, incidentally, had voted for him in large numbers. To be sure, Premadasa did initiate social welfare projects that seemed to embody Buddhist values. Some of these projects arose from his prior cooperation with Sarvodaya when he was prime minister under President Jayewardene. For example, the village development movement, Gamudawa, began during Jayewardene's government and was patterned after Sarvodaya's *gramodaya* or "village uplift" projects. Despite these highly touted social projects, however, it is significant that Premadasa did not actually base his economic or social policies on Buddhist principles. Perhaps even more than Jayewardene, Premadasa pursued the policies of an open-market economy. He saw no problem in professing simultaneously the virtues of Buddhism and capitalism. There was no conflict because Buddhism was to him a matter of individual morality and ritual practice. Even when he borrowed ideas for rural development projects from Sarvodaya, Premadasa largely omitted the explicitly Buddhist rationale. The government sponsored *shramadanas* that he promoted, for example, lacked the spiritual focus that was central to those held by Sarvodaya.

In the end, under Premadasa's regime the dominant interpretation of Buddhism came to resemble what Tambiah has termed "political Buddhism."[18] It was this chauvinistic, violent, political Buddhism that Premadasa employed as a rationale for his attacks on the Sarvodaya movement.

The Government's Attack on Sarvodaya

The clash between Premadasa's government and the Sarvodaya movement revealed the fundamental differences between the government's political Buddhism and the engaged Buddhism of Sarvodaya. This clash represents an extreme example of the difficulties that engaged Buddhism can encounter in coexisting with a system dominated by power politics and a market economy. Johan Galtung has pointed out that the state never likes to have rivals. He observed that "the state originally was the successor to the emperor and the emperor was the successor to God, and both God and the emperor were very jealous of all rivals."[19] This truth seems to have applied particularly well to President Premadasa who understood his identity to be the chief representative of both the religion and the state. Premadasa recognized that Ariyaratne posed a threat both to his spiritual leadership and to his political leadership, especially among the poor people of the villages who had been a major factor in electing him. Sensing this threat to his identity and his leadership and regarding himself as the rightful protector of the *dhamma*, Premadasa attacked Sarvodaya in general and Ariyaratne in particular. Premadasa's campaign of attacks invoked his own claim to be the protector of Buddhism. He charged that Ariyaratne and his movement were polluting the religion and endangering the Buddhist nation.

One of the most visible and forceful methods of attack used by the government was a well-planned media campaign that directly targeted the sources of Ariyaratne's and Sarvodaya's charisma and popularity, their commitment to *dharmic* values and their renunciation of materialism and wealth. Representing the viewpoint of political Buddhism, the government-controlled media used many different approaches to attempt to repudiate Ariyaratne's image as a Buddhist reformer who followed Gandhi, eschewing material wealth and regarding the spiritual truths of the *dhamma* as the only real wealth. Front-page stories in the government newspapers portrayed Ariyaratne as a false guru who used the *dhamma* only to enrich himself. One story compared Ariyaratne to another Sri Lankan man who had fraudulently posed as a guru in England. The story said both Ariyaratne and the false guru had "used the most sacred tenets of Eastern spirituality to pile up fortunes."[20] Another series of stories ran under a banner headline proclaiming that "Sarvodaya Sells Lankan Children Abroad."[21] The gist of this series of stories had been taken from an article that had appeared in a West German tabloid magazine some seven years earlier, and even that tabloid had eventually conceded that Sarvodaya actually was innocent of such charges. Nevertheless, the government press dredged up this charge to blacken Sarvodaya's reputation. Even though Ariyaratne issued an immediate denial and rebuttal, the accusation continued to appear in the press in various forms for the next few years. In its attempts to stigmatize Ariyaratne and Sarvodaya as Other and as threats to the national interest, some government press stories also charged Sarvodaya with misusing development funds to supply arms to the LTTE (Liberation Tigers of Tamil Eelam), the separatist Tamil force. One paper combined some of these themes by labeling Dr. Ariyaratne the "Maharishi from Moratuwa" and saying that "spiritual leaders of the caliber of Buddha and Christ, without setting up trust funds in their names" or funneling funds to aggressors have shown the way to change humanity.[22]

In addition to the media campaign, the government attempted to shut down the Sarvodaya movement by limiting its freedom and ability to function in the country. Key government ministries refused to assist Sarvodaya in any way, citing bureaucratic regulations that had not been a barrier previously. For example, the national radio and television stations ceased covering Sarvodaya events and canceled Ariyaratne's weekly educational radio program. The immigration department made it difficult for anyone connected with Sarvodaya to enter or leave the country. Other government departments such as the Criminal Investigation Department (CID), the Labor Department, the Bribery Commission, the Environmental Authority, and the Income Tax Department, enforced new or seldom used rules and summoned Sarvodaya officials for questioning. The CID, in particular, made countless visits to Sarvodaya centers and took many people into its offices for interrogation. These questioning sessions frequently went on for hours; in the worst case, two women were detained under extremely inhumane conditions for two months. In addition, the leaders of Sarvodaya received several death threats from individuals who came to their doors. Tightening the screws financially, the government and the Central Bank cancelled many of Sarvodaya's loans and compelled some foreign agencies to cancel their funding of Sarvodaya's projects. When asked by Sarvodaya workers to explain why they were carrying out these actions, government officials replied that they were doing these things on "orders from above."[23]

The capstone to the government's campaign of attacks on Sarvodaya was put in place when Premadasa appointed a Presidential Commission of Inquiry (of nongovernmental organizations). This commission was set up, at least in theory, to investigate wrongdoing by all NGOs in the country, but in practice its major function was to attack the Sarvodaya movement and Ariyaratne. Seeing it as a way to prove their innocence, the Sarvodaya leaders at first welcomed this commission. However, they soon recognized that the commissioners were also acting "under orders from above" and would be unable to give Sarvodaya a fair hearing. Faced with this direct threat and witnessing the suffering of the country under Premadasa's regime, Ariyaratne spoke out against the government and called for "nonviolent direct action within the law and nonpartisan people's politics." Ariyaratne charged that Premadasa had lost his *dharmic* mandate to serve as a Buddhist leader.

The most direct confrontation between Sarvodaya's engaged Buddhist approach and the government's political Buddhism occurred at Kandalama, a village near the ancient Buddhist cave temple at Dambulla. This confrontation demonstrated the way that the government sought to cast Sarvodaya as an Other as well as the ways that Sarvodaya fought back against the government also on Buddhist grounds. The confrontation concerned a proposal by a corporation to build a massive, four story, luxury hotel at Kandalama. This proposal had been approved by the government in the interest of increasing tourism. Having seen the disastrous impact that such tourist developments had on previously tranquil village areas such as Hikkaduwa, the local village population led by the Mahanayaka of the Dambulla temple, Venerable Inamaluwe Sumangala, appealed to the government to cancel the plans for the hotel. The monk and his followers argued that such a large hotel would adversely affect the cultural and moral environment of the community, disrupt the ecological balance of the semiwilderness area, pollute the water supply, and infringe on the sanctity of the ancient, sacred Buddhist shrine. Ven. Sumangala, who was also the chair of Sarvodaya's council of elders, appealed to Sarvodaya to assist him in this cause. Ven. Sumangala and Dr. Ariyaratne decided to hold a *satyagraha* or peaceful demonstration at Dambulla to protest this development project. A Catholic group, led by Father Oswald Firth, also joined the protest movement because they had recently fought the government over a similar development project in a Christian area at Iranawila, on the west coast of Sri Lanka. Therefore, on July 12, 1992, thousands of Sri Lankans, Buddhists, and Christians, many of them Sarvodaya followers, assembled at the Dambulla Raja Maha Vihara and peacefully demonstrated their opposition to the government's plans to build the tourist hotel. Buddhist monks and Catholic priests spoke against the hotel and against the government and then led the people in peaceful meditation.

The after effects of the demonstration at Kandalama were quite interesting, with both the government and Sarvodaya jockeying to be seen as the true representative of Buddhism. Premadasa's government, which had identified itself as the savior of the *dhamma* and the *sasana*, found itself after the *satyagraha* in the position of opposing the Ven. Sumangala and all his Buddhist followers who protested that a sacred Buddhist area would be violated by the hotel complex. Even worse, the government appeared to be opposing the Buddhists on this issue even though it had given in to the Catholics who had made a similar protest about a development project in their area. Sarvodaya and its allies had clearly put the government on the defensive, it seemed. Premadasa tried staging his own progovernment demonstration at Dambulla to explain how the hotel would benefit the people, but it was poorly attended and appeared clearly to be a defensive gesture. But then someone in the government discovered a photo that had been taken at Sarvodaya's *satyagraha* showing some Catholic nuns holding aloft a large cross in front of the Dambulla Buddhist cave temple. The government used this picture to regain the high ground as the defender of Buddhism. Posters displaying this photo appeared suddenly all over the country. The posters also carried the statement, "Sarvodaya businessman (*mudalali*) Ariyaratne and the rogue priest Sumangala took the cross to Dambulla." The government papers then carried the picture along with editorials denouncing this as an affront to Buddhism and proclaiming that "the organisers had desecrated a Buddhist sacred area and *polluted* a Buddhist environment by allowing other religionists to display a cross in the precincts of the Dambulla Raja Maha Vihara."[24] Other stories charged that Sarvodaya and the other leaders had been attempting to create ethnic strife by displaying Christian symbols in a Buddhist temple. The government papers cited monks who took the government's side. One Mahanayaka asked, "Will the Buddhist clergy ever be allowed to display the Buddhist flag and perform *satyagraha* in the Vatican?" Another Mahanayaka from Anuradhapura declared that the President "who created a separate Ministry for Buddha Sasana is doing a great service for the country. It is wrong to conduct such agitations when the president is making a genuine effort to develop all places of religious worship."[25] The government stories did not bother to explain that the Christians had gotten permission from the Buddhist leaders to carry the cross in the procession, and they did not cite the many monks and leaders of the *sangha* who approved of the *satyagraha*.

This incident can be seen to have exemplified some of the central issues in the conflict between Sarvodaya and the government of President Premadasa. It raised the question of who speaks for Buddhism, the government which holds the Ministry of Buddha Sasana and claims a *dharmic* mandate, or Sarvodaya and its followers. Implicit also were questions about Buddhism and economics: Could the free market development plans of a nominally Buddhist government be considered Buddhist economics, or did Sarvodaya's sustainable development ideas and proenvironment stance have a greater claim to be seen as Buddhist economics? Finally, Kandalama brought into clearer focus the question of the relation of religion and politics. The government attacked Ariyaratne and Ven. Sumangala for exploiting this issue for political purposes. Premadasa charged that Ariyaratne had abandoned his nonpartisan stance as the head of Sarvodaya by becoming involved in partisan politics. An editorial in a government-controlled newspaper chided, "Dr. Ariyaratne is no Gandhi. Nor is he a religious leader. He is at his best when he spins a story linked to a Buddhist theory to collect donations from gullible donors abroad. But on this occasion he and his followers who rushed to give a religious garb to a political protest have failed."[26] The government was willing to portray Sarvodaya as an Other of any stripe; previous newspaper articles had linked him to the Tamils and now this incident linked him to the Christians. Ariyaratne responded by arguing that a government that identifies itself with Buddhism and claims to be acting in the name of the *dhamma* should enforce a social and an environmental ethic rather than building luxury hotels that benefit only rich investors and foreign tourists.

Conclusion

What was the outcome and the significance of this clash of visions between Sarvodaya and the government of President Premadasa? The outcome might have been different had not President Premadasa met an untimely death at the hands of an assassin on May 1, 1993. It seems certain that Premadasa would have continued to pursue Sarvodaya and might have succeeded in his attempt to destroy the organization and its leadership. As it happened, however, the interim government that assumed power when the president died acted immediately to stop the persecution of Sarvodaya and to lift all restrictions against them. Having passed through a kind of political ordeal of fire, Sarvodaya emerged with renewed prestige in some quarters of Sri Lanka and the world. To be sure, however, the four and a half years of vilification by the government press and media damaged Sarvodaya's reputation in ways that will take time to repair fully. Sarvodaya could also still encounter opposition from future governments that advocate the kind of political Buddhism that Premadasa perfected. It is not likely that political Buddhism, which has been such a powerful force in Sri Lanka, has breathed its last.

The events that occurred, however, were significant in that they provided a clear contrast between these two contemporary reinterpretations of Buddhism: political Buddhism and the socially engaged Buddhism of Sarvodaya. If we use the term "Buddhist fundamentalism" to refer to the movements that emerged from the Buddhist revival, then both of these reinterpretations might be seen as variations of Buddhist fundamentalism, albeit variations manifesting quite different "family resemblances."[27] Political Buddhism focuses on its Buddhist identity, and from its Buddhist identity derives a charter to rule and protect the land, the race, and the religion. This Buddhist identity, however, is not understood to require the government to follow or enact Buddhist values. Thus, recent governments in Sri Lanka that proclaimed their Buddhist identity have, nevertheless, carried out military campaigns and pursued economic policies that have greatly widened the gap between the rich and the poor. Sarvodaya's socially engaged Buddhism, on the other hand, emphasizes Buddhist values over Buddhist identity. Sarvodaya's reinterpretation of Buddhism entails drawing on Buddhist philosophy and values to construct an integrated development process in which the political, economic, and social elements are coordinated with the spiritual, moral, and cultural values.

Ariyaratne says that Sarvodaya aims at both individual as well as national "awakening"; Sarvodaya's idea of a *dhammadipa* would mean creating a government whose policies on all levels conform with the *dhamma*. For Premadasa's government, on the other hand, *dhammadipa* seems to have signified only a cosmic or *karmic* heritage that had to be kept in balance through ritual performances and the production of merit. The differences between these two ideas of Buddhist government were manifest in the debate during the clash. Premadasa attacked Sarvodaya as an enemy of the nation for siding with the Tamils in its peace marches and for siding with the Christians in the demonstration at Kandalama.

Ariyaratne responded that by using violence against the people and by following economic and environmental policies that created structural violence the government had lost its "dharmic and moral legitimacy to rule this country."[28] Ariyaratne contended that the law of *dhamma* and the people's law were higher than the law of the state, so that when the law of the state violates the two higher forms of law the people have a responsibility to oppose the government. While the government was attacking him, Ariyaratne continued to speak out in Sarvodaya meetings throughout the country where he charged that the government had violated the *dharmic* law and generated violence in at least six areas.[29] When the government accused Ariyaratne of vitiating his claim to be a religious leader by becoming involved in political issues such as the debate over the tourist hotel at Kandalama or the government's conduct of the war, Ariyaratne responded that "what the government considers politics, I consider the welfare of the people and the protection of the *dhamma*."[30]

Thus, if political Buddhism and Sarvodaya's socially-engaged Buddhism represent variations of Buddhist fundamentalism, their interpretations reveal contrasting visions of the meaning of Buddhism for the contemporary world. Sarvodaya's critics have charged that the movement has had problems in actualizing its vision of Buddhist development, but that is a topic for another study and does not detract from the significance of Sarvodaya's vision. While political Buddhism has, as Tambiah has observed, invoked a Buddhism devoid of its "normative and humane ethic," Sarvodaya has advocated a Buddhist ethic as a comprehensive approach to such areas as politics, economics, and social organization. In this sense, Sarvodaya's interpretation of Buddhism has served a prophetic role in challenging the views and policies of the dominant, conservative political Buddhism. Sarvodaya's vision of socially engaged Buddhism and its contrast with a political Buddhism that follows Western economic and political models might be summarized with the following quote from Sulak Sivaraksa:

> Economists measure development in terms of increasing currency and material items, fostering greed. Politicians see development in terms of increased power, fostering hatred. Both measure the results strictly in terms of quantity, fostering delusion. From the Buddhist point of view, development must aim at the reduction of these three poisons, not their increase. We must develop our spirit.[31]

Notes

1. I have traced some of these different interpretations in my book, *The Buddhist Revival in Sri Lanka* (Columbia: University of South Carolina Press, 1988).

2. S.J. Tambiah, *Buddhism Betrayed: Religion, Politics and Violence in Sri Lanka* (Chicago: University of Chicago Press, 1992), p. 92.

3. See the discussion about the MEP in the Introduction to this study.

4. A.T. Ariyaratne, *The Power Pyramid and the Dharmic Cycle* (Ratmalana, Sri Lanka: Sarvodaya Vishva Lekha, 1988), 97.

5. A.T. Ariyaratne, "Political Institutions and Traditional Morality" *Dana* (vol. 14, no. 9, Sept. 1989), p. 16.

6. *Dharmic Cycle*, p. 73.

7. Ibid., p. 48.

8. Ibid., p. 95.

9. Sarvodaya's actual success in its outreach to the Tamil minority is difficult to assess. Since the escalation of the ethnic conflict, Sarvodaya has been largely cut off from its projects in the northern parts of the country. Sarvodaya has, however, been a major advocate of peace and Ariyaratne has traveled to the north on at least two occasions to meet with the Tamil militants.

10. *Dharmic Cycle*, p. 89.

11. Ibid., p. 177.

12. Cited in Steven Kemper, *The Presence of the Past: Chronicles, Politics, and Culture in Sinhala Life* (Ithaca, New York: Cornell University Press, 1991), p. 174. Jayewardene also said that he had a responsibility to assist other religions as well.

13. Kemper, *Presence of the Past*, p. 178, writes, "Jayewardene's conception of Buddhism as a religion of individual responsibility had several consequences, justifying both his disinclination to make Buddhism the state religion and his desire to remove Buddhist monks from political life and secular vocations."

14. Ibid., p. 169

15. Speech by Premadasa, Jan. 2, 1990 at the Malwatte Chapter of Siyam Nikaya, cited in J. van der Horst, "Presidency and Conceptions of Kingship," p. 6, paper presented at the Fourth Sri Lanka Studies Conference, Colombo, August 10–13, 1993. The language of this quotation reflects the kind of ideas that Premadasa learned from Sarvodaya, ideas about linking "government and the spiritual well-being of the people." Premadasa frequently used these ideas to bolster his own policies, but coming from him the words took on a quite different meaning.

16. For a thorough discussion of Premadasa's aspirations to be regarded as an Asokan Cakkavatti king, see J. van der Horst, *Who is He, What is He Doing?: Religious Rhetoric and Performances in Sri Lanka during R. Premadasa's Presidency* (Amstrdam: VU University Press, 1995).

17. Van der Horst, "Presidency and Conceptions of Kingship," p. 21.

18. Tambiah, *Buddhism Betrayed?*, p. 92.

19. Johan Galtung, quoted in an interview by Jehan Perera in *The Island*, 15 September 1992.

20. *Sunday Observer*, 28 April 1991.

21. Ibid.

22. *Observer*, 12 January 1992.

23. Notes from interview with Sarvodaya staff, August 1994.

24. *Daily News*, 21 July 1993 (italics mine). Many stories that the government papers ran during this period tried to accuse also Sarvodaya of polluting the environment. Some stories argued that the Sarvodaya headquarters complex polluted its area in Moratuwa.

25. *Daily News*, 23 July 1992.

26. *Daily Observer*, 20 July 1992.

27. See the discussion of Marty and Applegate in the Introduction to this volume.

28. J. Perera, C. Marasainghe and L. Jayasekera, ed., *A People's Movement Under Siege* (Moratuwa: Sarvodaya Book Publishing Services, 1992), p. 217.

29. These were the areas in which the government had created physical or structural violence: the environment; the economy that produced a widening gap between the rich and the poor; failure to nurture the traditional value systems; failing to protect the human rights of all people; limiting the freedom of the media to proclaim the truth; and militarization and physical violence against the people of the nation. (These items were cited in many speeches that Ariyaratne delivered, and are contained in *A People's Movement Under Siege*, pp. 150ff.).

30. Ariyaratne in a speech to *dhamma* school teachers in Hambantota, Sri Lanka, August 8, 1992.

31. Sulak Sivaraksa, *Seeds of Peace* (Berkeley: Parallax Press, 1992), p. 44.

Chapter 3

The Plurality of Buddhist Fundamentalism: An Inquiry into Views among Buddhist Monks in Sri Lanka

Chandra R. de Silva

In the last few years, a number of scholars have begun to analyze critically attitudes held by Buddhist monks in relation to society and polity in Sri Lanka. Their analyses have concentrated on how these attitudes, especially those which I here term "fundamentalist," have an impact on (and, in the opinion of many of these scholars, generally impede) the process of building a democratic and multiethnic society in Sri Lanka. The word *fundamentalism* has been defined in a variety of ways.[1] For the purpose of this chapter, and following the Introduction to this study, it will connote a desire to restore what are perceived as "original" or "ideal" values and behavior patterns, and an active campaign to reestablish institutional and social structures that promote such values and behavior. It also implies a rejection of many contemporary values and institutions as being essentially flawed.

In this chapter, I will reexamine the justification for labeling as fundamentalist some of the ideas of Buddhist monks in Sri Lanka. On the basis of writings by contemporary monks and through interview data gathered during the summer of 1993 and follow-up research in 1995–96, I will make two arguments: a) the variety of views relating to the ideal social and political order among Buddhist monks in Sri Lanka is often masked by the great concern for an appearance of a "unified" front; and b) the continuing tensions and contradictions between the Buddhist doctrinal tradition and twentieth-century nationalist ideology among Sinhala-Buddhist monks[2] illustrates not only a different kind of fundamentalism, but also provides clues on strategies that might be adopted to foster greater tolerance.

Let me begin with the idea of fundamentalism. Any fundamentalist doctrine needs to have a vision of an ideal moral and social order thought to have existed in the past. There is clearly such a vision among many Buddhist monks in Sri Lanka. This vision, in large measure based on the *Mahavamsa*, generally embodies the theory of a strong bond linking Buddhism, the polity, and the people of the country, the Sinhala. Along these lines, the Venerable Dheerananda, formerly a principal of a state school in the North Central Province, and currently a lecturer at the University of Peradeniya, has argued that:

> Although Buddhist monks were not very active politically early on, our sources indicate that they were active participants in influencing the ruler by the first century, BC, replacing the *brahmins*. But of course, they were impartial advisors, not political players. They advised the king on his duties and how the king should obtain popular participation according to the *dhamma*. They advised the people on how to order their livelihood in a Buddhist way. In some cases where there were problems such as the lack of water, the *bhikkhus* [Buddhist monks] advised the king to develop irrigation with the support of the people.[3]

The Venerable Nanaloka, a graduate of the University of Peradeniya and a *Prachina Panditha,* currently at Sarananda Pirivena, Anuradhapura, was more eloquent on the bonds between the monks and the (Sinhala) people. But he reiterated Dheerananda's claims:

> From ancient times, *bhikkhus* were regarded as the guardian deities of our nation. If the nation [*jathiya*] was faced with a threat, the monks saved it. The *bhikkhus* were the leaders of the nation. In time they became *kula devathavo*, that is, the peacemakers of the family. But with social evolution this status has disappeared. For this the monks are responsible, so are the people, especially our older monks are responsible because they have not devised a means of training the young.

Nanaloka then linked the guardianship of Buddhism and the polity to the Sinhala people:

> After the coming of Mahinda, the relationship between our *jathiya* [people or race, i.e., the Sinhalas] and Buddhism was like that between the bark and the tree. The tree cannot survive without the bark. Our nation had an extraordinary civilization because of Buddhism. If you look at the evidence from the archeological excavations we can see how

> our people were self-sufficient in food, and developed in their moral qualities [*adhyathmika gunadharma*] and physical states. After the coming of Mahinda, agriculture developed as a way of living. The cultivator would work in the fields all day and in the evening would visit the temple and discuss whatever problems he had. He would go to the temple for physical and mental relaxation. He received solace in the temple. The temple also had ceremonies for: the [first] cutting of hair; [first] eating of solid foods for children. [It offered also] advise for couples intending to marry; Angulimala *sutta* recitation for pregnant women; and *pansakula* for the dead. Thus from birth to death, there was a link with the temple. When a new well was dug, the first water was offered at *Buddha puja* [offering of food to the Buddha]. The first fruits of a tree, the first milk from a cow, were all offered in the same way. Our old authors such as Gurulugomi, Vidyachakravarthi, and Parakrama Panditha were sincere Buddhists, not just Buddhists in name. Thus people were bound to the *sasana* [Buddhist order].[4]

Much of the Venerable Nanaloka's vision fits well with Stanley J. Tambiah's definition of the elements of a traditional "Buddhist Polity," including:

> (1) Religion (*sasana*), i.e., Buddhism characterized in terms of the three jewels, Buddha, Dhamma and Sangha; (2) Kingship which was stressed in terms of such idealizations as the righteous ruler (Dharmaraja), the Buddha-to-be (Bodhisattva) and the wheel-rolling emperor (Chakkavatti); and (3) a "people"—the Sinhalese, the Mons, the Burmese, the Thai and so on—who received their stamp in terms of the above two features, and whose historical destiny was considered to be their preservation. The concept of a people with a historical conservationist destiny had other components as well—ethnic, linguistic, cultural—which were fused with the religio-political ideas.[5]

Fundamentalism, however, is more than a vision of the past. It involves an urge and perhaps even a program to re-create a lost social order, which was seen to have ensured prosperity in the "imagined" past. I use the word *imagined* in the sense of "constructed" rather than "fictitious."[6] I will highlight three aspects of the past, which many Buddhist monks would like to resuscitate. First, there is the perception of the distant past of the *Mahavamsa* as an idyllic period when people lived simple and moral lives. Second, there is the role of the *sangha* (order of Buddhist monks) in the polity, particularly as advisors to the ruler. The third and related aspect concerns the "restoration" of unity and harmony. Unity of the *sangha* is the first concern, while relations between the *sangha* and Buddhist laypersons is second. Finally, the concept of unity and harmony is extended to cover the entire region of Sri Lanka.

The picture of a prosperous, moral, and just society of old resonates in the minds of many Buddhist monks. Venerable Dheerananda explained that, in the past, Buddhist monks advised people even on matters of agriculture and economics, or:

> on the ways in which the produce should be utilized. One fourth for consumption, half for investment, and the fourth as saving. This was the rule in our old society. This kind of planning must have been the reason why there was so much prosperity and ability to build monuments. They also made the people "civilized" by teaching them good principles—abhorrence of killing and respect for life.

In urban areas especially, contemporary Sri Lankans have moved away from Dheerananda's ideal vision of society. His 1993 critique of contemporary society was adumbrated in the 1954 *Betrayal of Buddhism*, which explored the condition of Buddhism in the early postcolonial period. According to its authors "the real and final remedy was the replacement of Western materialistic, social and individual values and the establishment of genuine values founded on the Buddhist Dhamma."[7] Contemporary Buddhist monks likewise argue that Buddhist values can be fostered by admonishing the people. They also add that positive steps should be taken by the state to shut off avenues leading to wrong actions.[8]

The monks I interviewed all agreed that monks should foster certain Buddhist values and preach against vices, such as gambling, that corrupt those values. For the most part, they also agreed that these values should be enforced, doubtless part of a fundamentalist program. However, there are monks who have doubts about the practicability of this policy. Questioned about the feasibility of a state that would attempt to enforce Buddhist values, Venerable Rahula responded, "I would support it but it would be very difficult. For example, how would a Buddhist state promote fishing? What about pesticide manufacture? There would be unemployment and the government would fall."[9]

Monks view differently also the second aspect of the past that they would like to see resuscitated—namely, the proper nature of the relationship between the *sangha* and the polity. A few of the monks whom I interviewed advocated the withdrawal of monks from politics. One of them, who was more interested in developing internal peace through meditation,[10] claimed that even though, in ancient days, Buddhist monks involved themselves in politics, such involvement can only be divisive in the present:

> The Buddha did not advise the kings on war. We should not pressure the ruler. Pressure should come from the people. *Bhikkhus* should not go on

demonstrations. It is true that *bhikkhus* did participate in politics in the past. But this will really harm the people. While our task is to teach the religion we should not be distracted by other gains which attract us to politics.

There are groups of monks who favor retiring to the forest or to meditation centers,[11] but theirs was a minority view. Most monks are clearly for an interventionist position of the *sangha* in relation to social problems. Venerable Nanaloka, for instance, argued that "the Buddha preached political principles. Thus, there is no need to question Buddhist monks' involvement in politics. Politics is essential and there is nothing wrong in working with politicians to solve the problems of the people." The problem for Nanaloka was how to work with politicians within an adversarial political system without being dragged into partisan politics. Venerable Nanaloka himself expressed fears in this regard: "*Bhikkhus* have fallen due to politics. They lose their position of respect by participating in politics this way. This can be seen clearly. We should not be in particular parties. Politicians try to use *bhikkhus* to gain political advantage."

The scholar monk, Venerable Karagampitiye Jinarathana, current head of the Dharmendraramaya, Mt. Lavinia, argued against all political involvement for monks whatsoever: "*Bhikkhus* should not take part in politics. It leads to the loss of dignity of monks."

Venerable Bellanwila Wimalaratana, chief incumbent of the Bellanwila temple, near Colombo, expressed similar sentiments:[12]

My personal opinion is that *bhikkhus* should in no way participate in the party politics which prevail today. That means the distancing of the *bhikkhu* from the people because people look at *bhikkhus* as persons belonging to our political party [or theirs]. *Bhikkhus* should be able to advise all. *Bhikkhus* cannot control political parties with a lay leadership and become controlled by them. The *bhikkhu* will get only temporary benefits which disappear with the fall of parties from power. The strength of the *bhikkhu* is not in political backing but in learning, dedication and the like.

Venerable Bellanwila Wimalaratana also explained that the system tended to force Buddhist monks to establish links with particular politicians:

What has happened is that politics has penetrated everything; to have a plan approved to build a house, to get electricity, to build a road you need to go to the MP [Member of Parliament]. In this context, the *bhikkhu* has to go to the politician to have the temple built or to get something done in the village. Thus the *bhikkhu* has to go where the politician wants him to go in order to get things done.

The chief monk of the Isipathanaramaya, located in Colombo South, gave a slightly different twist to a similar view about the relationship between monks and the polity:

> Because this is a Buddhist country and a place where Buddhism has the foremost place,[13] politicians know that if they get the support of *bhikkhus*, it will help them. That is why they support certain temples. The alliance between the politician who patronizes a temple and the *bhikkhus* in it [once begun] cannot be broken [easily] by either side.

The problem for the chief monk of the Isipathanaramaya was not only that the "political" *bhikkhu* would threaten the esteem of the entire *sangha*, but that politicians were seen as unreliable. As another monk remarked: "Many politicians like to have *bhikkhus* support them to get to power. After that, they want to know why *bhikkhus* enter politics." Despite a difference of opinion, most monks linked their vision of the appropriate relationship between monks and the polity—whether for or against a strong alliance—with an "imagined" past.

The imagined past is not merely a charter for present-day intervention. As both Steven Kemper and Stanley Tambiah perceptively have pointed out, the imagined past is often evoked as a moral standard.[14] Some monks emphasized the difference between the "impartial advice" given by the monks of old and what was seen as partisan party allegiance in the present day.[15]

Inherent in this situation of a monk immersed in politics is the sense of contradiction aroused in many Buddhists when a renunciant enters into the sphere of worldly concerns. As Richard Gombrich and Gananath Obeyesekere point out:

> The strength of the monk's role lies in the fact that it is the opposite of the lay role. He is an image of detachment from worldly ties, from human social conflicts, from cross cutting kin bonds that enmesh every one of us in our social existence. . . . Thus, the question is not whether a monk can partake of affairs of the world, but *how*. A monk arriving in a Sarvodaya[16] camp and uttering a sermon of exhortation poses no problem, so long as he maintains his aloofness and goes back to his monastery. But if he gets involved in social and economic activity, which he is supposed to have renounced, he ceases to mirror our ideals.[17]

In other words, monks and laity alike stress the loss of respect that may accompany monks who are perceived as worldly.

The ideal for most monks, then, is to regain the imagined, past position of being respected, especially in their role as impartial advisors and counselors. Clearly, one way to do this is to restore traditional monarchy, but such an event is recognized as impossible. Some contemporary Buddhist monks have proposed alternative political systems where "Buddhist values" would be supreme and where politicians would be guided by the advice of Buddhist monks. The "alternative democracies" proposed by Venerable Madihe Pannasiha and Venerable Henpitagedara Nanasiha, for instance, would eliminate party political rivalries and seek to establish a common, agreed plan of development. The former has advocated a nonparty national election to select a group of leaders pledged to implement an ideal plan of development. Such a plan would be agreed upon beforehand by consensus by a group of nonparty experts. Venerable Nanasiha, on the other hand, has preferred to rely on 7000 village representatives who would work together to construct plans for development. Both plans have been explored elsewhere in some detail.[18] My interest here is whether these plans reflect fundamentalist values.

Both plans are clearly based on Buddhist referents. Moreover, both plans embody the Buddhist (and Socratic) idea that true knowledge brings understanding and that rational persons can arrive at consensus through discussion on what needs to be done. Venerable Nanasiha's scheme resonates with what is reputed to have been the political system of the Vajjian confederation in the time of the Buddha. Once more, and invoking the past as charter, the assumption is that if we assemble "good persons," they will be able to work together. In the sense that these plans propose blueprints that eliminate partisan political competition and restore an imagined harmonious polity, they might be deemed fundamentalist. Yet, as Martin E. Marty and R. Scott Appleby have pointed out:

> Fundamentalism has proven itself *selectively traditional and selectively modern.* Fundamentalists are not simply traditionalists or conservatives. In fact, they reject the clinging to tradition and the uncritical conservation of all that has emerged in the tradition, for they view tradition as a mosaic of compromises, as a body of accumulated adaptations to the demands of the specific historical, and thus contingent, circumstances. Fundamentalists do not object to innovation or adaptation in itself but to the elevation of these adaptations to a privileged status which in turn precludes the flexibility required in crafting a comprehensive response to contemporary challenges.[19]

Given these guidelines for assessing fundamentalist projects, and especially given Nanasiha's and Pannasiha's wholesale rejection of the modern, the two schemes are fundamentalist in that they look to the past (encoded in the

Mahavamsa) to solve the problems of the present. Few monks believe, moreover, that the two schemes are really practicable.

Let us now look back upon the concept of a Buddhist polity as it has evolved among the monks in Sri Lanka. There is general agreement on a "constructed vision of the past," when the ruler worked for the welfare of the people and the religion. There is agreement that the current political system is not working well.[20] Yet, the solution to the problem is not seen as replacing the current polity with a "Buddhist democracy," as advocated by Madihe Pannasiha and Henpitagedera Nanasiha.[21] In fact, contrary to what Tambiah states and what Kemper seems to imply, *bhikkhus* do not see themselves, and are not seen by others, as "alternatives" to politics and politicians.[22] There is a sense in which the Buddhist monks see themselves as truer representatives of the people than the politicians. As the monk Rahula (from Bentara Elpitiya) remarked: "A *bhikkhu* does not represent a family or a village but the whole country." In general, however, *bhikkhus* perceive themselves as the conscience of politicians, politicians who are notoriously vulnerable to bribes and temptations. The problem, then, is how to ensure the production of "good" leaders through a corrupt and divisive system. The answer (which echoed through many of the responses) was that first the *sangha* needed to be "united" and needed to speak with one voice to ensure that the political leadership heeded the advice of monks.

Clearly, however, there is acceptance among many Buddhist monks that the contemporary state should actively support Buddhism and that monks have a duty to advise those in power on matters relating to polity where religion and the state have a symbiotic relationship. As Ven. Palipane Chandrananda stated in March 1996 on the proposed clause in the draft constitution assuring the preeminence of Buddhism, "There is no need for the Constitution to give such place to Buddhism because Buddhism enjoyed this position from the time of the advent of Arahat Mahinda. What is expected of the government is to recognise this position."[23] Explicit constitutional recognition of the "foremost position" of Buddhism came in a clause in the First Constitution of the Republic of Sri Lanka in 1972. This clause was maintained and strengthened in the Second Constitution, of 1978.

In 1991 the primacy of Buddhism was further entrenched when President Ranasinha Premadasa set up a Supreme Council of Buddhist religious leaders to advise him. This council, comprised by a majority of Buddhist monks, continues to function to the present. Indeed, the resignation of chief monks of the *nikayas* (monastic fraternities) from the Supreme Council in January 1997, on the grounds that their advice on national policy was being ignored by the current president, Chandrika Kumaranatunga, was a public relations fiasco for the government.[24] The triumph of the principle that, in Sri Lanka, religion cannot be separated from politics may be seen in the draft of a new constitution composed by Kumaranatunga's People's Alliance in April 1997, which not only continues to provide that "The Republic of Sri Lanka shall give to Buddhism the foremost place" but also, for the first time, gives constitutional status to the Supreme Council of Buddhist leaders: "The State shall consult the Supreme Council in all matters pertaining to the protection and fostering of the Buddha Sasana."[25]

The willingness of President Kumaranatunga—who long represented a secular approach to politics in Sri Lanka—to accept and constitutionally reinforce an avowedly Buddhist advisory body is a reflection of the Buddhist fundamentalism and the political strength of those who believe that protection of Buddhism is the special obligation of the Sri Lankan state. Despite this, there are Buddhist monks who dissent from aspects of this policy. As Ven. Hevanpola Ratanasara explained, a clause granting Buddhism "the foremost place" was wrong because it is against Buddhist philosophy, it has no moral justification, and it is an infringement of the basic rights of other religions.[26]

This brings us to the question of "unity." The Sinhala word *eksathkama* denotes unity. The word *samagiya*, which is also sometimes translated as "unity,"[27] is better rendered as "harmoniously working together." All Buddhist monks whom I interviewed emphasized *samagiya*, and played down the division of the *sangha* into sects (*nikayas*). As the Venerable Bellanwila Wimalaratana explained, "Today, *nikayas* exist only as pupillary successions [*gurukula*]. We work together and receive alms together. Therefore, there is no division as such." Venerable Karagampitiye Jinarathana agreed: "The divisions in terms of *nikayas* are not there now in the way it was in the past. Now everyone works together except in disciplinary proceedings." Some of this emphasis accords with the present situation. Student monks in Sri Lankan universities often work together as a pressure group and are reluctant to criticize fellow monks when conversing with laypersons. When necessary, monks live for extended periods in temples that do not belong to their own *nikaya*.

But there are, nonetheless, real and pervasive divisions among the *sangha*. Some of the deepest divisions within the *sangha* are between the younger monks, who often come from poorer socioeconomic backgrounds and are exposed to secular education, and those who are older and have had a more traditional training under a mentor. Some of the younger monks, some of whom did not wish to be identified, were, in fact, very critical of leadership in the *sangha*. Nevertheless, despite occasional acrimonious debates in newspapers and on political platforms, there is a continuing reluctance by Buddhist monks to criticize other monks. In my series of interviews, monks were almost invariably more comfortable in responding to criticisms by others of individual monks or of groups of monks than in initiating critical comments themselves.

What is also significant, however, is that there is a vision of the past in which divisions were absent or at least minimal. Serious doctrinal differences within the *sangha* in the past are seen as having arisen due to influences from outside the country. This explains, in part, the extensive protests that arose when Venerable Palpola Vipassi accepted ordination from a Japanese Shingon sect in 1990.[28] Along these lines, monks also view Western, colonial domination as having opened up a gulf between Buddhist monks and lay Buddhists. As Venerable Nanaloka explained:

> The change in the old relationship was primarily due to the coming of the Europeans, especially the coming of the English. One of their devices [*upakrama*] was to break the connection between the Buddhist monks and the people because they felt that as long as that lasted they could not do what they wished. The center of education shifted from the temple to the church. Our people began to be attracted by Western culture and began to follow its norms and thus the old links were destroyed.[29]

In this case, the "far Other," the Christian European, posed the most formidable threat to the unity of the *sangha*, and the *sangha's* relationship to the laity.

In comparison with the Christian, often perceived by Buddhist fundamentalists as a far Other, Hindus are seen, at least by some monks, as a group that has not had its fair share, perhaps even as a potential ally. As a senior monk pointed out:

> In colonial, British times, the non-Hindu Tamils had many privileges—educational opportunities. They now bring up unnecessary issues such as privileges for Buddhism. Buddhism has not got a privileged position but its rightful position. Hindus have not obtained their rightful position because the second position [i.e., the position in Sri Lanka to which they are entitled] has been obtained by Christian churches. Anyone visiting Sri Lanka would think that Christianity is the second religion in the country and, in some areas, the first. I do not wish to have a religious confrontation, but the Hindus are the second most numerous group, yet Hindu culture does not get that place because of other forces.

In the course of his exploration of what he perceives to be the current, low position of Hinduism in Sri Lanka, the monk exonerated Buddhists from any responsibility:

> Hindu culture does not suffer because Buddhism has been granted special privileges. We respect Hindu deities. Hindu deities and Tamils walk in our processions. Sinhalas go to see *vel* [a festival for the god Kataragama] and go to Hindu *kovils* [temples].[30]

For the senior monk, Buddhist and Hindu culture share a healthy relationship. For him, Hindu tradition is a necessary component of Buddhism in Sri Lanka.

While the evocation of the term "Hindu" often elicited a sympathetic response, the term "Tamil" often did not. Of course, there were exceptions. Venerable Nanaloka of Sarananda Pirivena was forthright:

> But there is one thing which I need to state: granting their demands, except the one to break up the country for an Eelam state,[31] is fair. They are all citizens of our country. If there are human rights which are essential for us, they should have them, too. There is no distinction between Sinhala and Tamil in this respect. All of us must have rights. It is our duty to ensure this. But we will never agree to a division of the country. We do not say that a solution to this problem should come through war.

On the other hand, some certainly viewed the Tamils as aliens and as a disruptive force. As Venerable Karagampitiye Jinarathana remarked, "Just because they have come from Tamil Nadu and got together in one area, how can we give them a part of the country? They have India, that great country of India."[32]

The traditional emphasis on the need for harmony and unity certainly tends to make many Buddhist monks suspicious of what are seen as divisive political tendencies. This is clearly illustrated by attitudes toward the campaign for a separate independent Tamil state in Sri Lanka. Venerable Bellanwila Wimalaratana argued that:

> It is wrong to ask for a separate area whether for the Tamils, Muslims or Sinhalas. If it is said that this is our homeland [*nijabhumi*] or that it belongs to our kind [*vargayata himi*] the basis is wrong. People of this country must be able to live where they wish. Muslims could ask for a homeland saying that they need one to ensure their safety. Then we will have to live as separate races [*jathis*]. This is a very unscientific [*ashashtriya*] system.[33]

A number of monks advanced other practical reasons for their opposition. "This [a separate state] will lead to border disputes."[34] Another monk reiterated this claim: "I cannot agree to division. If we look at the population or the resources, we are too small for that."[35] The major reason, however, was a deeply felt belief that the division of the country would be disastrous for Sinhala Buddhists. There were also fears that an independent Tamil state in Sri Lanka would merge with breakaway Tamils in south India and form a large and potentially threatening state.[36] For instance, one monk claimed that "the Sinhala live only in Sri Lanka. We as Sinhalas do not like to give part of our country. We can live together with equal rights for all without dividing the country."[37]

The same fears of consequences relating to the loss of unity lie at the basis of opposition to devolution of power to Provincial Councils. The establishment of Provincial Councils was at the heart of the 1987 Indo-Lanka Accord, which itself was designed, among other things, to attempt to resolve the ongoing civil conflict between the Sri Lankan government and separatist Tamil groups. Elections to these councils were first held in the period April-November 1988. The idea of Provincial Councils, in general, and the idea of a single Northeast Council to cover the areas claimed as traditional homelands by Tamil groups, has roused strong opposition among sections of the Sinhala.[38] Many monks are opposed to the new effort at some devolution of power. According to one:

> There is no evidence that administration in this land suffered because of the absence of Provincial Councils. Because we could not give councils to the Northeast alone it was introduced everywhere. If we strengthen this system, and give the councils more powers, then we will give the Eelamists what they want.[39]

According to another monk, devolution of power will not have long-term effects:

> It will be a temporary solution. They are fighting for self-rule. According to the Provincial Council system, power is shared and resides largely with the center. So the Tamils will want all powers and when they get them, they will gain a situation in which they can invade the rest of the country. That is why it will be a temporary solution.[40]

Another monk made a similar point:

> I do not think that they are of much use, except for increasing expenditures. [question: "But if the Tamil leaders agree to the Provincial Councils as a solution?"] That is not a good idea. They are close to India and Tamil Nadu. That will be a cause for fear here. Sri Lanka has [historically] had troubles [*karadara*] from India.[41]

Similar fears of separatism were at the root of the opposition of the leadership of the Buddhist *sangha* to the 1995–97 proposals of the People's Alliance Government for a new constitution which would devolve power to "regions." Leading Buddhist monks argued consistently that unless the LTTE were defeated, making Sri Lanka a "union of regions" was the first step to dividing the country.[42] This opposition was widespread. Speaking at the Sharastananda Pirivena, Dehiwala, in February 1996, Ven. Maduluwawe Sobhita emphasized that "it is our duty to hand over a united country to the future generation. All communities must unite in this endeavour."[43] However, the argument of some of the leading Buddhist monks has been that the safeguarding of unity (*eksath bhava*) was dependent on the preservation of the unitary form of the state (*ekeeya rijjyaya*). This was also the conclusion reached on Tuesday, March 5, 1996, by some two thousand Buddhist monks assembled in Colombo to consider the government's constitutional proposals.[44] The government, in subsequent drafts of the proposed constitution, tried to emphasize their concern over the preservation of unity under a "devolved" political system.[45]

Despite these attitudes, there was recognition of existing discontent and the need for radical reform to regain the allegiance of the Tamils of the north and east. In the words of Venerable Bellanwila Wimalaratana:

> Let's not talk of a Northeastern Province but of new provinces. This would be fair. The Tamils have developed a distrust of Sinhala politicians and wish to protect their language and culture. They must be given room to do so, but there are some things that must be placed under the central government to protect the unitary [*ekeeya*] nature of the state.

The Venerable Nanaloka of Sarananda Pirivena was more explicit:

> We do not say that a solution to this problem should come through war. On the contrary, their requirements must be met peacefully. [question: "What about Provincial Councils and their powers, including police, education, and health? Some say that if these powers are granted it will effectively divide the country. Do you think so?"] I think that is the fear. This is our fear, too. But how else do we solve the problem, if we do not give them these powers? Then we will be withholding their rights. If I do not get my rights you have deprived me of them. My opinion is that though police powers are given, the power of the armed forces is with the central government. Is that not so? [my answer: "yes."] Then, they should be given these rights. If we can give them to the Western Province why can we not give them to the Northeast? What there is mainly is the fear that these people are different and will not act in our interest. We cannot solve the problem that way. It is a fear."[46]

The point that might be emphasized here is that within the paradigm of the desirability of the unity of the country, there can be very different attitudes toward minorities. Some Buddhist monks do exhibit a considerable amount of hostility and prejudice. Consider, for instance, the view of one monk:

> The only way to solve this is to settle people according to their proportion in the country in the Northeast Province. Then their power will end. This is more an Eelamist problem than an ethnic [*janavargika*] question. If it were an ethnic problem division will not solve it, because when their numbers increase, they will have to come to these [Sinhala] parts. They have not changed their laws. They have a law called *Thesavalai* (sic) according to which their lands cannot be sold to others. I saw this in the paper today; about claims that lands in Trincomalee were their lands. This was a threat [to Sinhala settlers]. If they think about it in that way, why do they live here [in Sinhala areas]? Those who are here, then, must be sent there [to the north]. But this will never be done. Therefore, these laws must be changed by the state. If those people can live anywhere in the island, why cannot the Sinhalas go there? If we change these things the problem will be resolved. But this will not be done and the problem will grow."[47]

On the other hand, there were some monks who placed part of the blame on the Sinhala people. Venerable Rahula, for instance, pointed out:

> When something happens in the north we clean the chicken coops of the Indian Tamils.[48] The Tamils in the north are badly treated: their jewelry is stolen and their women are harassed. I have this information from the perpetrators. We need a political solution. They are citizens of our country.[49]

The Venerable Nanaloka of Sarananda Pirivena, Anuradhapura, also expressed sympathy for the Tamil Other:

> The Tamils believe that our politicians deceived them. This might be true. Much of the economic burden of our country is shouldered by Tamils, especially their agricultural production. Thus, we should ensure a fair deal for them. It is possible that they did not get what powers they wished because of certain disagreements [*amanapakam*].[50]

Thus, among monks in contemporary Sri Lanka, there are a variety of views concerning the position of Hindu culture, as well as the rights of Sri Lankan Tamil people vis-à-vis Buddhist culture and the Sinhala people.

Indeed, as we have seen, these views are not uniform. Also, as we have seen, many monks' views reflect fundamentalist values inasmuch as they see Tamils and Tamil culture as a threat to Buddhist order. At the same time, however, there are as many monks who are sympathetic to what they consider to be the plight of the Tamil in contemporary Sri Lanka. Yet, they, too, harken back to the ideal past. While they do not share the fundamentalist values that view the Tamil as the threatening Other, they nonetheless exemplify Buddhist fundamentalism. Let me explain.

Peter Schalk has coined the word *dharmacracy* to describe what he sees as the fundamentalist views of Buddhist monks in Sri Lanka. According to Schalk:

> The concept of "dharmacracy" in Sri Lanka is put forward by the Maha Sangha and by other Sinhala-Buddhist groups on the conscious level as a protest against the "secularism" of the state, similar to the Visva Hindu Parisad's protest against the "secularism" of the Indian state. In Sri Lanka and in India these protests have become a threat and obstacle to peace between ethnic groups. In reality, however, this protest goes much deeper than only against the policy of the state on religious affairs.[51]

Dharmacracy assumes the acceptance of the primacy of Buddhism and the infusion of its values into all areas of political life. Schalk argues that in the Sri Lankan concept of dharmacracy, the democratic political system is replaced by the ideal of a ruler who fosters and protects the dominant religion. Dharmacracy also involves the politicization of religion. Buddhism becomes transformed into "a concept of the organic solidarity of the Sinhala race."[52] Schalk goes on to argue that "the Sinhalese concept of dharmacracy is fundamentalist in the sense that it is a conscious attempt to preserve continuities with an (imagined) past base, with the words of the Buddha"[53] and, I might add, with some interpretations of the *Mahavamsa*. If dharmacracy is inherently Buddhist fundamentalism, even sympathetic attitudes regarding the relationship between the state, the *sangha*, and the Tamil people are fundamentalist inasmuch as they are founded on the notion of the primacy, and the all-encompassing nature, of Buddhism in Sri Lanka.

The question as to whether the ideas contained in what Schalk calls dharmacracy are Buddhist has been addressed in part by Donald Swearer. According to Swearer:

> The primary "fundamentalism" extracted from the sacred "source texts" of Sri Lanka (the myths and legends) is properly speaking more reflective of, and at the service of, the nationalist rather than the Bud-

> dhist world view—although the two are inseparable in the rhetoric of the charismatic fundamentalist leaders. In other words, the specifically Buddhist character of the myths and legends is subservient to the personal and social identity both threatened and affirmed in the texts. Cultural identity in effect becomes a "a religious fetish, an idol, a thing which has self-contained magical properties," rather than a transcendent and transforming moral and spiritual ideal in terms of which all systems and institutions are judged as limited or only a partial embodiment.

Swearer then relates religious fundamentalism to nationalist goals:

> Religions thus harnessed to nationalism are often regarded as more pure and orthodox than the traditional forms they supplant; in turn, nationalism readily takes on the character of a fervid, absolutistic revival of religion. In the case of Sri Lanka, the search for national identity is prior and conditions the fundamentalism of the religion(s) incorporated into nationalism.[54]

Gananath Obeyesekere, in a recent essay, takes Swearer's argument one step further. He points out that the teachings of the Buddha do not provide a doctrinal justification for cultural identity, violence, and intolerance of others. There is no concept of a "just war" or a justification for kingly violence. The Buddha is no longer active and, in any case, the Buddha was seen as a totally benevolent figure. Buddhist doctrine and ethics are universal.[55]

Obeyesekere argues that while Sinhala leaders have used "Buddhist history" to justify the construction of a national identity drawn exclusively from Sinhala-Buddhist sources, there has been continual tension between the "benign" Buddhist doctrine and an uncompromising and exclusive Sinhala-Buddhist identity. Indeed, this is one reason that it is more accurate to talk of "Sinhala-Buddhist fundamentalism" rather than "Buddhist fundamentalism," in general.

While there are many monks who subscribe to Sinhala-Buddhist fundamentalist ideas, the links between tradition and contemporary attitudes are complex. There are many nuances within any one tradition and the concept of "dharmacracy" is, as we have seen, at one end of a continuum. At the other end are more tolerant and humane ideas, which are reflected in the views of some of the monks quoted in this chapter. One of the areas that needs more study and reflection pertains to the changing system of *pirivena* education available to Buddhist monks in Sri Lanka. Concerns relating to the linkage between the secular postsecondary education system and *pirivena* education, and the curricular content of the *pirivena* educational system were expressed by Buddhist monks of very different political and ideological persuasions. Currently, Buddhist monks do not receive a comprehensive education relating to the basic secular concepts prevalent in the society in which they live. The way in which this element is integrated into monastic education is likely to have a major impact on the Sri Lankan *sangha*, and through that impact, on many areas of political and social life in the country.

Notes

1. See Martin E. Marty and Scott B. Appleby, *Fundamentalisms Observed* (Chicago: University of Chicago Press, 1991), passim.

2. For an excellent analysis of this tension, see Gananath Obeyesekere, "Duttagamini and the Buddhist Conscience," in *Religion and Political Conflict in South Asia: India, Pakistan and Sri Lanka*, Douglas Allen, ed. (Delhi: Oxford University Press, 1993), pp. 135–60.

3. Interview at the University of Peradeniya. This was part of a series of 25 in-depth interviews conducted in July–August 1993.

4. Not all Buddhist monks were starry-eyed about the past. A chief monk of a temple in Colombo argued that political patronage has had adverse effects on the *sangha*: "The status of monks declined because of patronage. When the king built a stupa and handed it over to a monk, the monk became subservient (*gathi*). The Buddha has said that we should live like the bee who takes surplus honey without harming the scent or the color of the flower. This did not happen. When a bird flies he takes only his wings. The *bhikkhu* should have only the robe and the begging bowl. When this changed the *bhikkhus* fell under the sponsor."

5. S. J. Tambiah, "Sangha and Polity in Modern Thailand," in *Religion and Legitimation of Power in Thailand, Laos and Burma,* Bardwell L. Smith, ed. (Chambersburg: Anima Books, 1978), pp. 111–12. Tambiah explains that the traditional "Buddhist polity" should not be understood as a static model. In "normal" times, the political and religious spheres of authority did not interpenetrate extensively. "But in abnormal circumstances their relation changed in two directions: when a particular king did come to exercise strong power and his kingdom expanded and waxed strong, when he won wars, booty, and prisoners, and when he made attempts at a greater centralization of power, under such a king the Sangha too was built up as an ecclesiastical hierarchy and enjoyed royal liberality. But this resulted in the paradox that the Sangha that was organizationally strengthened was also thereby politically regulated." For a more detailed exposition, see S. J. Tambiah, *World Conqueror and World Renouncer* (Cambridge: Cambridge University Press, 1976).

6. Benedict Anderson, *Imagined Communities: Reflections on the Origin and Spread of Nationalism*, revised edition (New York: Verso, 1993), p. 6.

7. *The Betrayal of Buddhism: Report of the Unofficial Buddhist Committee of Inquiry* (Balangoda: Dharmavijaya Press, 1956), p. 101.

8. Stanley Jeyaraja Tambiah, *Buddhism Betrayed?: Religion, Politics and Violence in Sri Lanka* (Chicago: University of Chicago Press, 1992), pp. 118–22.

9. The idea that the fall of a government would have an impact on the very nature of the structure of the state is reflective of political experience in Sri Lanka.

10. On the growing popularity of the *vipassana* meditation movement, see George D. Bond, *The Buddhist Revival in Sri Lanka: Religious Tradition, Reinterpretation and Response* (Columbia: University of South Carolina Press, 1988), pp. 130–238.

11. See Michael Carrithers, *The Forest Monks of Sri Lanka: An Anthropological and Historical Study* (Delhi: Oxford University Press, 1983).

12. For more information on the temple, see George Bond, *The Buddhist Revival*, pp. 292–93, and John C. Holt, *Buddha in the Crown: Avalokitesvara in the Buddhist Traditions of Sri Lanka* (New York: Oxford University Press, 1991), pp. 216–17.

13. See below for more on Buddhism's "foremost" position in the constitution.

14. Steven Kemper, *The Presence of the Past : Chronicles, Politics and Culture in Sinhala Life* (Ithaca: Cornell University Press, 1991), p. 224; Stanley Tambiah, *Buddhism Betrayed?*, pp. 106–14.

15. Interviews with Venerable Bellanwila Wimalaratana, August 4, 1993; and Chief Incumbent, Isipathanaramaya, August 2, 1993.

16. For more on Sarvodaya, see George Bond's essay in this volume.

17. Richard Gombrich and Gananath Obeyesekere, *Buddhism Transformed: Religious Change in Sri Lanka* (Princeton: Princeton University Press, 1988), p. 255.

18. Steven Kemper, *The Presence of the Past*, pp. 214–22.

19. Martin E. Marty and R. Scott Appleby, ed., *Fundamentalisms Observed*, p. 825.

20. There was strong criticism of subservience to the politician "Other." Venerable Rahula (from Bentara Elpitiya) remarked that "I do not think that the current situation of *bhikkhus* being subservient to political parties is a good one. Bhikkhus should be able to speak their minds and criticize."

21. For summaries of their schemes, see Stanley Tambiah, *Buddhism Betrayed?*, pp. 114–23.

22. Stanley Tambiah, *Buddhism Betrayed?*, p. 122; Steven Kemper, *The Presence of the Past*, p. 210.

23. *Ceylon Daily News*, Internet Edition, 6 March 1996.

24. Buddhist monks participating in the deliberations of this body strongly urged the use of state funds and resources for such matters as the curbing of Christian missionary enterprises ("Minutes of the Uttareetara Anusasaka Mandalaya," Ministry of Buddha Sasana, Colombo).

25. Clause 7 of the draft constitution.

26. *Ceylon Daily News*, 22 January 1996.

27. Steven Kemper, *The Presence of the Past*, p. 212.

28. See Peter Schalk, "Articles 9 and 18 of the Constitution as Obstacles to Peace," *Lanka*, vol. 5 (1990), pp. 280–92.

29. Ven. Vijitha pushed this back somewhat earlier in time, "When the Portuguese came they found a great bond between the Buddhist monks and the people. Since their aim was to spread their religion, they found this link to be an impediment. So they wished to break this bond."

30. This modifies K. M. de Silva's assertion that, apparently by 1978, the Roman Catholics ceased to be seen as a threat to the Buddhists. See K. M. de Silva, "Religion and the State," *Sri Lanka: Problems of Governance*, K. M. de Silva, ed. (Kandy: International Centre for Ethnic Studies, 1993), p. 337.

31. An independent Tamil state in the north and east of Sri Lanka.

32. Interview on August 4, 1993.

33. Interview on August 4, 1993.

34. Interview with Ven. Dheerananda. Another monk in Colombo, who wished to remain anonymous, said: "A separate state is not essential. If we do that, from that moment we will have many problems including border disputes. Instead of that, we should have an environment where all can live where they wish."

35. Interview with Venerable Rahula on July 27, 1993.

36. Interview with chief monk at Isipathanaramaya, Colombo: "Their motive is to join with south India. Will they stop with a division?," he asked.

37. Interview with a monk on July 8, 1993, at Polonnaruwa.

38. On the agreement, see *Indo-Lanka Agreement of July 1987*, Shelton U. Kodikara Colombo, ed. (Colombo: University of Colombo, 1989). On opposition to the agreement, see C.A. Chandraperuma, *Sri Lanka: The JVP Insurrection, 1987–1989* (Colombo: Lake House, 1991).

39. Interview with Kottawe Nanda on August 3, 1993.

40. Interview with a monk at Polonnaruwa.

41. Interview with Karagampitiye Jinarathana.

42. *The Sunday Times*, 29 July 1995; "Sri Lanka Reassures Buddhists on Devolution Plan," Sri Lanka Net, July 30, 1995; Interview with Ven. Maduluwawe Sobhita reported in *The Sunday Times*, 17 December 1995.

43. *Ceylon Daily News*, Internet Edition, 7 February 1996.

44. *Ceylon Daily News*, Internet Edition, 6 March 1996. The importance of the distinction between *eksath* and *ekeeya* was explained to me by Ven. Bellanwila Wimalarathana, Chief Incumbent, Bellanwila Temple, at an interview on December 27, 1995.

45. Thus the preamble to the April 1997 draft constitution has the following: Wherein the territories constituting the nation shall form one indissoluble union, the units whereof will be characterised by such boundaries and limitation on their powers and authority as may be prescribed; Wherein the territorial integrity, independence and unity of the nation including its sovereign rights over land, sea and air shall be safeguarded."

46. Interview on July 8, 1993.

47. Interview on August 4, 1993.

48. This was a reference to looting the meager possessions of the Plantation Tamil workers.

49. Interview on July 27, 1993.

50. Interview on July 10, 1993.

51. Peter Schalk, "Articles 9 and 18 of the Constitution of Sri Lanka." Schalk adds: "I have invented the word "dharmacracy" as an analogy to the already existing concept of tora-cracy (not theo-cracy) in Jewish religion. The word "dharmacracy" comes also very close in meaning to the precolonial Buddhist concept of *sasana*, which was supposed to cover all sectors of society by its interpretations, not unlike the Muslim concept of religion *shari'a* or as *din*. It embraces not only *iman*, the content of the faith, and *ibadat*, the religious duties, but also *mu'amalat*, "transactions" which regulate the economic, social, and political life. *Din* covers then all aspects of political and civil society. I have invented the word "dharmacracy" because I needed a word which clearly indicated the conscious fusion of religion and politics."

52. Ibid., pp. 277–78.

53. Ibid., p. 278.

54. Donald Swearer, "Fundamentalistic Movements in Theravada Buddhism," in Martin E. Marty and R. Scott Appleby, ed., *Fundamentalisms Observed*, p. 650. Swearer quotes Bruce Kapferer, *Legends of People, Myths of State* (Washington, D.C.: Smithsonian Institution Press, 1988), p. 2.

55. Gananath Obeyesekere, "Buddhism, Nationhood and Cultural Identity: A Question of Fundamentals," in Martin E. Marty and R. Scott Appleby, ed., *Fundamentalisms Comprehended.* However, Tessa Bartholomeusz at present is engaged in a project on "just war thinking" in contemporary Sri Lanka. The project has been funded by a fellowship from the American Institute of Sri Lanka Studies.

Chapter 4

The Impact of Land Reforms, Rural Images, and Nationalist Ideology on Plantation Tamils

Oddvar Hollup

Introduction

With the growth in ethnonationalism and Sinhala-Buddhist "fundamentalism" in Sri Lanka, Sri Lanka's ethnic groups have become further polarized and alienated from each other. In this process, there has been a tendency to stress and exaggerate ethnic distinctiveness and cultural differences at the expense of cultural similarities which Sinhalas, Tamils, and Muslims share in common. Because the Sinhalas—the majority and politically dominant group—historically have failed to recognize (or at least have refused to consider) Sri Lanka a plural society in its implementation of a cultural policy and its definition of nationhood, the situation for Sri Lankan ethnic minorities generally has been one of negotiation and of accommodation.

In an atmosphere of Sinhala nationalism and Tamil separatism, supported by widespread incidents of ethnic violence, there has been a tendency of essentializing cultural differences by the use of cultural symbols and power. Both Sinhalas and Sri Lanka Tamils in different ways have made use of the past, history, and cultural heritage, to stress their right to rule over people and territory. In the process of creating two monolithic categories of people in Sri Lanka, another ethnic minority, the Indian Tamils or Plantation Tamils, with whom this chapter deals, have been "denied" a separate identity of their own. The Sinhalas do not recognize or make distinctions between the two Tamil communities—Plantation Tamils and Sri Lankan Tamils—casting them both as the monolithic Other. Plantation Tamils to some extent have been denied representations of their own because Sri Lanka Tamils in public discourse have attempted to represent Plantation Tamils' interests and grievances in order to suit and support their own claim for a separate state. The conditions under which Plantation Tamils have been living in terms of civil rights, the issue of statelessness and repatriation, together with the discrimination that followed, have been utilized by Sri Lanka Tamils in promoting their own interests and in legitimating their accusations against the Sinhala-Buddhist dominated state.

Plantation Tamils constitute mostly a low-status group of plantation workers who have been powerless, subjected to repatriation to India, and without proper political representation until recently.[1] Due to their low socioeconomic status, low level of education, poor living and working conditions, and their relatively marginal role in the society at large, they have had little opportunity to shape and define a distinct ethnic identity of their own. Most Sinhalas have regarded them either as "alien" or just Tamils, based on Tamil language and Hindu religion, not particularly different from the Sri Lanka Tamils living in the north and east of the island. This may explain why Plantation Tamils became victims of ethnic rioting in the central highlands in 1977, 1981, and during the holocaust of 1983.[2]

In this chapter I will describe the position of the Plantation Tamils and analyze some of the socioeconomic consequences of the nationalization of the plantations and the impact it has had on Tamil plantation workers. I will view these land reforms that affected the tea industry in the mid-1970s[3] in the context of nationalist ideology, the political rhetoric of Sinhala-Buddhist fundamentalism, representations of the rural order, and the social practice of state patronage.[4] Although Sinhala nationalism can be considered an important underlying factor that led to the nationalization of the plantations, it cannot be treated as a monocausal explanation. Nationalization took place partly as a response to the demands raised by the JVP (Janatha Vimukti Peramuna) insurgency in 1971 and the political pressure within the United Front government from the leftist parties, especially the LSSP (Lanka Sama Samaja Party).

The fact that Plantation Tamils were not integrated into the society at large until recently, due to lack of citizenship and poor electoral power, together with their relative social and geographical isolation in the plantations, contributed to and reconfirmed Sinhala perceptions considering them as Other—that is, as relatively recent immigrants of Indian origin. That their status should be other than that of the "coolie" was difficult to accept, hence their avenues for social mobility were severely restricted, except through trade in which Plantation Tamils flourished.

Sinhala Buddhist Nationalist Identity and the Construction of the Past in the Present

Both history and myth, as well as the invention of tradition—when used to reconstruct the past in the present—can be used to invoke "nation-ness" or "peoplehood." Such interpretations of the past and shared origin are often exploited by ethnonationalists to construct identity. The emergence of a Sinhala-Buddhist nationalist ideology in Sri Lanka, in fact, provides us with an illustrative example of how the past—that is, the interpretation of history and myth—has been exploited in constructing a common national identity and shared origin. As the case of Sri Lanka suggests, the establishment of a connection between the present conditions and the past can serve as an important means to political legitimacy.

Several scholars have stressed the importance of mythic traditions, derived from the monk-authored, fifth-century chronicle, the *Mahavamsa*,[5] in shaping Sinhala political consciousness and cultural identity. The *Mahavamsa* became the most potent ideological charter to unite the themes of people, territory, and religion, bound to each other in symbiosis as suggested by Seneviratne,[6] or in hierarchical cosmology, as Kapferer suggests.[7] The legends in the *Mahavamsa* serve to legitimate the Sinhalas' claim to be of Aryan race (as opposed to Tamils who are Dravidians) and the descendants of prince Vijaya, considering themselves as the first civilized settlers of the island. Another legend, about the hero king Dutugemunu who defeated the Tamil king Elara, has been used to legitimate the political dominance of the Sinhalas over the Tamils. The reactivation of this mythohistorical charter has been used to interpret present conditions and mobilize the masses and direct their anger and violence against Tamils, as Tambiah has claimed.[8]

Nissan and Stirrat have pointed out that both the Sinhalas and the Tamils justify ethnic violence in terms of opposing "histories,"[9] representing different views of the past. The past is presented as a struggle between two opposed and mutually exclusive entities, the Sinhalas and the Tamils, where the latter are portrayed as "enemies" and invaders from south India. For the Sinhalas, history justifies their claim and mission to rule over the island and to protect Buddhism therein. Although Tamils refer to the past to support their demand for a total autonomy for Tamil-dominated areas (their homeland), they do not link it to history and former kingdoms.[10] Rather they seem to value belonging to a great literary and religious heritage, rather than to a political history, as Daniel has suggested.[11] Daniel discusses two polar orientations a people may assume toward the past: history and culture. Sinhalas tend to privilege history whereas Sri Lanka Tamils privilege cultural heritage. And, although Sri Lankan Tamils more recently have started to focus upon history in their identity formation, the Plantation Tamils are seen to combine both stances towards the past in order to claim a distinct identity. They consider themselves both "new" (*pudd al*) and "old" (*palle al*) people, because they are recent immigrants, yet they can vaunt an ancient historical tradition.

Despite these different orientations toward the past, however, I would argue for the importance of seeing how they are constituted within relations of power. The question for me is not so much concerned with how Plantation Tamil identity is being shaped or influenced by Buddhist "fundamentalism" or Sri Lanka Tamil separatism (which is answered elsewhere in this volume), but rather how they are being denied a separate ethnic identity by "Others," including other Tamils. In short, in order to maintain and reproduce Otherness, it has become important to deny Plantation Tamils' representations of their own ethnic identity, an identity that is also shaped by Sri Lankan social realities. We cannot discount here, moreover, the impact that the plantation regime, the hill country, and the "memory" of village life in south India have had in shaping the identity of Plantation Tamils.

Plantation Tamils—A Separate Ethnic Group

Plantation Tamils (formerly known as Indian Tamils), descendants of Indian labor migrants to the plantations during the British period, make up less than 6 percent of the population in Sri Lanka. The majority (80 percent) are estate workers living on numerous tea and rubber plantations in the central highlands. Some are landless laborers and squatters in the north, while a minor segment are traders and merchants in Colombo and towns in the planting districts. Plantation Tamils constitute a distinct ethnic group, separated by caste, occupation, manner of speech (dialect), time of arrival to the island, political affiliation, and regional location from the Sri Lanka Tamils, who live in the northern and eastern parts of the island. Despite similarities in language (Tamil) and some religious practices connected with Saivite Hinduism, the Plantation Tamils have not identified themselves and their interests with those of the Sri Lanka Tamils. They have not supported the Sri Lanka Tamils' claim for an independent state, Tamil Eelam. Nor do they want a place for themselves in it where they have nothing (neither land, property, or attachment), and would be forced to labor under Sri Lanka Tamils. Sri Lanka Tamils have attempted to become spokesmen on behalf of the Plantation Tamils, and have made use of their grievances regarding citizenship, better living and working conditions, to support their own demand for a separate state. However, Plantation Tamils have come to view themselves as different from Sri Lanka Tamils merely because the latter have ill-treated them (often in humiliating ways) and have exploited their labor power. Plantation Tamil workers and their children for many decades have been a source of cheap labor (as servants) for both Sinhala and Sri Lanka Tamil middle-class people.[12] Some would probably suggest that Plantation Tamils are less distinct from Sri Lanka Tamils due to their cultural affinities and dependence on Sri Lankan Tamils' residential and political affiliations. Although Plantation Tamils regard themselves as different from Sri Lanka Tamils, this does not exclude that they may feel some sympathy for some of their grievances. Yet, this identification is more situational in character as, for example, the aftermath of the 1983 ethnic riots suggests. At that time, Sri Lanka Tamils and Plantation Tamils shared common experiences of destiny, and both became victims of arson, looting, and murder.

Plantation Tamils stress that they are living, and have to remain, in the up-country districts dominated by the rural Sinhala majority. Not only have they adapted themselves to particular ways of life in up-country estates, but they are used to the cool climate as well. The Tamil plantation workers have largely been confined—first economically and subsequently emotionally—to the estates. Plantation Tamils, of whom most are low-status plantation workers, to some extent have been geographically and socially isolated[13] compared to Sinhalas and Sri Lanka Tamils. Plantation Tamils have lacked integration into the wider society and have remained within the territorial boundaries of the plantations, constituting a relatively "captive" and immobile labor force. Until quite recently they have been politically marginalized, excepting the influence of their trade union, the CWC (Ceylon Workers Congress) and its president S. Thondaman,[14] who became a minister in the UNP (United National Party) government in 1977. However, the Plantation Tamils did not benefit much from new job opportunities created in the public sector, partly because they lacked higher education (and citizenship). More importantly, however, their lack of political patronage and the paucity of public sector activities in Tamil areas also have excluded them from the mainstream. As a consequence, Plantation Tamils have confined themselves to trade and commerce as a possible avenue for upward mobility.

Among Plantation Tamils there has been a gradual shift toward a stronger emphasis on ethnic identity that tends to transcend other social identities based on class and caste.[15] This tendency to stress ethnic identity has been influenced by the development of Sinhala-Buddhist fundamentalism, Tamil separatism, and the occurrence of ethnic violence. As a consequence, interethnic relations have deteriorated and ethnic identity has become the predominant identity by which the major ethnic groups try to distinguish themselves from the others. A claim to a separate cultural identity among the Plantation Tamils has not been accompanied by political demands for a separate territory and regional autonomy. With increasing ethnic antagonism and polarization, there has been a tendency among the majority Sinhala to consider the minor differences between the two Tamil minorities as irrelevant, creating a monolithic Tamil category. This process of singularization, this reconstruction of the past in the present, has created notions that Sinhala-Buddhist and Tamil-Hindu identities are mutually exclusive, "creating" two separate nations and ethnicities.[16] In this process of ethnic polarization, the Plantation Tamils have been denied their own separate ethnic identity, and have been lumped together with the Sri Lanka Tamils into one blanket category.

As is shown by other contributions in this volume, there has been an attempt among the Sinhala at constructing a "singular identity"—based on a common Sinhala-Buddhist cultural heritage. In the new conception of "being Sinhala," the Sinhala-Buddhist identity has come to dominate and has embraced other categories among the Sinhala population, whose identities based on caste and religion are suppressed or considered less relevant. In constructing a common Sinhala identity, the Sinhala-speaking people have put a greater emphasis on "race" and language, or shared origin, rather than religion.[17] It is through a common identification with a shared past and language that the Sinhalas all have come to see themselves as distinctive.

I have argued elsewhere that competition in trade, access to higher education, employment, land grants, and the like, are important factors explaining ethnic rivalry in Sri Lanka.[18] Since the Plantation Tamils are living close to Sinhalas, especially in the low- and mid-country situated tea and rubber plantations, they have become victims of acts of retaliation from Sinhalas who have responded to acts of violence carried out by Tamil Tigers in the north of the country. As a result, in Sinhala dominated areas, the Plantation Tamils have come to represent the accessible and recognizable Other to the Sinhala.

The creation of Plantation Tamil identity is also bound up with their struggle for the improvement of their political and economic position, the issue of repatriation and the granting of citizenship to those being classified as stateless. For instance, the implementation of the Sastri-Bandaranaike pact of 1967, which commenced in 1970,[19] and came to an end in 1983, did shape and influence the Plantation Tamils' relations toward Sinhala Buddhists and their nationalist ideology. They experienced the materialization of the nationalist ideology especially during the SLFP (Sri Lankan Freedom Party) rule between 1970 and 1977, which later led the Plantation Tamils and CWC to support the UNP in succeeding elections.[20]

The repatriation issue and the implementation of the land reforms in the plantations can therefore be seen as interconnected and related to the growth of Sinhala-Buddhist nationalism and fundamentalism. On the other hand, when these issues became politicized and were carried forward by Plantation Tamil leadership in the CWC and its president S. Thondaman, it acted as a reassertion of Plantation Tamil identity. Sri Lanka citizenship for the remaining Plantation Tamils has been a powerful political demand for the CWC and other trade unions, which the CWC sees as a prerequisite for increasing their electoral power in the central highlands. Both issues—the citizenship question and repatriation—have served to unite the Plantation Tamils, creating a sense of common interests vis-à-vis other ethnic groups. Despite a decision in 1988 to grant all stateless persons citizenship, the implementation has been slow and ineffective, and as a consequence some 318,000 Plantation Tamils remain stateless in Sri Lanka.[21]

However, the fact that many more Plantation Tamils have become Sri Lankan citizens and have achieved voting rights has increased their political representation, as indicated by their presence in the newly elected Provincial Councils. Since 1983, the CWC and the Plantation Tamils in the up-country plantation districts have exercised increased political influence through its strategic alliance with the then ruling party, the UNP. But with the increased political representation of the Plantation Tamils, Thondaman's sole leadership has been met with some challenges from newly emerging leaders—namely, Sellasamy and Chandrasekeran, the latter of whom broke away from the CWC to form his own party, the Up-country Peoples Front. These factors have changed the political landscape and contributed to make plantation workers a more politicized group, which the Sinhala-dominated political parties have to take into account when forming alliances to contest political power.

Representations of Village and Plantation in the Construction of Otherness

Village-estate relations have been interpreted and contrasted with each other in terms of a dual economy, in which the former represents a "hemmed-in" and "traditional" entity or sector, while the estate has been described as an "enclave" or modern sector (Snodgrass 1966). Meyer criticizes these representations and argues that they represent powerful reinforcing myths whose political implications are highly significant (1992b:200). This dichotomy between village and plantation, seen as self-contained units, is at best a social construction, because there is much evidence of flow between them.

On the practical level it is difficult to see them as separate. To illustrate, in the low country and in some mid-country estates, there are a substantial number of Sinhala resident laborers and many more commuting villagers. The images constructed of the village and the estate are closely interconnected with the nationalist rhetoric of the "positive" or "negative" impacts of the plantation system on villages.[22] These images or representations of rural life and estate are evident in the reports of the Kandyan Peasantry Commission,[23] which became important in shaping the views of nationalists. Its report portrayed a crisis in rural culture in which the kin-based, homogeneous, and reciprocal nature of "traditional village society" were being destroyed. Moore has noticed that the report stresses: the alleged harmony and unity of precolonial social and economic life; the integrating cultural role of Buddhism in this life; and the loss of "community" as a sociocultural phenomenon of the colonial era.[24]

Representations of the "negative" impact that plantations have had on the village economy include: the acquisition of village land; damaging effects on local ecology; and deforestation and absence of benefits to the village population. The "imagined" negative impact of the estates on villages accords with reality. Bandarage, among others, argues that "the plantation sector was developed at the expense of village agriculture and peasant subsistence."[25] According to these representations, the Kandyan Sinhalas have been deprived of their high land (and chena cultivation) while the expansion of the plantations is considered the direct, and indirect, consequence of stagnation in agricultural production and increasing rural poverty. In addition, estates have inhibited the possibility of village expansion. The Kandyan peasants have become embittered over the dominant role of the plantations and the monopolization of employment by the Tamil workers, whom they associate with the British plantocracy. Many Sinhala rural people believe that Tamil estate workers enjoy a better living standard (in terms of steady wages and the issue of food rations by the estate) than many of the Kandyan peasants. There is a tendency also to privilege external factors in order to explain the social ills, poverty, and exploitation among the Sinhalas, rather than focusing on class and caste differences within the rural social structure. These representations of the idealized rural order have become an important part of the Sinhala-Buddhist nationalist ideology and of fundamentalism, which to some extent can explain the rush toward legislation for land reform and nationalization of the plantations. It also explains at least partially the wide appeal of the "Sinhala-Only" language act and the privileging of Buddhism in the constitution. The symbols of the past thus have served as a charter for the proper social order for the present. Indeed, as Moore suggests, the rural past, with a stress on "community" and "harmony," has become a central theme in national political ideology.[26]

The idealized vision of rural life in nationalist rhetoric has come to be connected with the electoral power of the Sinhala peasantry and the well-established relationship (and forms of dependency) between the peasantry and the state (state patronage). The powerful symbols of this idealized vision of Sinhala cultural identity included: the tank; paddy fields; and the temple.[27] They have become indisputably associated with Sinhala-Buddhist identity. Jayawardena notes that "there was a harking back to an idealized village community of peasant owners, assumed to characterize ancient Ceylon, as constituting a valid model for Sri Lanka's modern development."[28] The same symbolic associations were revived by ministers during inauguration ceremonies of modern development projects—for example, the Mahaveli program. Along these lines, in a study of the politics of development rituals, Tennekoon has shown how interpretations of the past and the Sinhala mythohistory of legends have been reenacted in social practices of the present.[29]

Socioeconomic Consequences of Land Reforms on Tamil Plantation Workers

When the plantations became state property and changed management due to political interference on employment,[30] the number of workers on payrolls increased substantially, due to political patronage and poor management. Government policy was enacted to reduce unemployment among the youth in the estates and to provide employment for the unemployed Sinhala in the neighboring villages (Daniel 1993). As a result, there were more registered workers—that is, names on the payroll—than actual laborers. The immediate benefits of the land reform to local villagers was usually in the form of unproductive jobs such as watchmen or supervisors and allotments to build a house. The Usawasama (Up Country Cooperative Plantations Development Board) was one of the public-sector corporations that initially disposed over 68,000 acres. It became widely known for poor management, while it sacrificed agricultural output for immediate benefits to local villagers by allocating jobs and rights to pluck tea. When the UNP came into power in 1977, this land was transferred to the state plantation corporations.

One of the effects of land reform on the plantations was the fragmentation of the estate lands due to colonization schemes—that is, parts of the land were settled by poor and landless Sinhala villagers. In addition, there was wholesale neglect of agriculture and mismanagement of many of the estates that had been taken over, which threatened their economic viability (or profitability). Without work, many unemployed and homeless Tamil laborers fled into the cities of Kandy and Colombo. Nationalization of the estates and the eruption of ethnic riots in many mid-country estates in Kandy, Matale, and Ratnapura during 1977 and 1981 forced many Plantation Tamils to flee to the semiarid districts of Mannar, Vavuniya, and Mullaitivu in the north in search of social security. Here these refugees or displaced persons were transformed into bonded laborers while working as landless laborers for Sri Lanka Tamil absentee landowners. They cleared the jungle and set up small mud huts with thatched roofs, while living in conditions far more deplorable than on the estates.

Since a majority of the Tamil estate households rely on estate wages as their main and sole source of income, they are dependent on how much work (that is, number of days per month) the estate can provide them. This, in return, depends on the economic viability and agricultural maintenance of the estate to produce necessary yields. The land reforms have led to a great deterioration of the agronomic conditions in many mid-country estates (Kandy and Matale), which has resulted in less work and diminishing incomes for the Tamil estate workers. Increasing poverty and underemployment has led to some internal migration, to other and better maintained tea estates at higher altitudes (Nuwara Eliya or Hatton-Maskeliya). There has been also labor migration to the up-country estates in the decades since land reform. Plantation workers have been paid incentives up to Rs. 2,000 to move to one of the up-country estates, which have suffered labor shortages as a consequence of Indian repatriation schemes. Thus, more Sinhala villagers have found employment in low country estates.

With the nationalization of the estates there were not only changes in ownership, but also in management. The paternalistic pattern of managerial methods prevailing under the resident British planter underwent a change with their gradual departure during the 1960s and early 1970s. The land reforms introduced an almost entirely Sinhala management recruited from the upper- and middle-class wealthy landowning families in Colombo and Kandy. Their management style has differed in the sense that they have not shown any interest in the welfare and living conditions of the Tamil labor force. Management in estates has become subject to both communalism and political interference, something which has led to a replacement of estate managers following an election, where, for instance, an SLFP-supporter is replaced with a manager loyal to the UNP, and vice versa.

During the first years after the land reforms were introduced, there were also many experiments with corporate management that failed, including the alienation of estate land to make corporate farms. Tamil workers encountered severe problems when living on estates that came under the management of such cooperatives, for example, NADSA (National Agricultural Development and Settlement Authority).[31] The NADSA authorities resorted to methods of squeezing out the Tamil-speaking workers who found themselves in the position of vagrants. The workers in these estates were often faced with few days of work, as little as eight to ten days a month, which meant reduced income and often starvation: some workers complained that they did not get work or salary advances to buy their food provisions. Although many Tamil workers were ready to leave NADSA controlled estates and move to other estates, they were unable to do so because their pension and dues offered them for long service had not been settled. Other steps, thought of as progressive, such as the takeover of estate schools, land alienation, and greater estate-village integration, only served to increase the Tamil workers' sense of insecurity and disenfranchisement.

The nationalization of the plantations, accompanied by a further indigenization of management and staff where more Sinhala were recruited to jobs in the low- and mid-country estates, did not change for the better the Tamil workers' position and living conditions. Their low wages, poor working and housing conditions, deplorable health and educational conditions were not alleviated.

Herring has argued that although the best land was seized during land reforms, the major beneficiaries were not those at the productive base—that is, the noncitizen (or stateless) Plantation Tamils, or even the landless Sinhala laborers—but primarily the state through its increased control of both patronage resources and the national economy.[32] It can be argued that the main objective of the ruling elite (although contradictory to their own interests as plantation owners themselves) in carrying out the nationalization of the plantations was the redressing of grievances of the Kandyan peasantry. The elite had ideological reasons, backed by a moral and mythohistoric justification, for supporting the image of an authentic, family-farming and rice-based Sinhala society. They found the Kandyan areas most suitable for transformation.[33]

Conclusion

Land reform and the nationalization of the plantations in Sri Lanka must be analyzed in connection with the emergence of Sinhala-Buddhist fundamentalist ideology and political patronage. The ideology, based on mythohistorical interpretations of the past, helped to create greater homogeneity by constructing a "singular identity" among Sinhalas while at the same time excluding others. The past, in terms of the myths and legends of Sinhala-Buddhist chronicles, still plays an important role in the construction of national identity, supported by a fundamentalist ideology that conflates race, language, and religion. These interpretations of the past, when connected with rural images, representations of the estates, and construction of the Other, can be helpful in explaining the legislation of land reforms and the nationalization of the plantations.

Land reforms and nationalization of the plantations represent politically motivated means to build up electoral support, especially since the distribution of state resources has functioned as an important means of political patronage. The state, defined as a Sinhala-Buddhist one, became committed to support the Sinhala peasantry as a moral obligation. As a result, the land reforms were conducted in the name of the peasantry by the landed elite, rather than springing from demands and discontent among the peasantry. Although nationalist sentiments were mobilized in support of the nationalization of the plantations and can be regarded as an important underlying factor, it cannot alone explain the move toward state takeover. Indeed, one political force behind nationalization was the Marxist party LSSP, which was assisted by fear of peasant discontent by the SLFP-led government after the JVP uprising in 1971. This was a factor that led to a sudden rush toward legislation, but the fact remains that Sinhala-Buddhist nationalist and fundamentalist ideology was a moving force. This is indicated by the fact that the UNP, which had the support of landowning groups, also voted in favor of the land reforms in 1975.

Land reforms and nationalization of the estates has not succeeded in redistributing any significant amount of land to the rural poor. Neither has it transformed the agrarian structure, nor has it challenged the power and status of the landed elite, mainly because paddy lands were virtually exempted from the land reforms of the mid 1970s. Moore suggests that land policy, and the ideologies that support it, have in general focused much more on the control of land than on the cultivation or use of land.[34] The nationalization of individually and company-owned estates constitutes no exception in that respect. What is also evident by the common malpractice in the implementation of the land reforms is the effective exclusion of the Plantation Tamil population from any share in the process of alienation of land. In fact, the converse is true: they have been evicted from some of the mid-country estates in which they had labored for generations.

Buddhist fundamentalist ideas as implemented in Sinhala nationalist ideology and practical policies, such as the citizenship issue and repatriation, together with experiences of ethnic rioting, have shaped the identity of the Plantation Tamils. Plantation Tamils have become more consciously aware of the fact that they constitute a separate ethnic group with needs, interests, problems, and grievances of their own, not to be confused with those of Sri Lanka Tamils, some of whom demand a separate state in the northern and eastern provinces.

Notes

1. The Plantation Tamils' poor political representation is partly due to their disenfranchisement in 1948, when the majority were denied Sri Lankan citizenship. After an agreement in 1967 between India and Sri Lanka, some 400,000 were repatriated to India while the remaining were gradually granted Sri Lankan citizenship. With the recent introduction of Provincial Councils in 1987, the Plantation Tamils have improved their political representation.

2. O. Hollup, "Ethnic Identity, Violence and the Estate Tamil Minority in Sri Lanka," *The Round Table*, 1992, 323.

3. The land expropriated by the government during the nationalization comprised 63 percent of the total tea acreage and 32 percent of the rubber acreage. The land reform of 1972 was directed toward local proprietors where 226,629 hectares were nationalized. In 1975 some 395 large estates comprising 168,758 hectares of land was expropriated from foreign and local companies.

4. Successive governments have under various agencies (Land Reform Commission, NADSA, etc.) used the policy of state-aided land grants and settlement schemes (colonization) of landless peasants to increase electoral support. Hence these distributions functioned as a form of political patronage.

5. B. Kapferer, *Legends of People: Myths of State* (Washington, D.C.: Smithsonian Institution, 1988); G. Obeyesekere and R. Gombrich, *Buddhism Transformed* (Princeton University Press, 1988); J. Spencer, ed., *Sri Lanka: History and the Roots of Conflict* (London: Routledge, 1990a); S. Tambiah, *Sri Lanka: Ethnic Fratricide and the Dismantling of Democracy* (University of Chicago Press, 1986); and S. Tambiah, *Buddhism Betrayed? Religion, Politics and Violence in Sri Lanka* (University of Chicago Press, 1992).

6. H.L. Seneviratne, "Identity and the Conflation of Past and Present," *Social Analysis*, vol. 25 (1989).

7. Kapferer's (*Legends of People*, 1988) ontological interpretations have been criticized by S. Kemper, *The Presence of the Past: Chronicles, Politics and Culture in Sinhala Life* (Cornell University Press, 1992); and D. Scott, *Formations of Ritual: Colonial and Anthropological Discourses on the Sinhala Yaktovil* (University of Minnesota Press, 1994).

8. Stanley Tambiah, *Sri Lanka.*

9. E. Nissan and R.L. Stirrat, "State, Nation and the Representation of Evil: The Case of Sri Lanka," Sussex Research Papers in Social Anthropology, no. 1, 1987.

10. D.-Hellmann Rajanayagam, "Tamils and the Meaning of History," in *The Sri Lankan Tamils: Ethnicity and Identity*, C. Manogaran and B. Pfaffenberger, eds. (Westview Press, 1994), has pointed out that in the 1920s and 1930s Sri Lanka Tamils began to write histories of the Jaffna kingdom to assert their identity, not only vis-à-vis the Sinhala but also vis-à-vis the Tamils of south India. For more on this, see the Introduction to this volume.

11. E.V. Daniel, "Three Dispositions towards the Past: One Sinhala Two Tamil," *Social Analysis*, vol. 25 (1989).

12. O. Hollup, *Bonded Labor-Caste and Cultural Identity Among Tamil Plantation Workers in Sri Lanka* (New Delhi: Sterling Publishers Private Ltd., 1994).

13. The relative social isolation of Tamil estate workers was supported by the particular characteristics of the plantations as a "total institution": see E. Goffman, *Asylum* (New York, 1961), which broke down the boundaries between three spheres of life—notably work, residence, and recreation. Almost all aspects of social life were conducted within the same territorial boundaries.

14. O. Hollup, "Trade Unions and Leadership among Tamil Estate Workers in Sri Lanka," *Journal of Contemporary Asia*, vol. 21, no. 2 (1991).

15. The importance of caste identity has undergone a radical transformation over time among the Plantation Tamils. For more, see R. Jayaraman, *Caste Continuities in Ceylon* (Bombay: Popular Prakashan, 1975); H.P. Chattopadhyaya, *Indians in Sri Lanka* (Calcutta: O.P.S. Publisher, 1979); and O. Hollup, *Bonded Labor*, 1994.

16. Stanley Tambiah, *Sri Lanka.*

17. R.L. Stirrat, *Power and Religiosity in a Post-colonial Setting: Sinhala Catholics in Contemporary Sri Lanka* (Cambridge University Press, 1992).

18. O. Hollup, "Ethnic Identity."

19. According to this pact, some 650,000 Plantation Tamils were to apply for Indian citizenship and passport and, in due time, were to be repatriated. This process of repatriation started in the late 1960s and terminated in 1983 due to the ethnic riots and breakdown in ferry transport over the Palk Straits. During this period some 400,000 Plantation Tamils were repatriated.

20. The CWC which has, until now, been the sole representative of the Plantation Tamils, was an allied partner of the UNP for 15 years until the 1994 elections. It is only quite recently that their control with plantation votes has become contested by other trade unions and political parties such as the Up-country Peoples United Front.

21. B. Olsen, "Human rights issues in Sri Lanka," in P. Baehr, and H. Hey et al., *Human Rights in Developing Countries Yearbook, 1994* (Boston: Kluwer Publishers, 1994).

22. A. Bandarage, *Colonialism in Sri Lanka: Political Economy of the Kandyan Highlands 1833–1886* (Berlin: Mouton, 1983); R.J. Herring, *Land to the Tiller* (New Haven: Yale University Press, 1983).

23. One of the central themes in this representation of village-estate relations was that the British dispossessed the Kandyan peasantry of their lands to give them over to European planters. See E. Meyer, "From Landgrabbing to Landhunger: High Land Appropriation in the Plantation Areas of Sri Lanka during the British Period," *Modern Asian Studies*, vol. 26, no. 2 (1992a): 322.

24. M. Moore, *The State and Peasant Politics in Sri Lanka* (Cambridge University Press, 1985), p. 243.

25. A. Bandarage, *Colonialism in Sri Lanka*, p. 325.

26. M. Moore, *The State and Peasant Politics.*

27. Ibid., and J. Spencer, *A Sinhala Village.*

28. Lal Jayawardena quoted in Stanley Tambiah, *Buddhism Betrayed?*, p. xii.

29. S. Tennekoon, "Rituals of Development: The Accelerated Mahaveli Development Program of Sri Lanka," *American Ethnologist*, vol. 15. no. 2 (1988).

30. Although management before the nationalization was basically Sinhala, the major change that occurred after the land reform was the selection of SLFP supporters as managers without necessarily a planter background. They were previously cooperative managers, teachers, or local administrators without any prior knowledge of tea cultivation and how to run an estate.

31. NADSA was started by the munificent offer and aid of the World Bank for the sole purpose of giving a better future for the plantation workers and increase productivity. However, it seems that many of these allocated funds were misused or ineffective.

32. R. Herring, *Land to the Tiller*, p. 270.

33. The Kandyan Sinhalas tend to regard themselves as the pure Sinhala Buddhists and carriers of old tradition from the ancient kingdom, in contrast to low-country Sinhala who became Westernized, Christianized, and exposed to capitalism in the early days of colonial impact.

34. M. Moore, *The State and Peasant Politics*.

Chapter 5

In the Shadow of Violence: "Tamilness" and the Anthropology of Identity in Southern Sri Lanka[1]

Pradeep Jeganathan

> One . . . three . . . seventy
> Hundred . . . two hundred . . . two hundred
> and fifty:
> This counting will never end
> For before it has ended
> You come again
> With bombs and bullets
> To increase the numbers to be counted.
> If only someone could come and see
> The beauty of this moment!
>
> The rioters will come again:
> We wait expectantly.[2]

In an important article published recently, Gananath Obeyesekere echoes the concerns of this volume of papers: the question of Otherness in Sri Lankan Buddhist society.[3] Obeyesekere is rightly wary of "defining the Other as a radically exclusive conception," since the example at stake—the Tamil Other in relation to the Sinhala Self—has been historically both a sought after ally and hated enemy, wife or invader. Such a conception stands, then, in close relation to the theme of these chapters collected here: the complicated place of Otherness in Buddhist Lanka, and in particular the "near[ness]" of the Tamil Hindu Other to the Sinhala-Buddhist Self. I have found this conception of "otherness" instructive. Indeed, the evidence I will produce in this paper will support this framing, even though the order of my categories are reversed: the Tamil Self in relation to Sinhala Others is my concern. Yet, I want tell that story of Othering a little differently from the way it has been told before me. In so doing I hope to rethink not only the place of "Tamilness" in Sinhala-Buddhist society, but also the anthropology of identity in the Sri Lankan ethnographic field.

Given my concern with "Tamilness," my anthropological objects in this chapter will be a set of signifying practices that are constituted by and constitutive of the Tamil Self. There is, as there must be necessarily, a large terrain of practices that are imbricated in the production of a particular identity, and Tamilness is not an exception. My analysis, then, will only attend to one moment in this larger terrain of practices, and so will be necessarily incomplete. That said, let me specify the character and kind of the signifying practices that concern me, which I shall do negatively, at first. I will not be concerned in this chapter with what might justifiably be posited as conventional practices of the Tamil Self, such as ritual practices of faith and worship, or the intra- and intercaste interactions.

I will, on the contrary, focus on a set of signifying practices of Tamilness that are only visible in relation to the presence of violence in the ethnographic landscape of Lanka. An examination of these practices, I suggest, will allow for a foregrounding of a particular aspect of Tamil identity that has emerged in recent years, which is crucial to understanding that identity more generally. Tamilness in southern Sri Lanka, I will argue, is produced in the shadow of violence. Or, in other words, in anticipation of violence. So this paper examines a repertoire of practices that are produced by Tamils given an anticipation of violence. I will call these practices "tactics of anticipation." They will be the primary anthropological object here.

Before moving further with the positivity of that anthropology, I will attempt to clarify and locate my analytical categories in relation to other recent approaches to the anthropology of identity in Sri Lanka. First of all, I want to suggest that choosing a framing that encompasses violence as a category is not idiosyncratic: it is not a product of my particular research interests—which center, undoubtedly, on the place of violence, and its perpetration in urban Sri Lanka. On the contrary, the framing is increasingly pervasive: to write of Lanka today is also to write of violence. If the subject is Sri Lanka, violence must, and does, appear. I claim, however, that violence will appear in my text differently from its appearance in the general scholarly discourses on Sri Lanka. How, then, does violence appear in scholarly discourse on Lanka? What is the form of that appearance? What is its analytic place? My answer, which I will produce succinctly first, and expand on later, is this: violence, not always, but usually—that is to say, in the dominant form of its appearance in the literature—takes on the form of a "problem." Its very presence in the well-known and well-worked ethnographic field of Lanka is in itself a problem. It is that problem, that question of its very emergence, that motivates explanation.

Let me clarify these claims further by returning to Obeyesekere's article, with which I started. Primarily, of course, his paper is part of an important collection of texts on fundamentalism, and produces a brilliant response to that project. In the course of that response, violence emerges as a categorical presence in Obeyesekere's text, repeatedly and quite centrally. This emergence is not recent; in many articles by Obeyesekere published in the last decade, violence appears as a category, that must, given its very emergence, be explained.[4]

In these papers, violence is inserted into an analytic that produces the answer to the question: What is the logic of this *emergence* of violence? Specifically, in this particular paper of Obeyesekere, violence emerges as "problem"—needing explanation—in relation to the perceived nonviolent nature of Buddhism. Take this key sentence: "Here then is the partial answer to the question of how Buddhism, a religion of radical nonviolence, has produced in our time an intensity of political violence."[5] The production of violence is to be explained because, in Obeyesekere's view, it sits nonintuitively in relation to "nonviolent" Buddhism. Now one kind of violence that is at stake here is interethnic or Sinhala Buddhist/Tamil Hindu political violence. Let us read the explanation that Obeyesekere advances for the emergence of this kind of violence.

It is "Buddhist history," Obeyesekere argues, in contrast to the Buddhist "doctrinal tradition," that is "associated with . . . violence and the intolerance of others." In a colonial context, this Buddhist history is intertwined by the religious reformer Anagarika Dharmapala, with the doctrinal fundamentalism produced a few years earlier by the American Theosophist Henry Steele Olcott.[6] What emerges here is a new Buddhist history; a discourse where "passion, physical and polemical violence" can "reign." Given a concern with the presence of violence, the discourse of Buddhist history must be located in relation to "Tamil-Hindu history." "This Buddhist history, redefined and elaborated in various ways, exists in confrontation with the very recently invented yet equally polemical Tamil-Hindu history."[7]

It is by tracking this confrontational relationship then—that is to say, the relationship between the Sinhala Self, and Tamil Other—that for Obeyesekere the "why" and "how" of the problem of the emergence of violence can be addressed: "Here [in this confrontation] reigns . . . violence . . . and demeaning of the Other."[8] In this problematic the anthropology of two of the key identities at stake in the Lankan ethnographic field—the identities of "Sinhalaness" and "Tamilness," and the crucial relationship between them—are then examined to produce an answer to that vexing and ever-present question: How or why has violence emerged in the Lankan ethnographic field?[9]

I can see, I want to stress, that there are considerable analytic gains that have been made by Obeyesekere in the pursuance of this problematic. But I also want to suggest that a fresh perspective may lead to other kinds of analytical gains in relation to our understanding of Lankan identities. It is in that spirit that I want to think this problem anew, examining the relationship between "Tamilness," and Sinhala sociocultural life by working through a different set of analytical moves. Reversing the common location of violence as a category that must be explained, given its emergence, I will situate it as unavailable for explanation.[10] I shall do so because I think there is the possibility of losing the density, the opacity, the very presence of the object—violence—by attempting to explain its emergence. The shadow of violence, then, will hover over this text—its very density casting a long, dark, fuzzy pall over it. There will be no "getting beyond" violence in this paper; no explaining it away. Rather than be explained—and thereby be worked upon—the category of violence in this paper, since it is unavailable for explanation, may help hence in the analytical work of the paper itself. The presence of violence in this text, then, will be used to foreground a set of particular signifying practices of Tamilness.

The kind of violence at stake in this chapter is urban collective violence—what might be called riots—that have taken place with some regularity in southern Sri Lanka.[11] At the end of July 1983, Tamils living in southern Sri Lanka experienced a week-long moment of direct, overwhelming violence.[12] That week remains an extraordinary punctuation point in our modern history, the profound significance of which, I believe, we are yet to fully understand.[13] Tamil Sri Lankans, who were living in the south of the country during the violence, found their lives changed forever, as they found their "Tamilness," remade first in relation to this violence, and then repeatedly, in its wake, in the months and years after.

Valli Kanapathipillai, in her pioneering efforts, has examined, sensitively and closely, the (female) survivor of this violence, tracing the effect an event of violence had on particular life histories, and telling of particular reconfigurations in the wake of that event.[14] This kind of work is rare in the Lankan ethnographic field, as it positions violence as unavailable for explanation, just as I would like to, instead of positioning its emergence as a problematic in itself. But my explicit concern with the analytical place of violence is not Kanapathipillai's; the place of violence is not thought through anew in her work, emerging rather through the received anthropological category of the survivor. This analytic category of the survivor is produced through (oral) biographies of the survival of direct violence.

As such, then, the place of violence in Kanapathipillai's work is that of a "cause." It is through this causal relationship that the "survivor" is produced: the "survivor" exists because she has experienced violence. Such efforts are now familiar in the anthropology of violence,[15] for they operate in relation to an object that is always already visible to the ethnographic eye sensitive to the effects of violence, an object whose existence is indisputable to the ethnographer because it is marked out prior to her arrival in the field, an object, in other words, that is always already available to an anthropology of violence.

I want to draw a distinction between Kanapathipillai's work, and my own here. My concern is with the anticipation of violence, not with the experience of survival and the survivor of violence. There is, therefore, an analytic distinction to be drawn between our objects and, subtle though it may seem, I would plead its importance. By refusing to position violence in a direct causal relationship with the categories of my investigation—Tamilness in southern Sri Lanka—I am able to both think the texture of the relationship between the categories of "violence" and "Tamilness" in a way that may have not been possible before.

But, even in so doing, the riskier, uncharted nature of my undertaking may become apparent. The signifying practices of "the anticipation of violence" are not, it seems to me, to be as coherently available to the ethnographic eye, or to the anthropological project, as might be practices of survival. The practices I want to think through here are both ever-present and ephemeral. They may seem visible, but then may fade away; they may shift position, but seem always to be centered; they may disappear quickly, and reappear even more strongly and suddenly. The practice of anticipating violence, I want to suggest, flitters across the landscape of Lanka like a shadow cast on a cloudy day by the setting sun. The production of such a category does not come easily to anthropology; it will emerge only through and within my analysis, spreading through it darkly and pervasively.

Three chronological and interlocking clusters of practices provide a grid on which my analysis rests. First, I explore narrations of the anticipation of violence that are located within the space of the July 1983 riots. Second, I mark the explicit production of "tactics of anticipation" in expectation of more civilian-directed violence in the south, in the years after 1983. And third, I comment on the self-conscious production of these tactics of anticipation by southern Tamils, for circulation through the metropolitan West. Throughout, my analysis will draw upon extensive, recent ethnographic research carried out in Colombo.

An introductory digression that sketches out networks of social power in Patupara,[16] a neighborhood in which I lived and learned about for two years, will be necessary before the position of Tamils, and the location of "Tamilness" in that community, can be delineated. Patupara is a small lane that leads up from a vast, and uninhabited marshy plain—to a major road that falls on to Galle Road.[17] Up until the 1950s, Patupara was a footpath cutting across the farms of the Pereras, a Sinhala-Christian family, who had bought land in the area in the early part of this century.[18] While the Pereras had capitalized their grass fields, with coconut trees and a coconut processing mill, and sheds of cattle that stood on the high land surrounding Patupara, the lower reaches of the fields, especially where the path trailed off into the great marsh, was, in the rainy season, a small lake of water. It was here that the now middle-aged Perera brothers had come down from their exclusive public school, "to do a spot of fishing," during the holidays. But old Mr. Perera passed on, Colombo expanded south, and country, slowly but surely, became city. The farm ceased to function, and the value of the land was transformed into urban real estate.

Property, which had existed in an abstract, jural sense since the seventeenth century, began to take on the yet newer inflection of the urban: a "novel social space" simultaneously defined by "unprecedented proximity," and "privatization."[19] Land is now measured in perches, not acres. The new plots of land became the grounds of new family homes: the bungalow, self-contained with a defined boundary marked by a wall or fence, had come into being. Here, "spatial distance reflected social distance."[20] Some of the Perera children built family homes on their shares of land and others sold parcels to other bourgeois families.

Importantly, this was simultaneous with Patupara's transformation into a "real" road from its early beginnings as a footpath. The chief quality of a "real" road, in my use here, is its representability on the maps of the Municipal Council, where Patupara (the road) emerges uncertainly in the late 1960s. The road was then tarred, its drains measured, municipal taxes levied, and crucially, bourgeois families who lived down the road got "real" addresses: numbers and street names, marking the privatization of space. A road is a vector of capital.[21] The road challenged, but did not completely displace, the claim of the "Walauwe"—the manor house of the Pereras—to be the symbolic center of the community. The road is where the grocery stores and the public taps are: one cannot, therefore, avoid the road if one lives in the community. It defines my basic unit of analysis.

Yet, the transformation of the value of land was inevitably uneven. In the days of the farm, the workers had lived where they worked. These old, retired workers—their children now factory workers, in the main—were gifted small pieces of low-lying land in inconvenient spots: on the banks of storm water drains, or near garbage dumps. Their always small shacks, which in contemporary Sri Lankan urban-planning discourses are called shanties, are now crowded together, sandwiched between the bungalows. Since many of the gifts had been informal in the naturalized relationship between the "lord" and his "servants," the time-consuming and expensive survey plans and "deeds of gift" were not drawn up for the workers.[22] The land parcels of the workers, a product of modernity, lacked the complete realization of commodification: exchangeability. In fact, a worker lived on a small plot at the overarching sufferance of his/her lords with whom lay the ultimate possibility of denying the gift, and declaring the workers "squatters."

If we turn now to two particular plots of land, the specificities of the intersections of authority and ethnicity will be apparent. The first of these plots—about 0.75 acres in extent—had been marsh, overgrown with shrubs. Michael Perera who owned it (wanting to raise cash) sold the entire plot to a real estate development company—a subsidiary of an enormous conglomerate of intersecting, publicly-quoted, holding companies. Earth-filled trucks, bulldozers, and power rollers transformed that piece of marsh into "buildable land" in a matter of weeks. The company, building a high, white wall around the entire plot—so that the shanties around its edges could not be seen—blocked it out with colored markers into eight perch plots and settled down to sell it off at ten, yes, ten times what they paid for it. The snag, however, was the Carolis family. They occupied 7.5 perches at the eastern end of the plot, steadfastly maintaining that John Hamu had given them the land before he died. John Hamu, one of the Perera brothers who had been both an alcoholic and a leftist, indeed might have given them the land, except it was not ever his to give: it was his brother's. Neither Perera persuasion, nor company offers of money (well below selling price) worked, and the Carolis family did not move. So, now, the white wall zig zags at the east end of the land.

This issue of the Carolis land had soured relationships with the Pereras considerably. All the Perera children now thought of Carolis' family as those who were "squatting on Michael's land." Carolis, in turn, had stopped visiting the Pereras at Sinhala *Avurudhu* (New Year). And, there was yet an added dimension to this relationship that further complicated it: Carolis' daughter Leela had married a Tamil, Muttiah. Now Muttiah and his family lived on the same plot of land that Carolis was "squatting" on; upon marriage, they had built a new shack, abutting the old one. It was not the marriage, as much as the growing family that resulted from it, that made it imperative that the land not be handed over to the Pereras or their nominees. And Muttiah, a newcomer to the intricate relations between this particular master and his servants, was caught in an uncomfortable middle. His Tamilness had never figured explicitly in the dispute, but he had felt, as he told me later, that it might.

The question of property was crucial in the case of another Tamil family that had lived in the neighborhood for a decade. The Josephs were a middle-class family that had rented a house from one of the Perera brothers. A few years before the riots they had been asked to leave by the landlord, but they had stayed on, citing the high rentals in new houses and apartments. The house the Josephs occupied was rent-controlled, and Sri Lanka's strong tenant protection laws made it nearly impossible for the Pereras to force the issue legally. Here, too, the question of the Josephs' Tamilness had not been directly addressed by the Pereras, who in any event liked to think of themselves as cosmopolitan people whose best friends, as the old cliché goes, were Tamils.

Then came the riots. That massive anti-Tamil violence that shook urban Sri Lanka for one week in July 1983. This paper is not about the political economy of that event or its ideological place in a Lankan national space. I would like to set those questions aside to consider another question that will take us to the heart of this paper—the texture of "Tamilness" in the midst of that violence, and its remaking in the years after. Muttiah, who talked to me about those times during the two years I lived in Patupara, narrates that waiting vividly.

Many of these conversations took place under particular circumstances that are constitutive of methodological sites, that are crucial to my ethnographic representations here. These were particular moments during the long calm of the early 1990s, when Tamils like Muttiah expected another riot to be around the corner. One such important moment was in mid-1992, when a militant bomb, in the north of the country, blew up nearly the entire commanding staff of the Sri Lankan armed forces. A big military funeral was planned the next day at the national cemetery in Colombo. In 1983 the long week of violence had begun after a similar military funeral. We seemed to teeter, briefly but palpably, at the edge of a space for violence within which a riot could take place.

It was at times like this, when Muttiah would speak to me of 1983—and seeing as he did its sharply etched shadow across his life—that he produced in his narratives a rich texture of detail that was not available at other times. These narratives are not, then, merely about the past. And they do *not* in my representation here serve as "evidence" produced in an effort to investigate the "event." On the contrary, these narratives—like all history—are about the past as well as the present; about recollections as well as anticipation. They are made, like Tamilness itself, in the shadow of violence.

"I didn't know what would happen," Muttiah remembered, "maybe they would come for me, just me, or they would burn the house, also. If it was just me, it would be all right, but without the house we would have nowhere to live. I thought if I wasn't in the house, when they came, things would be all right. So I left." Suddenly, Muttiah, who usually saw himself as the protector and master of his family becomes, in his own eyes, its liability. It was his own "Tamilness" that made him want to banish himself from their midst, acting as if his presence was a taint on their being. Even as he left home, warning his wife and two daughters to be careful, he stopped by the Josephs, to warn them of the impending danger. This was unusual; in the ordinary course of events, Muttiah—who drove a garbage truck for the Municipal Council—had little to say, except in submissive greeting to Joseph, who had a white-collar job in the city. What is more, Muttiah would trace his ancestry to India, within a depth of a few generations, while Joseph would to Jaffna, marking himself and his family as "Sri Lanka Tamil" on a census form. But here and now, in the face of violence, class and origin did not matter as much as they might have on another day: Muttiah opened the gate to the Josephs' house, and knocked on the door.

Only Joseph was home: his family had been sent away that very hour, with a few documents they had thought were invaluable, to a Sinhala friend's house in another neighborhood. Joseph had stayed behind, as he told Muttiah, "as the man of the house to keep the house safe." There is an obvious reversal of movement here, when Joseph is contrasted with Muttiah's own departure from home; here Joseph is not a liability, rather, despite his "Tamilness," he remains a true patriarch, a protector of hearth and home. But what I find significant here is the nexus of masculinity and ethnicity that emerges in each case, and that emerges in others I know of, as well. To wait for a riot is to wait in a space for violence, at its shifting, porous boundaries. A space for violence is a space of danger, one in which particular masculinities can emerge.[23] And, in Muttiah's subordinated, sacrificial leaving home in an attempt to save the house, to Joseph's desire to face down any intruders single-handedly, we have similar but different plays of masculinity and ethnicity at the boundary of a space of violence.

But Muttiah talked Joseph out of it. Exercising the rare authority of street wiseness that his working-class status gave him, Muttiah told Joseph that it was unwise to stay; so unwise that he could risk death. Joseph capitulated slowly, but then, in the inevitable unraveling of the logic of bourgeois order in the face of violence, asked for time to put a few belongings into a bag. And, as Muttiah waited, Joseph scuttled about the house first picking up one, and then another, possession, commodity, heirloom, keepsake, or knick-knack, only to put it down again in confusion. Such uncertainty is familiar, I would argue, to Tamilness in Sri Lanka; to be a Tamil is to both remember and anticipate the destruction of property so treasured by bourgeois society. The many Tamils who have safe deposit boxes, deep in the vaults of banks in York Street, live in the vise of this anxiety, of not knowing what in their lives must fit into a box two feet by three. It is not—as Joseph's dilemma demonstrates—easy to know what from one's home, that terrain of lived detail made over years, must be fitted into a box or shoulder bag.

They went off together, Muttiah and Joseph, to hide, deep in the marsh, until the danger had past. They walked far, until their bodies had sunk in up to their waists, shrouding their heads with banana leaves. Joseph, who had rarely been near the marsh before, and certainly not this far, had been appalled by the grime and the stench, but Muttiah knew it was their safest bet. What Muttiah remembers about that day is the smoke. First, it looked like a rain cloud darkening the sky, but then it grew larger, blackening not just the sky but the earth, as well. It filled the air with the smell of charring and tiny particles of ash. By tracing the movement of smoke, they could tell the neighborhoods that were on fire, and those that were yet untouched. They waited in the marsh for the fires to come to them.

A common Tamilness emerges here in this example, between Muttiah and Joseph—despite differences of class—as it did among thousands of southern Tamils in that week. Two men who, even though they lived a few hundred yards from each other yet had never done anything together, and who had, in every sense of the phrase, "kept their distance" from each other, now crouched close together. It was, of course, a momentary proximity, yet it is worth noting that it is ethnicity, with its ability to promise equality in the face of its impossibility, that does that work.[24]

On that day, in a complex set of events that I have described and analyzed elsewhere, the Josephs' house was attacked and looted by a group of neighborhood toughs.[25] I suggest here that the violence perpetrated in this neighborhood depended on a particular, unstable class alliance between the men who carried out the violence, and the Pereras, the overlords of the neighborhood. The Josephs had been marked as enemies in local, working class memory before the riots, in a way that Muttiah or his family had not been. So the Tamilness of the Josephs was made to matter, by both the toughs and the Pereras, while with Muttiah, local working-class solidarities were too strong for rupture. As the leader of that particular gang of thugs, Gunadasa, told me one night, nearly ten years later, when I asked him about Muttiah: "he had nothing to be afraid of, we would never touch one of our own." But Muttiah was not to know that, with any certainty. All of us, if we are Tamil, live in anticipation of violence to come.

My larger point is this. There is, in the shadow of violence, a repertoire of signifying practices that is positioned in relation to that shadow, that are very centrally about "Tamilness" as such. In this chapter I will call these practices "tactics of anticipation." These tactics are not merely produced in relation to one event of violence—July 1983—they are produced in relation to a chronological series of events of violence, the last being the July violence.

For Tamils in southern Sri Lanka the violence of 1983 was sudden and extraordinary, but not unexpected. The Muttiahs and the Josephs, like so many other Tamils in the south, did not know when and how violence would be upon them, or even perhaps, what shape it would take. But they would have known it was coming; all they could do was wait. The possibility of violence would have been real before 1983, given that Tamil civilians had experienced collective violence, years ago in 1958, and more recently, in 1977 and 1981.[26] But it is the overwhelming nature of the last riot that makes this very history of violence visible. And that visibility, now—after 1983—acquires a new depth, not of ten years but of forty.

I will try to both distill and reinforce my point here with recourse to a well-crafted literary text that concerns itself with "Tamilness" in southern Sri

Lanka: "Rasanayagam's Last Riot."[27] In this play—which is set on the 25th of July 1983—Rasanayagam's "Tamilness" is constructed in relationship to what I have called "tactics of anticipation" that are available to him. He visits (the Sinhala) Philip Fernando, an old university roommate, on occasions when a riot is imminent. Their friendship is then made manifest during these regular interludes of violence. Rasanayagam is, on each occasion, sheltered from the "mob" in the streets outside. On these occasions of sheltered intimacy with the Fernandos, Rasanayagam—apart from his case of belongings—also brings bottles of liquor with him, the number of bottles corresponding to the possible duration of the violence:

SITA [FERNANDO]: *I must say Rasa and you do some marathon boozing, whenever these riots take place!*
PHILIP [FERNANDO]: *What do you expect, confined here days on end with all the murder going on around us!*
SITA: *But still, it is bad to drink so much!*
PHILIP: *Don't exaggerate Sita, how frequent is that, '56 '58 '61 '74 '77 '81 . . .*
SITA: *Don't play the fool, Philip you are trying to make a comedy of the whole thing.*[28]

The string of dates "'56 '58 '61 . . ." that emerges here throughout the play is repeated in this and other forms. As such, it is a succinct marker of the intense visibility of prior events of violence, that the current riot—now available to be added to the end of the list—makes available as chronology. "Tactics of anticipation," then, can be produced in relation to this visible chronology of violence. In the play I am reading here, many parts of Rasanayagam's Self are produced through these tactics: so the bottles of alcohol that fill his bag, in each successive visit, and the "boozing" it produces, are gentle parodies of that repertoire of practices.

The most succinct example of a "tactic of anticipation" emerges in this text both as farce and tragedy. It is what might be called a "master" tactic of anticipation, the kind of tactic that is learned by us Tamils, so that they may be mobilized when confronted, during a riot, by a Sinhala mob, during a riot. Rasanayagam has learned, over the years, to pronounce the Sinhala word *baldiya* (bucket) the Sinhala way, as opposed to what might be thought of as a distinctively Tamil way of pronunciation: *valdiya.* The point for Rasanayagam is this: when he is confronted with a Sinhala "mob" who present him with a bucket and ask him to "name" it, he is able to perform his Tamilness as Sinhalaness, given the "tactics of anticipation" he has learned. He continues to perform these tactics throughout the text, negotiating the line between the serious and the parodic, until finally, as it were, he refuses in one profound moment to do it any more—to perform his Tamilness as Sinhalaness—and is then killed by a "mob" that has surrounded him. I have dwelt on this text to bring into relief the remaking of "Tamilness" in the wake of 1983. The story of Rasanayagam's life and death focuses on the central importance of a repertoire of practices, tactics of anticipation, for those Tamils who have lived on. The simple point is this: to be a Tamil in southern Lanka, after 1983, is to produce one's identity, one's Tamilness, in relation to the anticipation of violence. To live as a Tamil, then, is to learn such a repertoire of tactics.

Muttiah and his family, who stayed on in Lanka, then, are such Tamils. Like many working-class Tamils in Colombo, they could not muster the capital, symbolic and otherwise, to plan migration.[29] When I got to know Muttiah and his family in the early 1990s, the consequences of this position had slowly but subtly manifested themselves. His children were becoming Sinhala and Buddhist. Such an assimilative movement in working-class, urban Sri Lanka has a history as old as migration itself, with the intensive movements of Indian Malayali labor in the early twentieth century and subsequent intermarriages, being a good example.[30] In fact, Muttiah's own marriage to a Sinhala woman had not provoked a social crisis on either affinal side, and the relationship, as noted before, did not provoke comment in ordinary community life. Yet, the emerging configuration of Sinhalaness and Tamilness in the lives of Muttiah and Leela's children seemed to have undergone remarkable shifts in the space of a decade. There are five children in question here; two girls born five and three years before the riots, and three others born in rapid succession after a long hiatus, in the four years following 1983. The elder two, young women, when I knew them, had been given two names each, one with a Sinhala ring to it, and another with a Tamil ring. Such names, of course, are official appellations only invoked at sites of governmental power such as the school, hospital, or the courts. But urban working-class people take such institutions seriously, and the question of a name, and the practice of naming have similar importance.

With the first two children, "he [Muttiah] named them his way, and I named them my way," said Leela, when I asked her. Then the couple had just put in the two names in the certificate of birth, that crucial piece of government paper. But the other three children, including the much awaited boy child who was the reason for the couple's remarkable fertility, had but Sinhala names. "He still names them his way," said Leela, "but we don't write the names on the certificate." Muttiah, she said, thought it would be a way to avoid trouble in the future.

The presence of violence, in relation to tactics of its anticipation, emerges also in relation to the practice of "religion" in southern Lanka, central to the concerns of this volume. I shall use the "tactics of anticipation" practiced by the Muttiah family in relation to "religion" to comment on the place of "Tamilness" and also the anthropology of identity in southern Sri Lanka. The ethnographic terrain I shall use to do so is one that Jonathan Walters has recently called a "multireligious field"—that is to say, a field where the practices of "multireligion" can be thought through.[31]

The specific field in question here is that of the "Vel festival"—where Hindus and Buddhists perform public acts of faith as a "sacred spear" moves between two temples in the city in a complex ritual procession. The Vel festival itself can be seen both historically and anthropologically in relation to the multireligious field of Kataragama, which has, of course, drawn significant scholarly attention.[32] I could, given the framework this rich literature provides, and my concern with the presence of violence in the Lankan ethnographic field, proceed to analyze the interactions of "Buddhists" and "Hindus" in this field in an attempt to understand the "how" and "why" of political violence in Lanka. But I will not. My efforts, as I have already suggested, take me in a different direction. What I want to point to is the place of this multireligious field in relation to the anticipation of violence. Observing the festival in the summer of 1993, for example, what was dramatically apparent was the shrunken nature of the celebrations. An event that had flowed and overflowed along the main thoroughfares of Colombo producing an orgy of petty consumption for the middle- and working-classes, that rivaled the spectacular displays of faith that accompanied the fulfillment of vows by the believers, had retreated almost entirely into nonpublic spaces, the grounds of the temples themselves.

After 1983, the hoopla of Vel—not the movement of the spear itself, but its associated practices—could not be public, out there on the city streets anymore. It had to be contained inside a demarcated and defined boundary. Given that the festival had not even been held for several years after the riots, it would be possible to argue that there is here a clear cause and effect relationship: Vel was not held because of the riot. But to my mind—as I have suggested before—this causal relationship does not sufficiently illuminate the ethnographic field in this case. I want to think of the multireligious field as produced in anticipation of violence. In this reading the revived, but now nonpublic and withdrawn, nature of the event is a sign of its self-effacement, a way of positioning it as something other than a public celebration of Tamilness and Hinduness, which would be unwise given the constant anticipation of the possibility of violence.

In the period before the riots, the Muttiahs regularly attended the Vel festival in the city. But they do not do so anymore, and that annual event is only a distant memory for the elder children; the family hasn't been to "see Vel" since the riots. They have felt, and this was expressed with some subtlety to me, that to go and "see Vel" might not be "safe." They were right in their anticipation. In July 1993, when I visited the temples concerned with Vel and spent time there, anthropologizing that ethnographic field with a senior and distinguished colleague, a bomb exploded in that very space just minutes after we had left. Tamils I talked to believed that the bomb had been planted there by the army, as a disapproving warning against even limited celebrations of Tamilness.

Leaving events like Vel behind, the Muttiah family have moved cautiously into the sphere of Buddhism. Most inhabitants of Patupara are nominally Buddhists, but as in many urban neighborhoods only the very old and the very young display any interest in regular temple visits. What matters for everyone else is the observation of festivals like Vesak and Poson, with great energy and display. The older Muttiah children have begun to participate in these events, and the younger children now go to *Daham Pasal*, the Buddhist "Sunday School" at the local temple, with other neighborhood children. It is not my suggestion here that all working-class Tamils have moved to assimilate Sinhala-Buddhist socio-cultural practice after the experience of collective violence. On the contrary, there are other communities where spaces of "multireligion," and "multiethnicity" operate with success.[33] Yet, the options Muttiah's family have exercised are not idiosyncratic; rather, in my experience, they are becoming increasingly common.

I turn now to another aspect of the reproduction of Tamilness in the face of collective violence, by way of another Tamil family that moved to Patupara after 1983, the Pathmanathans. They made no bones about it, they were Jaffna Tamils, their interests in Colombo were commercial. They were not wealthy, but hoped, I think, to get there some day. The family, who had recently moved to Colombo from the north, had found it very hard to find adequate housing, especially since their son, Ravi, was seventeen. Young Tamil boys were under suspicion in the city, and cordon and search operations were frequent, while all Tamils were stopped routinely at check points everywhere. No landlord wanted to be accused of harboring a Tiger, and the few who would agree wanted inflated rents. The Pathmanathans' accommodation in Patupara was such an arrangement, but Pathmanathan thought it was a good deal, since the neighborhood was "quiet," and "safe." They were outsiders in the neighborhood, with no social links to other families in Patupara, such as the Pereras, who were central to the lives of many. They had little idea that anything at all had "happened" in Patupara in 1983, accepting on face value the bland, oft-repeated assertion that everything had been "fine." But still Pathmanathan liked the location of the house they rented because it was hidden from the road, and therefore shrouded his wife's Hindu ritual practices—which were carried out indoors—from Sinhala eyes. The possibility of violence, the position of the Pathmanathans in relation to it, remained an unsaid, but not an unthought, denominator in all this.

After the Pathmanathans had lived for about a year at the place, the landlords, no relations of the Pereras, decided to raise the rent on the house. Now this was understandable since price inflation in Colombo had to be countered; yet, the rise was steeper than might have been expected. For the Pathmanathans, who had rented the place on the understanding that the rent would be constant for two years, the demand seemed unjust. They refused to pay, until one day, not altogether by accident, they heard about the Josephs: the long-standing dispute the Josephs had over the rented house with the Pereras, and their sorry plight after the violence. This story was merely hinted at, not told in stark cause and effect tones or terms; but it struck right at the heart of life. Nearly ten years after the riot, the possibility of renewed civilian-directed violence was real as it was terrifying. The rules of the game, between landlord and tenant, were suddenly suspended: the Pathmanathans paid up silently.[34]

Things changed for the Pathmanathans after that; they grew cautious and wary; said little and walked quickly. For the old man and his wife, this was just another burden to bear, just another facet to their being in a Sinhala land. Their son, Ravi, however, responded differently. I realized this one night in mid-1992, when a militant bomb, in the north of the country, blew up nearly the entire commanding staff of the Sri Lankan armed forces; a moment I have marked before. I note, once again, the peculiarities of this methodological site: a moment framed by an event of violence, which then positions "Tamilness" firmly in the shadow of violence. The anticipation of violence, then, is both intense and representable in these particular moments, which are always experienced in relation to a chronology of events of civilian-directed violence that might be represented as a string of dates—'58, '77, '81, '83; on that night I wondered if '92 would be added to that list. Old Pathmanathan and his wife were, of course, worried, and I tried to reassure them that things would be all right.

But Ravi disagreed. There was going to be a riot, he said, and it is going to make 1983 look puny. As we argued late into the evening, it became increasingly clear that there was a great deal at stake for Ravi in this discussion. He, unlike his parents, was not in mortal fear of a riot. He had his papers in a bank vault, and a few clothes in a case. He lived in anticipation of a riot, not with helpless anger, but with clear foresight: it would help him to leave Lanka and migrate to the West. Ravi's cousin Bala was in Canada; he was doing well with his own grocery store, and would take Ravi in. Except he had little chance of obtaining political asylum, given the relatively peaceful conditions in southern Sri Lanka. Ravi wanted a riot. It was then, and only then, that his Tamilness would be worth something in the West. Ravi is not alone; there are many like him. The possibility of violence has loomed large for southern Tamils for too long for such a response to be unthinkable. But the possibility of violence is not enough for a visa: for embassy doors to open, people must die.[35]

A consideration of Ravi (and similarly positioned Tamils) is crucial to understanding the practices I have been calling "tactics of anticipation" in this paper, both politically and analytically. The proximity of Tamilness to the possibility of violence, is not for me, and should not be in general, sign of its political righteousness, or its positioning on a moral high ground. If this were so, then the narratives I have produced, and the ethnographic field I have constructed here, would merely be part of the growing story of Tamil "suffering" that is now told repeatedly in different contexts. Ravi's intervention demonstrates the complexity of such narratives of "suffering." It is my contention that "tactics of anticipation" can also be politically positioned, produced as they are in a field of power. Practices of the anticipation of violence, and humanist narratives of "suffering" that are associated with them, I want to stress, can be both self-conscious and interested, and produced performatively in different contexts. Hence, my effort to encompass a series of very differently situated practices of anticipation as *tactics,* which allow, finally, for the Tamilness of Ravi to emerge in relation to the Tamilness of Joseph, Muttiah, Pathmanathan, and that extraordinary fictional figure, Rasanayagam.

My conclusion is this: a life that is always already to be lived under the shadow of violence—in other words, the very proximity to violence of Tamilness—can itself be objectified and made available to the repertoire of practices I have called "tactics of anticipation."

Undoubtedly, my efforts to write of "Tamilness" in southern Sri Lanka have been incomplete, leaving untouched much of the internal content of that Tamilness, for example, its ritual practices, or its kinship patterns. Or, in other words, the anthropology of objects that are already visible. But the writing of that anthropological account has not been my intent. Rather I have tried a different approach. First, an approach that places violence in the center of analysis, positioned as unavailable for explanation and then, second, one that works through that categorical centrality of violence in its entirety, treating the relationship between violence, and the practices of its anticipation, not as an object always already known through a causal logic, but one that emerges slowly, producing with its own labor its analytic weight; taking seriously—in other words—the necessary repositioning of my received understanding of the anthropology of identity in the Lankan ethnographic field.

This analysis does not, then, rework the relationship between the Tamil Self, and the Sinhala Other, with view to explaining, or understanding, the emergence of violence in the Lankan ethnographic field. On the contrary, the relationship of the Tamil Self, to the Sinhala near Other, has been analyzed through the category of violence, and has therefore emerged as mediated by an irreducible and ever-present possibility of violence. But my point is not that this relationship to violence—apart from specific repertoires of practices—is an exclusive feature of Tamilness. There do not, upon reflection, seem to be Lankan identities that cannot be and should not be understood in relation to violence, which has been both pervasive and overwhelming in recent years. If so, there is a more general suggestion that arises from my work here: Sri Lankanist anthropologies of identity, like Tamilness itself, may have to be rethought in the shadow of violence.

Notes

1. Significant support for this work has been provided by a Century Fellowship awarded by the University of Chicago; a research fellowship funded by the John D. and Catherine T. MacArthur Foundation; an International Dissertation Fellowship awarded by the Joint Committee on South Asia of the American Council of Learned Societies; the Social Science Research Council funded by the Ford and Andrew W. Mellon Foundations; a Visiting Fellowship provided by the International Center for Ethnic Studies; and a Dissertation Fellowship awarded by the Guggenheim Foundation. I would like to thank Chandra de Silva for asking me to contribute to this volume and Tessa Bartholomeusz, Malathi de Alwis, Qadri Ismail, David Scott, and Jonathan Walters for commenting with such care on earlier drafts of this essay.

2. Manazir Aashiq Harganvi writing during the Bhagalpur riots. Translated and quoted by Gyanendra Pandey, "In Defense of the Fragment: Writing about Hindu-Muslim Riots in India Today," in *Representations* 37, Winter 1992:48. I am indebted to, and operate in a space created by, Gyanendra Pandey's path-breaking work in this essay and also in the "The Prose of Otherness" in *Essays in Honour of Ranajit Guha: Subaltern Studies 8,* David Arnold & David Hardiman, eds. (Delhi: Oxford University Press, 1994.)

3. Gananath Obeyesekere, "Buddhism, Nationhood, and Cultural Identity: A Question of Fundamentals," in *Fundamentalisms Comprehended*, Martin E. Marty and R. Scott Appleby, eds. (Chicago: University of Chicago Press, 1995), pp. 239ff.

4. Most notable in its immediacy in this regard is Obeyesekere's "The Origins and Institutionalization of Political Violence," in *Sri Lanka in Crisis and Change*, James Manor, ed. (New York: St. Martin's Press, 1984). See also, for example, Obeyesekere's more comprehensive and moving, "A Meditation on Conscience," *Occasional Papers*, Social Scientists' Association: Colombo, 1988.

5. "Buddhism, Nationhood," p. 235.

6. Ibid., p. 250.

7. Ibid., p. 251.

8. Ibid.

9. I have not, of course, done any justice to the dazzling historical and ethnographic dexterity of the section of Obeyesekere's argument that concerns me. Nor will

it be possible, in this chapter, to contrast this intervention to others which have operated similar problematics in the Lankan ethnographic field. For example, Stanley Tambiah points to a question, asked by others: "If Buddhism preaches nonviolence, why is there so much political violence in Sri Lanka today?," in *Buddhism Betrayed? Religion, Politics and Violence in Sri Lanka* (Chicago: University of Chicago Press, 1992), p. 1; Jonathan Spencer writes, in the immediate wake of the violence of 1983, "I found myself desperately trying to make sense of that familiar paradox—the perpetration of evil by apparently nice, decent people," "Popular Perceptions of the Violence: A Provincial View," in *Sri Lanka in Crisis and Change*, James Manor, ed., p. 187; and Bruce Kapferer proclaims, "Here is a reason, extraordinary as it may seem, for the sudden, almost inexplicable, transformation of a normally peaceful people into violent and murderously rampaging mobs," in *Legends of People, Myths of State: Violence, Intolerance, and Political Culture in Sri Lanka and Australia* (Washington, D.C.: Smithsonian Institution Press, 1988), p. 101. For an examination of the category of religion that is necessarily pertinent to these questions, see David Scott's "Conversion and Demonism: Colonial Christian Discourse and Religion in Sri Lanka" in *Comparative studies in society and history* , vol. 34, no. 2 (1992): 331–65, and "Religion in Colonial Civil Society: Buddhism and Modernity in Nineteenth Century Sri Lanka," in *The Thatched Patio*, 7, no. 4 (1994): 1–16.

10. As an aside, let me be clear here that I am not arguing for the impossibility of producing an analytic of violence, or for that matter, for understanding its "causes." Such work is both important and possible, but is not my task here.

11. By separating out this kind of violence, from other, important and devastating episodes of violence that Lankans have experienced in recent years, I can note the importance of both considering the kind and quality of violence under investigation, and also the importance of work that would locate other kinds of violence at their analytical center. In this regard I have found Malathi de Alwis' work on the southern Mother's Front inspiring. See "Motherhood as a Space of Protest," in *Appropriating Gender: Women, the State and Politicized Religion in South Asia*," Amrita Basu and Patricia Jeffreys, eds. (New York: Routledge, 1997).

12. I will, throughout this chapter, operate with the dual categories of Tamil[nes]s in "southern Sri Lanka." While this usage is primarily geographical, it can also mark a political distinction between "southern Tamils" and "northeastern Tamils," in the logic of contemporary Tamil nationalism itself. My understanding of this distinction is indebted to a categorically acute argument produced recently by Qadri Ismail, "Nation, Country, Community: The Logics of Sri Lankan Tamil Nationalism," in *Community/Gender/Violence: Essays on the Subaltern Condition*, Partha Chatterjee and Pradeep Jeganathan, eds. (Oxford: Oxford University Press, forthcoming). Ismail's own reading of southern Tamil identity, in relation to the logic of Tamil nationalism, is an important complement to my efforts here.

13. There is, of course, sophisticated and multifaceted literature that has advanced our understanding considerably. A comprehensive overview is available in Stanley Tambiah's, *Ethnic Fratricide and the Dismantling of Democracy in Sri Lanka*

(Chicago: University of Chicago Press, 1986). For a reading of the political economy of the violence, see Newton Gunasinghe,"The Open Economy and its Impact on Ethnic relations in Sri Lanka," in *Sri Lanka's Ethnic Conflict: Myths, Realties and Perspectives* (Delhi: Navrang, 1984); and Sunil Bastian, "The Political Economy of Ethnic Violence in Sri Lanka: The July 1983 Riot," in *Mirrors of Violence: Communities, Riots and Survivors in South Asia*, Veena Das, ed. (Delhi: Oxford University Press, 1990). Important anthropological accounts of the practices of violence at stake can be found in Bruce Kapferer, 1988, and Jonathan Spencer "Collective Violence and Everyday Practice in Sri Lanka," in *Modern Asian Studies*, 24, no. 3 (1990a): 620.

14. Valli Kanapathipillai "July 1983: The Survivor's Experience," in *Mirrors of Violence: Communities, Riots and Survivors in South Asia*, Veena Das, ed.; and "The Survivor Ten Years after the Riots," paper presented at the conference "July '83: Ten Years After," International Center for Ethnic Studies, Colombo, July 1993.

15. See for example, Veena Das' "Our Work to Cry, Your Work to Listen," in *Mirrors of Violence*, Veena Das, ed., which describes the survivors experience in the wake of the 1984 Delhi riots. See also *Critical Events: an anthropological perspective on contemporary India* (Delhi: Oxford University Press, 1995).

16. All proper names relating to and including Patupara are fictitious.

17. A four-lane highway that connects the capital of Colombo to the southern city of Galle along the southwest coast.

18. Colombo is a colonial city that takes shape in relation to European colonial power during and after the sixteenth century. For a historical account of its spatial organization, see Michael Roberts, "The Two Faces of the Port of Colombo," in *Brides of the Sea: Port Cities of Asia from the 16th–20th Centuries*, Frank Broeze, ed. (Honolulu: University of Hawaii Press, 1989), pp.173–87; and for a comprehensive demographic account see Bernard Panditharatne, "The Functional Zones of the Colombo City," in *The University of Ceylon Review*, 19(2), 1961:138–66. For the historicization of the construction of space in South Asian cities, see Anthony D. King, *Colonial Urban Development: Culture, Social Power and Environment* (London: Routledge & Kegan Paul, 1976); and on building forms, see King's *The Bungalow: The Production of Global Culture* (London: Routledge & Kegan Paul, 1989).

19. Derek Sayer, *Capitalism and Modernity: An Excursus on Marx and Weber* (London: Routledge, 1991), p. 45.

20. Anthony D. King, *The Bungalow*, p. 35.

21. For a sensitively wrought description of capitalization catalyzed by a new road in a Sinhala rural community, see Gunadasa Amarasekere's Sinhala novel *Karumakkarayo* (Colombo: Gunasena, 1953).

22. "Lord," here, will be my gloss for the Sinhala *Hamu*. I see the relationship of "Lord" to "servant" as a modern reactivation of an archaic form. See Newton Gunasinghe's brilliant ethnography, *Changing Social Relations in the Kandyan Coun-*

*tryside (*Colombo: Social Scientists' Association, 1990), for a theorization of such relationships; also Tamara Gunesekere's *Hierarchy and Egalitarianism: Caste, Class and Power in Sinhalese Peasant Society* (London: Athlone Press, 1994), for recent ethnographic details in a rural context.

23. I draw here on an argument that I have expanded on in "A Space for Violence: Politics, Anthropology, and the Location of a Sinhala Practice of Masculinity," in *Community/Gender/Violence: Essays on the Subaltern Condition*, Partha Chatterjee and Pradeep Jeganathan, eds.

24. I have tried to think through this problem in other work. See "All the Lords Men?: Ethnicity, and Inequality in the Space of a Riot," in *Collective Identities, Nationalisms and Protest in Sri Lanka* [2d edition, volume 2] Michael Roberts, ed. (Colombo: Marga Institute, forthcoming).

25. "All the Lords Men?: Ethnicity, and Inequality in the Space of a Riot," contains both a detailed ethnographic account, and anthropological argument about this event.

26. There is no significant literature on any one of these events. But see, on "1958," Tarzi Vittachi's, *Emergency '58 : The Story of the Ceylon Race Riots* (London: Andre Deutsch, 1959), a comprehensive journalistic account that also serves as a preliminary administrative history of the event, and James Manor's "Self-Inflicted Wound: Inter-Communal Violence in Ceylon, 1958," in *The Collected Seminar Papers of The Institute of Commonwealth Studies*, University of London, 30, 1982:15–26, which only hints at the sociological complexities at stake; and Edmund Leach's "What the Rioting in Ceylon Means," in *The Listener* (June 1958):926, which is only of incidental interest.

27. Ernest Macintyre, *Rasanayagam's Last Riot* (Sydney: Wordlink, 1993).

28. Ibid., p. 4.

29. After the violence, the Josephs, their house and home in ruins, emigrated to Australia from a refugee camp. As such, they joined hundreds of thousands of Tamils who have made their way out of Sri Lanka to metropolitan nations in the last twelve years. See, for a reading of such migration, Valentine Daniel, "The Nation in Sri Lankan Tamil Gatherings in Britain," in *Pravada*, vol. 2, no. 6 (1992): 12–17.

30. For a close reading of debates surrounding these "mixed" working-class marriages in a different historical period, see Kumari Jayawardena, *Ethnic and Class Conflicts in Sri Lanka* (Colombo: Center for Social Analysis, 1986).

31. See Jonathan Walters, "Multireligion on the Bus: Beyond 'Influence' and 'Syncretism' in the study of Religious Meetings," in *Unmaking the Nation: The Politics of Identity and History in Modern Sri Lanka*, Pradeep Jeganathan and Qadri Ismail, eds. (Colombo: Social Scientists' Association, 1995), p. 29 and passim.

32. James Cartman has suggested that, given fear of cholera epidemics in the late nineteenth century, the Vel festival comes into being in the wake of the regulations

and restrictions imposed by colonial authorities on the festival held in Kataragama. See *Hinduism in Ceylon* (Colombo: Gunasena, 1957), p. 124. For an account of the ritual relationship between Kataragama and Vel, see Don Handelman, "On the Desuetude of Kataragama" in *Man* (n.s.) 13:157. For ethnographic accounts of Kataragama, see Gananath Obeyesekere, "Social Change and the Deities: Rise of the Kataragama Cult in Modern Sri Lanka," in *Man* (n.s.)12 (1977): 377–96, and "The Fire Walkers of Kataragama: The Rise of Bhakti Religiosity in Buddhist Sri Lanka," in *Journal of Asian Studies* 37, no. 3 (1978): 457–76; and Bryan Pfaffenberger "The Kataragama Pilgrimage: Hindu-Buddhist Interaction and Significance in Sri Lanka's Polyethnic Social System," in *Journal of Asian Studies* 36, no. 2 (1977): 253–70.

33. I think through such a community in another work, "Traces of Violence, Spaces of Death: National and Local Identity in an Urban Sri Lankan Community," a paper presented at the 24th annual conference on South Asia, University of Wisconsin at Madison, November 1995.

34. Such situations are not uncommon; Kanapathipillai, 1990, has also noted an instance of the inflection with violence of a landlord-tenant relationship, as has Sumitra Rahubadha, in her enormously popular novel *Sura Asura* (Colombo: Kosala Prakashakayo, 1986).

35. It is not only Ravi who anticipates this possibility. There is more at stake than desire of Lankan Tamils to migrate seeking a better life for themselves. Immigration itself is part of a globalized circuit of capital with its own logic and imperatives, and large-scale migrations of Tamil political refugees to the metropolis from Lanka after 1983 have inserted "Tamilness" into those circuits. On the one hand are the many hundreds of thousands of Tamils in north America and Europe who live in the "half-light" of migration. They are not quite in yet; so they could be sent back. Every so often, bureaucrats will look down at the files, and wonder if Lanka could be reclassified as "safe." This would spell disaster for those who have paid tens of thousands to immigration "brokers" who got them to the West, where they thought the good life was at hand. On the other hand, of course, are the "brokers" who have a good thing going. There is something to be made off every refugee. They too live in anticipation of violence. A consideration of this ethnographic field, however, is beyond the scope of this paper.

Chapter 6

Sufi and Reformist Designs: Muslim Identity in Sri Lanka

Victor C. de Munck

Introduction

Scholars dishearteningly have observed that the second half of the twentieth century is marked by a proliferation of infranational civil wars along the fault lines of schismogenic "primordial loyalties" (Tilly 1993; van Creveld 1991; Wiberg 1991). Tilly (1993:1) writes that "the 20th century stands out from all its predecessors for the scale at which agents of states, including armed forces, have deployed violence not only against other armed forces but also against unarmed civilians. We live in a bloodthirsty time." Wiberg (1991:337) comments that "close to half the current major armed conflicts in the world have the ethno-national contradiction as one important component." Garnett (1988) provides the statistic that, in 1980, 23 percent of the 600 billion dollars spent in world military expenditures was accounted for by developing nations such as Sri Lanka. Sri Lankan government defense spending in 1995 was 32 billion rupees ($592 million). Since the anti-Tamil riots of 1983, the civil war in Sri Lanka has claimed an estimated 50,000 lives (Reuter Feb. 1, 1996).

This paper does not directly address the issue of violence, although, like a steady drumbeat, it certainly occupies the minds and hearts of the people about whom I write. Rather, here I explore first the rise of Islamic fundamentalism in Sri Lanka. By Islamic fundamentalism I mean the construction of an Islamic/Muslim identity based on a "memory" of a heroic Arabic past and an avowed ideological commitment to Islamic doctrinal practices and beliefs. In regard to Islamic fundamentalism, my main premise is that it is a macroidentity that is being constantly contested and shaped by local and global forces. Macroidentities (such as Sri Lankan ethnic and national identities, in general) are cobbled together out of local microidentities on the basis of perceived and asserted claims of historic and cultural commonalities. In the case of Islam in Sri Lanka, the Sufi tradition, which I explore below, counts as one such microidentity, which itself is negotiated constantly.

Second, I argue here that macroidentities in Sri Lanka and elsewhere are designed by elite leaders or organizations that have a vested interest in constructing macroidentities. Islamic fundamentalism in Sri Lanka reflects one such macroidentity, fashioned by the elite, that asserts historical and cultural ties with a larger identity—namely, pan-Arabic. Describing an Islamic fundamentalist ("macro") identity, however, does not simply mean aggregating a list of normative beliefs and practices shaped by elite leaders. Macroidentities, if they are to be accepted and have motivational force, must have something to say—must be useful—to individuals in the context of their real life experiences. "Reality" is "relativized to context" and, therefore, interpretations of what it means to be a Muslim shifts with context (Quinn 1985:294). In this sense, microidentities, constructed out of the intersection of shared experiences, shape and influence the interpretation of macroidentities.

By providing an ethnographic account of Muslim contentions over what constitutes an Islamic/Muslim identity, I hope to show how identity can be differentially interpreted, manipulated, and contested depending on context. That is, identities are "sites of unceasing struggle" in which the symbolic markers of identity are contested relative to their oppositional contexts (Ishmail 1995:56). In the global context, Islamic/Muslim identity is constructed in opposition to similar levels of contrast (for instance, Christian, Western); at the Sri Lankan national level, Islamic/Muslim identity is contrasted with Sinhala Buddhist and Tamil Hindu ones; and at the local level an Islamic/Muslim identity is contested between Sufi and orthodox versions of that identity.[1] The boundaries between these three conceptual levels becomes porous as individuals enter and are affected by national and global contexts and events.

In developing this argument, I will show how historical and contemporary processes at the local, national, and global levels have had an impact on Muslim villagers in the Sinhala-speaking community of Kutali.[2] Kutali, a village of approximately a thousand Muslims, is located in the Moneragala District of the Uva Bintenne.[3] In excursions to other Muslim communities in the south, east, and west of Sri Lanka, I have witnessed similar debates between adherents of Islamic orthodoxy and Sufism over what constitutes a true Muslim. I believe that my accounts of the contest over identity in Kutali can be generalized and applied to Muslim communities throughout Sri Lanka. Nationalist and global processes in Kutali and elsewhere in Muslim Sri Lanka have led to the emergence of a new pan-Islamic fundamentalist identity that seeks, through its adherents, to subvert a more localized Sufi-Muslim identity and establish itself as the sole legitimate version of identity for all Sri Lankan Muslims. As we shall see, the contest between proponents of these two ideologies has produced schismatic divisions within the village.

In contrast to the Catholic community of Sri Lanka, which, as Stirrat in this volume persuasively describes, has come to invoke ethnic, over religious, identity, Sri Lankan Muslims actively identify themselves as distinct from both the Tamil and Sinhala (and Burgher) communities on the basis of religious differences.[4] This is so despite internal discord among Muslims concerning what exactly constitutes the proper content of a Muslim religious identity. The difference in marking identities between Catholic and Muslim communities is due, in part, to the ethnic-religious conflation of the category "Muslim." While "Tamil" and "Sinhala" refer solely to ethnic groups, even though who "belongs" to those groups is often contested on the basis of religion, as the Introduction to this volume suggests, "Muslim" in Sri Lanka is a marker for both religion and ethnicity.

Managing Neutrality: A Viable Option?

De Silva (1986), Spencer (1990), and I (1994) have each stated that Sri Lankan Muslims have "managed" to maintain a neutral stance in the ongoing "interethnic fratricide" between Sri Lankan Tamils and Sinhalas. This observation was based on the strategical pragmatics of Muslim ethnic politics grounded in their minority status vis-à-vis both the Sinhala and Tamil populations of Sri Lanka.[5] I (1994:276) quote a Muslim villager who expressed this sentiment by stating that "In Tamil areas I am pro-Eelam, in Sinhala areas I am pro-Sri Lanka." The use of "Sri Lanka" is significant, for it denotes how ethnicity, notwithstanding the Muslim mode of drawing boundaries, has come to be the dominant mode of defining the nation, and the exclusion of Muslims as part of that nation.[6] The statement also expresses the alacrity with which Muslims may switch allegiance depending on circumstances. However, in both the Sinhala and Tamil context, as described by the Muslim villager, the Muslim is defined as being subordinate, and in an accommodating role, in relation to the dominant Other.

Unfortunately, references in scholarly literature to the accommodative policies of the Muslim elite connote a unity within the Sri Lankan Muslim community that elides fundamental differences both between eastern and western Muslim elites and between Muslim elites and the Muslim peasantry and urban poor. For the eastern Muslim elite, "managed neutrality" entails an accommodation within the Tamil majority. For the western Muslim elite, it entails an accommodation within the Sinhala majority. And for the villagers of Kutali, managed neutrality involves a consciously cynical and ad hoc acceptance of either Tamil or Sinhala hegemony depending on the situation. In all three situations, "managed neutrality" is constructed not as an affirmation of identity but as a defensive reaction to their subordinate and minority status.

However, managing neutrality has become increasingly more difficult in light of the hundreds of east coast Muslims who have been killed and the thousands left homeless since the onset of the third phase of the civil war (Ishmail 1995:92). Attempts by the LTTE (Liberation Tigers of Tamil Eelam) to gain the allegiance of north and east coast Muslims, in their struggle to create a sovereign state, have failed. The vast majority of Muslims seems to support the People Alliance's proposal for peace and blame the LTTE for starting this third stage of warfare. At the same time, there has been a resurgence of Islamic fundamentalism that leads some Muslims to look past the current exclusionary image of "nation" to a pan-Islamic image of community, much as they did at the turn of the twentieth century.

Splitting Identities: The Fundamentalist and Sufi Options

I think it is accurate to state that most Sri Lankan Muslims do not perceive themselves as full citizens of the Sri Lankan nation as it is presently formulated. Obeyesekere's (1979) infamous equation—"Sri Lanka=Sinhala=Buddhism"—retains its saliency in contemporary discourses on Sri Lankan nationalism. At the same time, Sri Lankan Muslims are divided as to what constitutes an "official" Muslim identity. On the one hand, there has been a strong South Asian Sufi tradition that retains its vigor, particularly among the urban poor and Muslim peasantry. On the other hand, Sri Lankan Muslims also identify themselves with the Arab world and seek to "remember" and affirm those connections in part through adherence to Islamic orthodoxy.

The rise of Islamic fundamentalism among Sri Lankan Muslims is linked to Muslim exclusion from that totalizing conception, discussed by Obeyesekere, of what it means to be a Sri Lankan. Muslim elites organize *jamatis* (meetings) to promote an Islamic identity that supersedes nation-state boundaries. At the same time, more "traditional" Sufi designs for Muslim identity are being undermined by leaders of Islamic orthodox movements.

A Brief History of Sri Lankan Muslims and Kutali Village

Sri Lankan Muslims (or Moors) trace their history back to Arab and Persian traders who arrived along the south Indian and Sri Lankan coast in the eighth century.[7] The Buddhist kingdoms of Sri Lanka encouraged Arab merchants to remain through intermarriage and the transfer of *nindagam* (feudal) lands with the expectation that the merchants would increase overseas commerce (Arasaratnam 1964; Dale 1980).

In 1505, Muslims opposed the entrance of the Portuguese into Sri Lanka in part because the Portuguese posed a threat to their control over overseas trade. The Kotte King Bhuvanekabahu VII sought the allegiance of the Portuguese to gain the upper hand over his brother, Mayadunne, who ruled the Sitawaka kingdom. As a result, many Kotte Muslims fled to Sitawaka and, when Sitawaka fell in 1593, they sought refuge in Kandy where they were welcomed by King Senarat. In 1617, King Senarat signed a peace treaty with the Portuguese in which he was initially urged to sever relations with Muslims. A compromise was reached by which the Muslims would be permitted to continue their trading activities as "friends" of the Kandyan kingdom.[8]

The Dutch attempted to curtail the Muslims' trading and retail activities by prohibiting them to travel to the western seaboard without first registering themselves. The Dutch prohibited Sri Lankan Muslims from buying property or possessing houses within the Fort and the Pettah merchant district of Colombo (Abayakoon 1976:95–96). Kandyan Muslims were supported by the king who relied on them for transporting local products and trading them for luxury goods and weapons. According to Goonewardena (1976:129), "The Moors had a virtual monopoly (on internal trade). They supplied salt, cloth and dried fish to the Kandyan villages and in return bought areca nuts and certain surpluses in food provisions for sale in Dutch territory."

In 1802, when the British arrived in Ceylon, trading opportunities increased for the Muslims. Muslims took advantage of the introduction of coffee plantations in 1820 by expanding the *tavalam* (bullock-cart) trade, transporting supplies to and from the plantations. The Muslims supported the British against the Nayakkar dynasty that ruled Kandy. According to lore, Kepitipola, the leader of the Welassa Rebellion against British rule, used the local *devale* (shrine for Buddhist deities) for a hiding place. A Muslim informed the British of Kepitipola's hiding place and Muslims were instrumental in his eventual capture. As a result of Muslim involvement in Kepitipola's denouement, tensions arose between Sinhala and Muslim in the area and many Muslims from neighboring towns (e.g., Medagama and Bibile) fled to the relatively isolated community of Kutali. The increasing politicization of ethnicity was more evident at the national level.

This sort of politicization made its way into the late nineteenth-century scholarly debate over what constituted "ethnicity." In 1888, Ponambalam Ramanathan, a leading spokesman for the Tamils, read and published a paper titled the "Ethnology of the Moors of Ceylon." He intended to demonstrate that Sri Lankan Muslims and Tamils shared the same cultural heritage. Along these lines, he argued that Muslims were of Tamil descent and should therefore be identified as Tamil-Muslims. His claim—that Muslims were Tamil converts to Islam—infuriated the Muslim community. Through the leadership of M.C. Siddik Lebbe, a Kandyan proctor and journalist, and Arabi Pasha, exiled from Egypt to Ceylon by the British in 1883, the Sri Lankan Muslim elite and urban middle class, particularly in Colombo, united in their efforts to establish a distinct Arab-Muslim identity. Through their efforts, the first Muslim college, Zahira College, was established in 1892 in Colombo. The Sri Lankan Muslim elite began to claim and express their Islamic identity by learning Arabic, wearing "fez" caps, and donning Arabic dress, including the veil for women. At the same time, I.L.M. Abdul Azeez began the first Muslim newspaper, *The Muslim Friend* (Thawfeeq n.d. 134). As president of the Moors Union, founded in 1900, Abdul Azeez fashioned a rebuttal to Ramanathan by claiming that the "Ceylon Moors" are descendants of Arab merchants who were, "according to tradition, members of the family of Hashim . . . less war-like and given to the peaceful pursuit of trade" (cited in Ismail 1995:68). As Ismail (1995:69–70) notes, Abdul Azeez discursively constructed a Muslim identity based on racial ancestry, and a religious-economic affiliation with the Hashimites (the tribe of Mohammed), peaceful immigrants involved in trade. This construction further served to differentiate Muslims from Tamils who, according to Sinhala populist constructions, entered the country as invaders. As Ishmail (1995:70) further observes, Azeez's image of Muslim identity is patriarchal because it lacks mention of Tamil wives who married the Arab merchants, thus presuming that "Arab men gave birth, by themselves, to the Sri Lankan social formation." These efforts by the Muslim western elite to develop a dynamic and distinct Muslim-Islamic community paralleled ethno-religious revivalist movements within the Tamil and Sinhala communities. The process of intraethnic consolidation also kindled interethnic discord and rivalry. For instance, in 1915, Anagarika Dharmapala wrote that:

> The Mohammedans, an alien people . . . by Shylockian methods became prosperous like Jews. The Sinhalese [were] sons of the soil, whose ancestors for 2358 years had shed rivers of blood to keep the country free from alien invaders . . . The alien South Indian Mohammedan comes to Ceylon, sees the neglected villager without any experience in trade . . . and the result is that Mohammedan thrives and the son of soil goes to the wall. (quoted in *The Circle* 1995, S. Ranjit)

Response to the 1915 Sinhala-Muslim riots also exemplifies this theme of intraethnic discord and its aftermath. Sinhala reaction to the incident that sparked the riot was organized and violent. Throughout May and June of that year, "groups of Sinhala men . . . attacked the property of Muslim traders and in some places destroyed mosques" (Ismail 1995:82). The colonial government declared martial law and Buddhist leaders (among them D.S. Senanayake, independent Ceylon's first prime minister) were accused of inciting the riots. In the Ceylon Legislative Council, Ramanathan made a plea in defense of the Buddhist leaders arguing that a "grievous injustice" had been done to them (i.e., imprisonment). In this debate the violence perpetrated against the Muslim community became a side issue, overshadowed by criticism of British colonial rule. The message was not lost on the Muslim community: they had become the "Other" relative to both the Sri Lankan Tamil and Sinhala communities.

Thus perceived as the Other, Muslims have been complicit in forming this identity for themselves by seeking to create distinct Muslim-Islamic institutions in Sri Lanka. Their intent has been to create a unified Muslim community with specific interests and institutional needs within the context of the Sri Lankan nation-state. In fact, since the turn of the century, the Sri Lankan Muslim urban elite and professional class, in order to perpetuate an identity distinct from the Tamils, has established newspapers, schools (*madrasas*), a Wakf board to oversee mosque activities and organization, a Kathi court for adjudicating divorces, and cultural associations (e.g., Moors Islamic Cultural Home). Yet, despite the push for a separate identity, and with the exception of the 1915 riots, the overarching history of Muslims with Sinhala and Tamil communities can be characterized as one of accommodation, motivated in the contemporary context by fear of being the target of state-sponsored violence. However, such a "history" of the Muslim relationship with Sinhalas omits the majority of Muslims who are neither elites or professionals, but agriculturalists.[9] The story of Kutali, an "old" Muslim village, situated in a Sinhala-dominated region, provides an alternative, perhaps metonymic, reading of how contemporary Muslim identities are locally formulated and contested among both the elite and subaltern.

The Origins and History of Kutali

The origins of Kutali are unclear. According to Adam Marikar (the retired trustee of the village mosque), Kutali was founded by two Muslim merchants in the late 1700s. Adam Marikar told me the following story: the Kandyan king's son had sculpted the imagined face of the woman he intended to marry in a block of wood. The king displayed this carving and offered a reward to the person who found this girl. The two merchants, traveling by *tavalam*, saw near Kutali a girl resembling the carving. As a reward, the merchants were bestowed much of the land on which present day Kutali is situated. One cannot help but note how this story parallels Muslim elite versions of Muslim identity (formed in relation to trade and as an accommodation to Sinhala rulers).

In contrast to neighboring Sinhala villages and hamlets where the homes and small shops (*kadees*) are dispersed and where rice paddy fields lie adjacent to dwellings, Kutali is a nucleated village, with the paddy fields surrounding the dwellings and shops. Villagers noted that the village was consciously planned so that they could defend themselves against attack by neighboring Sinhala.[10] It must be added that relations between Kutali Muslims and their Sinhala neighbors are amicable and, in the collective memory of the villagers, there has been no threat or outbreak of interethnic violence. All villagers, however, fear and recognize the potential for an eruption of ethnic violence. The clusters of tightly packed dwellings surrounded by paddy fields provide them with a physical and psychological defense against such a potentiality.

In 1914, a *Moulana* (a Muslim who claims direct descent to the Prophet Mohammed) from Dikwella (near Matara in the southern tip of Sri Lanka), traveled to Kutali and to other Muslim villages in the south central interior on a personal campaign to revitalize Islamic practices among the Muslim peasantry. The Moulana, a merchant, began an annual village festival called the *Burdha Kandhoori* (sometimes spelled *kanthuri*). According to his great grandson, the current Moulana, the objective of the festival was to rid rural Muslims of Hindu and Buddhist practices that had filtered into their religious customs. He explained that the festival was established to revitalize Muslim customs and traditions:

> My grandfather's father started this work in 1914. Earlier there was no Burdha Kandhoori. . . . In those days there was no religion and people had no knowledge of the proper way of reciting prayers, so my grandfather would travel to twelve Muslim villages yearly and teach villagers the proper ways of worshiping. The villages, of which Kutali was one, would put on a feast to honor him . . . being a Moulana is like a caste . . . we are from the blood of the Prophet, no? My daughters must marry other Moulanas, but boys can marry anyone because the blood is passed through patriliny. However, even sons should marry the daughters of Moulana families; all my six sons did so. People respect me because I am of the blood of the Prophet and through me they worship Him.

Though this description frames this annual festival as an event wrought by an individual, it must also be seen as part of the larger historical process of ethnic revival occurring in Sri Lanka at the turn of the twentieth century. The Burdha Kandhoori begins with the arrival of the Moulana and culminates in a large *kandhoori* (festival) on the eighth day, when he departs. Since 1914 the festival had continued unabated until 1980 when it was abruptly canceled for one year. Amid turmoil and much debate, it was recontinued in 1981. Villagers explained that the reason for the cancellation of the festival in 1980 was due to the trustee and other *marikars* (mosque administrators) pocketing funds collected before and during the festival.[11] The mosque trustee and his supporters argued that the cancellation was due to a drought that left the villagers unable to donate the requisite cash and foodstuffs necessary to hold the festival. However, there had been droughts in previous years and the festival never had been canceled.

Moreover, there are always allegations of corruption against the trustee and *marikars*. While poverty and corruption are necessary conditions, they may not be sufficient conditions for the cancellation. Instead, I believe the inroads made by the Tablighi Jama'at to instill Islamic orthodoxy and eliminate Sufi practices and beliefs among Sri Lankan Muslims has caused villagers, particularly young and educated village leaders, to refute or question the legitimacy of the Burdha Kandhoori as an Islamic practice.

The Sufi Tradition

Embedded in this sociopolitical history there has been a strong Sufi tradition that centers around devotional recitals (*maulid*) in honor of a saint (*Wali* or sometimes called *Andawer*, "god"). Two of the most prominent saints in Sri Lanka (and elsewhere in south India and the Maldives) are Qutub Mohideen Abdul Qadir al Jilani, an Iraqi saint and scholar born in 1092, and Shahul Hamid Nagore Meeran Sahib, born in northern India in 1532.[12] Abdul Qadir is said to have come to Sri Lanka and meditated for eleven years at Dafter Jailani, situated fifteen miles south of Balangoda.[13]

Annually, during the eleventh month of the Islamic calendar (Rabhi-ul-Akhir), there is a monthlong *maulid* (anniversary celebration) for the saint at this site and shorter twelve-day *maulids* in Muslim communities.[14] I attended the *maulid* for the month in 1981, living and interacting with the thousands of Muslims who had come on pilgrimage from Sri Lanka and India. Dafter Jailany is situated in the forest, approximately 2500 feet above sea level. A number of Sufi "hermit" mystics (*murshids*), including a woman, had taken up permanent residence in the area.[15] During the festival month I witnessed, there were long lines of pilgrims desiring to receive the blessings of the *murshid*. A few of the *murshids* had (and have) devoted acolytes who care for them throughout the year. The mystics and the festival at Jailany were, and continue to be, central to the construction of a Sufi identity.

Kutali villagers identify themselves both as Sunnis and as members of the Qadariya Tariqa (order or sect of Sufis). Though there is no official *pir* or *sheikh* (leader) who organizes and maintains the sect as an active order, there are weekly Thursday evening *dikhr* (devotional) services held in honor of "Mohideen Andawer." I observed similar services in Kalmunai (on the east coast) led by a *pir* and attended by both women and men; the women were separated from the men by a curtain. During *dikhr* recitals some participants enter trance states that are explained as the individual entering a state of spiritual grace (*fana*) in which they are attuned to the spiritual vibrations of Allah.

Each night, at Jailany, there is a procession around the shrine (*dargah*) of the saint led by a group of Rifa'i *fakirs* (also referred to as *murids*). Rifa'i was an Iraqi twelfth-century saint said to have followed in the "footsteps" of Mohideen Abdul Qadir. The Rifa'i *fakirs* are known by Sri Lankan Muslims for their ecstatic and extreme forms of devotional practices. Led by a *khalifa* (one of many titles for a leader of a Sufi order), the *fakirs* dance in elaborate militarylike fashion and as the tambourine playing and chanting becomes ever more intense, slash and pierce themselves with swords, maces, and long sharp metal skewers, in a manner reminiscent of Hindu and Buddhist worship at Kataragama. Members of the audience also participate.[16] These actions are intended both to reflect the faith of the *fakir* and participant, and the sacred power of the saint.

It is precisely the sacred states of the saint and the supernatural power that can be harnessed by devotees that lies, as we shall see, at the center of the debate over the acceptable parameters of Muslim religious practices and beliefs. At both the Kalmunai and Dafter Jailany festivals, there had been a small group of Muslims who handed out pamphlets and told interested bystanders that the worship of saints was a form of idolatry and, therefore, heresy (*haram*) according to the Shari'a (Islamic law). These Muslims were members of the Tablighi Jama'at, a group that perceives itself to represent orthodox Islam, as we shall see. The group provides the emerging dominant view of Islamic identity that extends the boundaries of identity from a local to a global context.

A Sufi Design for Identity

A Sufi design for identity, as used here, is defined both by the worship of saints and by the social establishment of a *Tariqa* (a Sufi order) constituted by a *pir* and his followers (*murid*). Though there is no *pir* in Kutali, there are weekly *dikhr* recitals: a Sufi practice in which the names of Allah are recited repetitively in devotion to the saint; the Moulana serves as a *pir* during his stay. Similar to Hindu and Buddhist folk deities, the saints, Mohideen and Shahul Hamid (among others), represent supernatural funds of power that can be tapped for aid through devotional practices and offerings.

The village mosque (*pali*) is called the Mohideen *pali* and there is a small till box at the gate along the street where villagers can put coins in for vows (*muradi* or *barre*).[17] The *labbai* (a term villagers use to refer to the village "folk priest,") or *vede mahatteyya* (folk healer who specializes in snake bites) are called on by villagers, after the harvest or at critical times in their lives to offer vows and give a *narsi* (also called *pukka* or *dana* and refers to food offerings) for the saint.[18] Simply exclaiming "Ya Mohideen" suffices to enlist his aid in times of trouble. This became clear to me when, in 1982, I took an ill villager to the hospital in the middle of the night on my 1952 Java motorcycle. On our return, there had been a downpour and one of the causeways was flooded. The light of the motorcycle reflected against the water so that it looked like pavement. As we motored into the flood, my passenger screamed out "Ya Mohideen" and, knee-deep in water, we managed to extricate ourselves. The story made the rounds and was cited as proof of Mohideen's power and attentiveness to individuals in distress.

The role of saints pervades everyday life in Kutali. They are distinguished from *Nabis* (prophets) or the *Rasool* (the Prophet Mohammed) who, according to one *maulavi* (a Muslim trained at a *madrasa* in Islamic doctrine and Arabic), are "dead and gone having fulfilled their task but Allah gave the saints the power to intercede on our behalf." The worship of saints is not confined to the exigencies of daily life but extends to devotional practices. The Thursday evening *dikhr* rites, performed on behalf of Mohideen, as we have seen, are in practice a recital of the various names of Allah. The participants congregate, light camphor incense, and proceed in unison to chant the various names of Allah with the intention of attaining inner harmony with the sacred (*fana*). Stories of the miracles and the devotional practices of Mohideen and Shahul Hamid circulate among Muslims and are told, much as *hadith* stories about the life of the Prophet Mohammed are recounted, as instructive parables.

Specifically with regard to the offering of vows, saint worship among Sri Lankan Muslims is similar to Tamil and Sinhala folk practices directed toward deities. In both forms of worship, the saint or deity is perceived as a supernatural intercessor who can act in behalf of the community or individual who offers the vow. The supplicant offers small coins or small tin images, and a ritual specialist communicates the vow, while the supplicant gives a food gift (*narsi* or *pukka*). Muslims recognize the parallels, but for those who believe in saints, the categorical differences distinguish them from the Tamil and Sinhala populations. Much like Buddhist folk deities, saints are perceived as hybrid entities—half human/half supernatural—who, because of their human qualities, are conceptualized as a bridge to the realm of the sacred. As villagers say, they function as a sort of idealized government attending to the needs of the powerless (see Gilsenan, 1973, for a similar account of saints in Lebanon).

Indeed, Muslim villagers explicitly recognize the ritual and functional parallels in their worship of saints and local Sinhala-Buddhist worship of the gods. For example, village elders have told me that Mohideen Andawer is the same as the Buddhist god Saman Deviyo, while Shahul Hamid is considered to be identical to Natha Deviyo. As those of us who are familiar with Sri Lankan Buddhist cosmology know, both gods are considered to be among the four protector deities of the island. Such conflation suggests the upward mobility of the Muslim saint. More importantly, it suggests that Sinhala-Buddhist culture has contributed in significant ways to the definition of minority identity in Sri Lanka, one of the themes of this book.

This conflation of Sri Lanka's religions and cultures is most pronounced in the premiere Muslim village festival, the Burdha Kandhoori, which occurs a month or so after the rice paddy harvest in April and May. A letter of invitation is sent by messenger to the Moulana in Dikwella sometime in January. He acknowledges the letter and informs the *marikars* of the date of his arrival. A month before he arrives, the *marikars* convene and divide up the labor to prepare for the Burdha Kandhoori. Villagers are enlisted in cooperative labor teams to clean up the village: they clean up homes and shops, whitewashing them with lime; women make colorful reed mats for the mosque; all gather foodstuffs and donations in the village; and local leaders make the rounds to collect donations from Sinhala villagers and wealthy merchants in the region (including Sinhala shop owners). Stories of the miraculous power of the Moulana are told and retold by Muslims and Sinhalas alike.

Sinhalas of the region are invited to attend the grand feast (*kandhoori*) that marks the culmination of the festival. Their participation in the festival explicitly is intended to preserve neighborly relations between Kutali villagers and the regional Sinhala people. Because of the parallels between the Burdha Kandhoori and Buddhist folk festivals, the Sinhala participants perceive the Moulana as the functional equivalent of the *kapurala* (Buddhist folk priest) whom they enlist to petition the gods for support.

Most villagers accept, without question, that the Moulana possesses supernatural power. But the source of his power, as the Moulana states, stems from his blood tie to the Prophet. Indeed, villagers perceive the Moulana as the symbolic embodiment of the Prophet. During the eight-day festival, the Moulana visits homes, charms water to heal the sick, resolves dowry and marriage problems, and arbitrates various other disputes. He also has the power to remove *marikars*, including the trustee, from office. During his stay in Kutali, he is the unquestioned religious leader of the village.

On the eighth, and final, day of the Burdha Kandhoori, approximately two thousand Sinhalas and Muslims stream into the village. A loudspeaker is rented through which music is broadcast and donations are announced. In 1981, the Mosque trustee estimated that more than one hundred chickens, twelve goats, and ten oxen were slaughtered for the final feast of the festival. The street by the mosque is lined with petty entrepreneurs selling costume jewelry, silver and gold bracelets, brass pots, saris, sarongs, and other wares. Sinhalas and Muslims from the area arrive by bus, rented vans, private vehicles, bicycles, and on foot. A merry-go-round and swings are set up on the mosque grounds for the children. Guests and hosts, Muslims and Sinhalas, rich and poor, sit on the ground in groups of five eating from large metal *sabans* (bowls). The *sabans* are filled with rice, vegetables, and meat curries. The five people around the *saban* dip their hands into the communal bowl and eat. After the feast, adults congregate in small groups chatting, watching the children play, and generally enjoying themselves. The women and children eat in the rice cooperative building across the street. Sinhalas and Muslims alike form a line, waiting to meet with the Moulana who will bless them or charm some water that they will store and drink only when they are ill. The general tenor of the day is one of communal harmony and camaraderie. While historically the Burdha Kandhoori had been intended to differentiate Muslim from Sinhala religious practices and ideology, on this day markers of religious-ethnic distinction elide in the figure of the Moulana.

After the feasting is over, the Moulana delivers a final benediction. In 1981 it went as follows:

> O Allah, let our sins be forgiven for those who are here and for all villagers. All the people want to pray and I beseech you to help them pray. O Allah, we are very poor and uneducated, therefore send us the means to become rich. O Allah, we want to die with lots of merit. O Allah, bless our request. O Allah, give us plenty of rain and good harvests, give many things to our village. O Allah, we hope for an abundance of rain and good paddy and *chena* [swidden] harvests. O Allah, we hope for better education and more comforts. O Allah, please grant our requests.[19]

This benediction is attuned to the specific needs of a Muslim peasantry. But Sinhala villagers are also present and treat the Moulana as a holy man. The ethnic-religious distinctions between Sinhala and Muslim peasantry are both muted and marked during this festival. There is, from my observations, no sense or expression of ethnic-religious discord but, rather, a sense of "collective effervescence," bringing both communities together in the presence of the embodiment of "the sacred." Despite the evident syncretism of this festival, evident both in the reference to "merit" (*pin*) and to the charming of water with *mantrams*, villagers view the proceedings as a symbolic display of the power and veracity of Islam. Whatever else the festival does and "means," it unites Muslim and Sinhala, legitimizing a socioreligious identity of historical depth and power. It unites them, too, because both, to paraphrase Radin (1957:246), live in a "blaze of reality" where the whimsy of nature and health can only be controlled by enlisting sacred power.

It is during the annual *maulids* and the Burdha Kandhoori that village microidentities based on their petitioning of the saints for prosperity, health, rain, and comforts, coalesce into a more encompassing macroidentity. These microidentities are delineated at critical junctures in the lives of people. They are contingently triggered whenever a child is ill, when paddy seeds are broadcast, a shop is opened, a woman goes into the forest to collect reeds to make mats or firewood, or a man goes hunting. At these times, villagers remember Mohideen or Shahul Hamid (also known as Meera Saibo). In making a vow or simply calling out "Ya Mohideen" whenever they need protection or guidance, villagers are engaged reflexively in the reproduction of social practices.

Stories of the saints are told as instructive tales, much as *Jataka* tales of the Buddha are told by Sinhala villagers. There is no orchestration of microidentities; rather, they are triggered as a consequence of everyday exigencies, hopes, and misfortunes. Muslim villagers respond to these situations in similar fashion. The reiteration of these similar actions, interpreted and motivated by shared beliefs, provide the sociocultural elements for constructing and organizing more inclusive (macro) identities. Through the participation in collective and scheduled rituals such as the Burdha Kandhoori, *maulids* and weekly *dikhr* prayer, these elements are assembled and organized into a Sufi identity. The trustee, *marikars*, and the Moulana benefit from their respective roles in these rituals. Their position as leaders is made visible and concrete; the leaders gain prestige, and they have the opportunity to make money. The mosque and villagers pay the Moulana for his services, the trustee an annual stipend, and the *marikars* receive cash donations to hold the festival. It is in their interest to construct and to organize a macroidentity out of the shared experiences and common concerns of villagers.

Despite the popularity of saint worship, there are village Muslims who are troubled by it, by the syncretism of Sufi practices, and by the villagers' idealization of the Moulana as the contemporary embodiment of the Prophet. In Kutali, these Muslims are mostly young (under thirty) and have been educated at high schools in towns on the east coast or in Badulla. They form a small but active group recruited by the Tablighi Jama'at. In 1979, 1981, and 1982, they were passive onlookers at the Burdha festival. They did not directly oppose the festival, but were instrumental in its cancellation in 1980 and in the construction of a new pan-Islamic identity that presages a return to orthodoxy and discredits the worship of saints and the recruitment of Sinhala-Buddhist *kattadis* and *bhikkhus* for curing illnesses.

The Tablighi Jama'at: The Construction of Muslim Orthodoxy

The Tablighi Jama'at was founded by Maulana Muhammed Ilyas in 1926 in the town of Mewat, near Delhi (Durrany 1993:22). Ilyas was a Muslim reformer who campaigned for Muslims to abandon non-Islamic accretions. Foremost among these was saint worship. Van der Veer (1992:555) illustrates this point when he writes of the Tablighi Jama'at in Surat (a port town in Gujarat) that,

> Public confrontations on religious issues are carefully avoided. Nevertheless, some of their propaganda clearly stands against Sufism, as is well understood among both Sufis and non-Sufis. They do not concern themselves with Hindu participation or Hindu influences in Sufi practices. Their main theme is that Sufi conceptions of hereditary saintliness and saintly power are innovations (*bida't*) that have led Muslims astray.

Van der Veer (1992:549) refers to the Tablighi Jama'at as the "main Muslim opponent" to Sufism in Surat.[20] Durrany (1993:147; 151) goes further by defining the Tablighi Jama'at as a fundamentalist movement whose members preach that "worldly constitutions and the government are imperfect and subject to change and corruption" and promotes "the establishment of an Islamic social order." These characterizations of the core goals of the Tablighi Jama'at accord with my own observations. The movement's followers oppose Sufi practices and imagine the establishment of a pan-Islamic identity that supersedes national boundaries.

The expressed goals of the Tablighi Jama'at platform are to reform and recruit Muslims into their movement. The Tablighi Jama'at is a religious, and not a political, movement. However, these goals have political, antinationalist, consequences. By espousing that Muslims should be committed to a transnational "realm of Islam" (*dar al Islam*) and that "worldly constitutions and the governments are imperfect and subject to change and corruption" (Durrany 1993:151), the Tablighi Jama'at provides Sri Lankan Muslims with a potent alternative identity to Sri Lankan Sinhala-Buddhist nationalism. If religion is, for Muslims, the dominant mode for defining identity in Sri Lanka, then the appeal of the Tablighi Jama'at is that it fashions an identity that supersedes nationalist Sinhala and Tamil discourses of identity.

It must be emphasized that the members of the Tablighi Jama'at are purposefully nonconfrontational in their opposition. During the Burdha Kandhoori and *maulids* for Mohideen and Shahul Hamid that I witnessed, village members of the Tablighi Jama'at did not express public disapproval, but their position is well known by their silence and nonparticipation in these ceremonies. The Tablighi Jama'at claims to represent orthodox, "pure" Islam and, by implication, Sufi practices and beliefs are defined as impure accretions—"abominations" or "danger," to use Mary Douglas's (1966) terminology. This dichotomous conceptualization of Muslim identity has intensified debates within the Muslim community over what it means to be a genuine Muslim.

From 1914 to 1980 the Moulana was the unquestioned authority on Islam. In the nationalist fervor of the first half of the twentieth century, religious-ethnic revival movements occurred within the framework of the nation, perhaps because the "framework" for the nation had not yet been properly formulated. The Burdha Kandhoori and Sufi practices of Sri Lankan Muslims are a pastiche of Hindu-Buddhist and Islamic practices and beliefs, but from the point of view of the "ordinary" Muslim, they serve as a distinctive socio-religious complex that confirms their own unique connections to funds of sacred power.

In rejecting this connection, the Tablighi Jama'at proposes an alternative, global prescription for what it means to be a Muslim; one that confers power through connection to a transnational Islamic identity. At the same time, such a rejection necessarily entails a rejection of local histories, dislocating villagers from their past. The past that is "significant" to the Tablighi Jama'at is not Sri Lankan or even South Asian, but rather an Arabic past—the time of the Prophet and his companions. In referring to their activities, the *jamatis* (missions or meetings) state that they are imitating the devotional practices of the companions (*sahabah*) of the Prophet Mohammed. The symbols used by the *jamatis* to invoke their image of a Muslim identity are taken from Islamic events that connect Muslims cross-culturally with a common cultural heritage.

The Tablighi Jama'at recruits members by organizing *jamatis* in Muslim communities throughout Sri Lanka (and elsewhere in South Asia). Three to four times a year a group of five to ten Tablighi members visit Kutali for a few days. Typically, the members are professionals (retired judges, lawyers, businessmen) from Colombo who travel by car or van; they are always males. Occasionally, Tablighis include members from Pakistan, Bangladesh, and India. The international flavor of these *jamatis* and the high status of the members impress, and occasionally irritate, villagers. The village lacks a police department, post office, or medical facility. Except for the Moulana and the *jamatis*, no "important" people visit the village. The arrival of Muslims from Colombo and other countries symbolically expresses the villagers' affiliation with a national and international community. The intent of the Tablighi is not only to recruit villagers but to instill, visit by visit, an image of genuine, orthodox Islam that overwhelms the more localized identity formulated by the Moulana.

During their visits, the members of the Tablighi sleep on reed mats in the Mohideen mosque. During the day, much like Christian missionaries, they go door to door to lecture on Islam and the Tablighi. They make a special point of meeting with a congregation of women who, behind a curtain, listen to a Tablighi member exhort them to adhere to doctrinal Islam—to pray five times a day (*salat*) and practice *purdah*. In the evening the Tablighis participate in prayers and deliver sermons. These sermons are well attended; the mosque is usually full. Interspersed in the sermon are repeated appeals to recruit villagers by asking them to stand up or raise their hands if they are willing to participate in locally organized *jamatis*. Despite the exhortations by the Tablighi leader, most villagers sit in uncomfortable silence. This is in stark contrast to typical meetings at the mosque where villagers are always boisterous.

This contrast came to the fore when, during a Tablighi visit, a poor elderly villager died. The *marikars* and other interested villagers adjourned secretly at the deceased's house to consider the funeral arrangements. The group decided to delay the funeral until after the Tablighi members left. They did not want the Tablighi members to see how poor and "backwards" the villagers were. The Moulana, on the other hand, is privy to "backstage" arenas and behavior. The difference in villagers' perceptions of the Tablighi Jama'at members as "outsiders" and the Moulana as "insider" is, I think, reflective of the difference between "local" and "global" knowledge. The relationship between the Moulana and the villagers is a localized relationship, built-up over time in face-to-face meetings and dinners where villagers tell the Moulana of their problems and he seeks a religious solution for them. The members of the Tablighi Jama'at are not concerned about developing this type of relationship. Their goal is to reform Muslim practices so that across Sri Lanka and the world, these practices will be uniform. They have no interest in establishing local ties or learning local knowledge; their concerns are universal rather than local.

Only a few villagers (approximately 10–20) were active members of the Tablighi Jama'at. These few, however, were tremendously influential. There were four *maulavis* (Islamic scholars trained at Muslim schools, *madrasas*). The three youngest (between the ages of 18–25) were leaders of the local "branch" of the Tablighi Jama'at. The fourth was in his late thirties, and was married to the trustee's sister and, although a supporter of the Tablighi Jama'at, took a less active role than did the other three *maulavis*. As *maulavis* and Tablighi Jama'at members, these three behaved as religious virtuosos: they attended and frequently led prayers; they did not swear and behaved modestly in public; and they gave sermons at the mosque, particularly during Jummah (Friday afternoon) services. They attempted to provide an example, through their behavior, of a new Muslim-Islamic identity.

After the Tablighi leaves, male villagers often gather at local shops (*kadees*) to exchange stories and jokes about the Tablighi. On one occasion, a man was telling the story of a Tablighi member who came to his house. He had seen him approaching and had told his son to answer the door and tell the Tablighi member that he was not at home. The boy had gone to the door and said, "my father told me to tell you he is not at home." Just then, one of the young *maulavis* arrived and, after the villagers had a good laugh, made a statement that it was a sin to disparage the Tablighi Jama'at; he reprimanded the villagers. Unlike typical shop debates, where villagers are quick to respond, the villagers were silent after the *maulavi's* comments. Their silence, I suggest, was not only borne out of their respect for the *maulavi*, but out of their tacit recognition that the Tablighi Jama'at metonymically represents true Islam and that all criticism of the Tablighi is, by implication, a criticism of Islam and, therefore, heretical. The frequency of their visits, the missionary zeal of the Tablighi Jama'at members, and the effective silencing of public criticism seem to me to foreshadow the eventual replacement of a syncretistic Sufi identity with a more "puritanical" Muslim identity. Since 1982, the Tablighi Jama'at has continued to recruit members and, in Sri Lanka, has emerged as the largest Muslim reform movement.[21]

As we have seen, in 1980 the Burdha Kandhoori was canceled for the first time in the collective memory of the villagers. Though there were charges of corruption in 1980, in 1981 the festival was resumed largely because villagers believed that the ensuing drought was a consequence of their not holding the festival. The problem lies deeper than corruption and weather. In discussions with the Moulana in 1979 and 1981, he told me that other villages had recently canceled the festival. In its historical context, the Burdha Kandhoori and the Moulana represent a distinct Sufi-Islamic identity that contrasts with Buddhism and marks religious and ethnic boundaries.

Today, the culturally relevant contrast is with the Tablighi Jama'at which provides a "nationalist" Islamic identity vis-à-vis Sinhala and Tamil nationalisms. The context has shifted from one that frames distinctions within localities to one that frames distinctions within, and between "nations." The cancellation of the Burdha Kandhoori in disparate communities suggests a gradual erosion of a community-based Sufi identity. The arrival of Tablighi Jama'at members by caravan into the community from outside—some from other countries—is intended to mirror the original historical spread of Islam. The representatives of the Tablighi Jama'at, their actions and preaching, express an identity and a connection to a global community that is more powerful and inclusive than one that Sufism can offer. In a time of interethnic fratricide, when Muslims feel excluded from both Tamil and Sinhala nationalisms, the building of a powerful pan-Islamic identity that looks back to its own glorious past, provides a solution to their dilemma.

Conclusion

Muslim identities in Sri Lanka recombine and change over time and space so that, at best, I have managed to describe two very general "designs" for Muslim identity. By conceptualizing identities as designs, I have emphasized how agents (the Moulana and the Tablighi Jama'at) design identities within local contexts. Agents do not operate in historical and cultural vacuums; they do not create designs *ab nihilo*. Sri Lankan Muslims don't just decide to "buy" one or the other potential identities sold at the ideological marketplace. Identities are formulated by agents out of the shared symbolic and experiential "lived worlds" of agents and audience.

By virtue of their religious, cultural, and linguistic differences, Kutali Muslims distinguish themselves from neighboring Sinhala communities. However, the day-to-day lives of Muslims and Sinhalas in the area historically have been (and are) much the same: they share common travails and interests. Their lives revolve around the same quotidian and seasonal cycles. Malaria, tuberculosis, drought, birds, and other animals that can ruin their crops do not make ethnic distinctions. The commonality of experiences has led to historically companionable relations between the two communities. Muslims and Sinhalas visit each other, exchange labor. The Muslim *vede mahatteyya* is called to cure snake bites by Sinhala families, while the Buddhist *kattadi* is summoned by villagers to cure various illnesses. Muslims set up shops during the annual festival at the nearby Bandara-Kataragama *devale* (a shrine for Buddhist folk deities). In short, ethnicity has been historically muted as a salient symbol of difference in lieu of the commonalities of their experiences. This is not to say that enmities did not (and do not) exist, but they were (and are) expressed in terms of interpersonal, or interfamilial, rather than interethnic, disputes.

The Burdha Kandhoori originated within the national context of religious revivalism and the emergence of an independent nation-state. The parallels of Muslim and Sinhala-Buddhist folk practices were ritually and conceptually untangled. The Moulana's genealogical tie to the Prophet Mohammed and his embodiment of Islamic funds of sacred power, the invocation of Muslim saints, and the practice of *maulids* and weekly *dikhr* rites offered Muslims their own effective and affective religious counterparts to Buddhist (and Hindu) ritual practices and beliefs.

The emergence of local ritual practices and identity discourses aimed at differentiating Muslims from Sinhalas in the early decades of the twentieth century were not merely coincidental with national events. Claims of ethnic distinction were partly propelled by fears of assimilation. Ramanathan's assertion that Muslims are Tamil converts and his subsequent support of Sinhalas during the Sinhala-Muslim riots of 1915 deepened divisions between these two communities (Mohan 1987:21–23; Weerasooria 1971:25).[22] The competition over trade between Sinhala and Muslim (coastal Moors) merchants coupled with the riots furthered the efforts by Muslim leaders at the turn of the century to create a Muslim identity. The Burdha Kandhoori, though a local development not directly motivated by events in Colombo and Kandy, was part of this national engagement of Muslims to shape a distinctive Muslim community.

The collective "remindings" of Sri Lankan history in modern ceremonies celebrating the nation do not include Muslims (Tennekoon 1988; Brow 1988). For Sri Lankan Muslims, their memories of a heroic past are traced back to the time of the Prophet. The preaching of the members of the Tablighi Jama'at, the willingness of these rich and urbane Muslims to sleep in the mosque on reed mats, recall the simple and pure religious life of the Prophet. In the identity politics of Sri Lanka, local events and interests are now directly related to national and global events and interests. The Tablighi Jama'at, more than the Moulana, resonates with the villagers' expansion into a world beyond the village boundaries.

Ahmed (1988:228) writes that nationalism "has created ambiguity and tension among Muslims" in India primarily because nationalism entails loyalty to the state and to a national culture that excludes Islam. Along these lines, within the contemporary discourse on Sri Lankan identity, Muslims have the option to accept the hegemonic ideology of the Sri Lankan state that reduces them, they argue, to second-class citizens or, in the present context, to construct an identity that transcends the nation-state. A more utopian (but less foreseeable) option is to do away with unitarian identity politics. For Sri Lankan Muslims, the Tablighi Jama'at offers them an alternative to Sri Lankan nationalism by involving them in a commemoration of their Islamic heritage and offering them full citizenship in a pan-Islamic "nation." It offers them a response to national level identity politics that does not mark them as the subordinate and minority group but, rather, as the dominant majority group. Despite the increasing prominence of Islamic "fundamentalism" in Sri Lanka, most Sri Lankan Muslims are not "fundamentalists," but, I would conjecture, seek inclusion in a Sri Lankan nationalist identity that does not stigmatize their "far Other" identity.

Notes

1. Since the 1980s, the dominant mode of reckoning Sri Lankan *Muslim* identity is religion. However, as Ishmail (1995) has shown, the saliency of identity markers is not immutable and has shifted from "race" to "language" to "religion." For more on this, see Bartholomeusz, Hollup, and Stirrat in this volume.

2. Kutali is a pseudonym that I have used in other publications and continue to use both for obvious reasons and for the sake of continuity. Kutali is a Tamil word that means "friend" and reflects, in my imagination, the way I hope villagers and I view each other.

3. The main period of my fieldwork was between June 1979 and February 1982. I returned for a month in 1992 and have remained in correspondence with villagers.

4. In this paper, I use "Muslim" as an inclusive term and do not address minority ethnic Muslim groups, particularly the Malayan Muslims, partly because they are a very small minority within the Muslim community and partly out of lack of my own knowledge. The first Malays came in the thirteenth century and the largest contingent came as exiles from Indonesia in the eighteenth century. At the turn of the twentieth century Malays formed 75 percent of the police force and 100 percent of the Colombo fire brigade (Thawfeeq n.d., 144–45). However, since then, the Malay community seems to have largely disintegrated as a cohesive entity, largely through intermarriage. There is a Ceylon Malay Research Organization headed by Mr. Murad Jayah.

5. Muslims comprise only about 7 percent of the Sri Lankan population compared with 18 percent and 74 percent for Tamils and Sinhalese, respectively.

6. Obviously this also applies to the villager's use of "Eelam."

7. "Moor," of course, is a Portuguese term. I use "Muslim" because Sri Lankan Muslims refer to themselves as "Muslim" rather than "Moor." There is also some evidence that pre-Islamic Arab traders arrived in Ceylon as early as the sixth century (Rachid 1976:190).

8. Chandra R. de Silva (1996, personal communication) notes that a "compromise formula" was reached in which King Senerath "promised to be a friend of friends of the Portuguese and enemies of their enemies."

9. In 1911 the majority of Sri Lankan Muslims were "small farmers cultivating their own lands" (Denham 1911:466, cited in Ishmail 1995:78). Samarasinghe and Dawood (1986) state that 35 percent of Muslims were agriculturalists and 28 percent traders in 1973 (cited in Ishmail 1995:78).

10. This was a "scripted" response provided by many villagers. Though this explanation may be accurate, the village plan is similar to that of other Muslim villages

and may also be part of the Muslim "image" of the community as centered around mosque and business (e.g., Lynch 1974).

11. There are four *marikars* in the village, with one voted trustee, or head *marikar*. The position of *marikar* is traditionally hereditary, but in 1957 the Wakf board that oversees all Sri Lankan mosques declared there should be open elections for the *marikar* and trustee posts every three years. In fact the elections still follow along hereditary lines, thus the elder brother and father of the present trustee had been trustees prior to him.

12. Qutub is a Sufi title that means "axis" or "pole star," suggesting that devotees of the saint order their lives and devotions around his teachings.

13. This is, it should be noted, a legendary claim lacking (to my knowledge of) historical evidence.

14. *Maulid* can be used both to refer to the anniversary or the recitals on behalf of the saints.

15. The woman mystic resided permanently in a spacious and well-kept two-room cave. She was approximately 30–35 years of age and attended to by a man of about fifty years who brought her food and water, and regulated the traffic of pilgrims who came to her for advice. Within the Sufi tradition it is not unusual to have female saints or *pirs*.

16. On a personal note, the piercing of flesh is more intense and "extreme" than I have witnessed at the Kataragama festival or other Hindu and Buddhist rituals accompanied by piercing. To provide an example, one of the *fakirs*, a young man in his twenties, took what looked like a fencing sword and pierced his abdomen lengthwise with the point sticking out the other side.

17. *Muradi* is the Arabic term that is sometimes used for giving vows, more often villagers use the Sinhala term *barre*.

18. The offering of vows in Kutali, and the procedures that accompany the giving of vows, including the recital of *mantrams* and the tying of amulets (*yantrams*) for protection, parallel Buddhist and Hindu customs. Probably because of the village's relative isolation from other Muslim enclaves and their close association with the surrounding Sinhala population, villagers use a mixture of Sinhala, Tamil, and Arabic colloquialisms to refer both to the ritual specialists and the procedure for offering vows. *Vede Mahatteyya*, for example, is a Sinhala term, but is used by all villagers to address and refer to the local "folk doctor." Both the *labbai* and *vede mahatteyya* statuses are traditionally inherited but they can also be achieved by someone willing to undergo the fairly rigorous training necessary to perform these roles. In 1982, none of the sons of either the *vede Mahatteyya* or *labbai* were interested in becoming apprentices and their particular skills are likely to be lost.

19. I am indebted to A. "Singer" Muthulingam for this translation.

20. In referring to the Tablighi Jama'at as an "opponent," van der Veer conceptualizes this movement as a superorganic entity, analyzing it as an agent of change, or, in my borrowed terminology, as a "design."

21. Personal communication, A.A. Salaam. I do not have statistics on the number of members and I hope to do a more detailed study of the Tablighi Jama'at next year.

22. On August 11, 1915, Ramanathan stated in the Legislative Council that "a great and grievous injustice has been done to the Sinhalese" (quoted in Mohan 1987:23).

Chapter 7

Sinhala Anglicans and Buddhism in Sri Lanka: When the "Other" Becomes You

Tessa J. Bartholomeusz

Introduction

As Oddvar Hollup comments in his essay, language, race, and ethnicity, rather than religion, as had been the case until recently, are the most important identity markers for Sinhalas and Tamils in contemporary Sri Lanka.[1] This observation provides a useful starting point for analyzing the Sinhala-Anglican community in Sri Lanka. Over the past few decades, it has constructed an identity to suit its neocolonial world. In that world, being "Sinhala"—the majority identity on the island—means being empowered. That empowerment has been eloquently discussed elsewhere.[2] In this chapter, I analyze at what point the majority of Sri Lankan Anglicans saw themselves as a separate religious community. In addition, I explore why today they identify themselves with Sinhalas, rather than the British, despite the Sinhalas' association with Buddhism. As we shall see, Sinhala Anglicans, much like other Sinhala groups, have been forced to show their loyalty to the nation through the revival of a shared "history," and language, rather than through religious affiliation.

The Creation of the Sinhala Anglican Tradition in Ceylon

Unlike India, which had a thriving Christian community before the advent of colonization,[3] Sri Lanka (Ceylon) became a permanent home to Christianity only after it was colonized by the Portuguese in the early 1500s.[4]

Though the Dutch later brought Protestant Christianity to the island, the Anglican Church did not become part of the religious mosaic of Sri Lanka until the British period. The first Anglican missionaries arrived in 1818 and set about preparing Ceylonese candidates for the ministry.[5] In this early British period, large numbers of Buddhists and Hindus converted to Anglicanism, at least nominally. This is not surprising: as is well known, colonized peoples often adopt the religion of colonizers as a strategy to advance in social institutions. British Anglicans in Ceylon were painfully aware of this phenomenon and tried with little success to safeguard Anglican liturgy from the influence of nominal Christians, both Sinhala and Tamil.[6] The British indeed had converted the "far Other," or Buddhists and Hindus whose cultures and traditions were perceived by the British as being totally alien. Yet Anglicans had the task of making sure that their converts had fully relinquished their former religious affiliations.

In fact, until the 1880s few attempts were made to adjust Anglican Christianity to fit the particular milieu in which it had begun to take root in the island. The British introduced Anglicanism to Sri Lanka, basing it solely on the British model. One of their main concerns was to ensure that Anglicanism remained aloof from Buddhist influence. In other words, they strove to create a separate religious community, distinct from Buddhism, Hinduism, and even other forms of Christianity. This entailed, among other things, carefully training "native" clergy;[7] prohibiting amendments to the English Prayer Book;[8] and serving as a watchdog agency that critiqued the British government's patronage of Buddhism, Hinduism, and the Anglican Church. Regarding the latter, British Anglicans domiciled on the island in the 1890s were scandalized to learn that the British governor of Ceylon regularly listened to the *Jayamangala Gatha*, or a Buddhist *sutra*, at government functions.[9] Though on one such occasion they granted that the governor believed the *Jayamangala Gatha* to be an "address of welcome,"[10] they pointed out that the verses were "distinctly religious and characteristic of Buddhism."[11] Therefore, Christians had "just grounds of complaint at their use."[12] The *Jayamangala Gatha* came to symbolize the ever-present threat of Buddhism and the "Other" to Anglican Christianity.

British Anglicans in Sri Lanka remained suspicious of Buddhism and its influence on converts to Christianity throughout the nineteenth century. Nineteenth-century British Anglicans were well aware that many of their converts confessed Christianity but practiced Buddhism, especially during crises. In one such instance in the 1870s, they agonized over what to do when they discovered that a "native" (Sinhala) priest had granted a Christian burial to a convert who had listened to Buddhist chanting on his deathbed. After much consideration, the Anglican community decided to suspend the priest.[13] The case made public the private concerns of many British Anglicans in Ceylon regarding converts. It was also serious enough to warrant a pastoral letter from the British bishop of Colombo, Reginald Copleston. In that letter, the bishop discussed the problem of lapsed Christian converts, coining the term "Buddhist Christianity."[14] British Anglicans in the 1870s used the term to describe the half-hearted conversion of Buddhists to Christianity. Priests used the burial case as material for sermons and began preaching with new vigor the dangers of complicity with Buddhism; that there could be "no communion between light and darkness."[15]

Along these lines, the Anglican Church in Ceylon warned its parishioners against marrying Buddhists, which amounted to "forsaking Christ."[16] Despite the British clergy's attempts to create a separate community modeled solely on British Anglican forms, it did not remain aloof from Buddhism. The process of mixing has created a remarkably sophisticated and cohesive new manifestation of Christianity that, as we shall see, many colonial British of the 1870s and earlier would not have condoned.

Though the Anglican clergy assiduously attempted to safeguard Anglican tradition from Buddhism, they were not insensitive to Buddhism's influence upon newly converted Christians. In 1876 the English archdeacon of Colombo reminded his clergy that "Christianity can scarcely be embraced without persecution and loss of caste and family and home."[17] He warned his clergy not to dismiss as dishonest and ungrateful the "native races" that nominally accept Christianity and continue to practice Buddhism.[18] Rather, he admonished the clergy to take pity on them and help them heal their "spiritual disease."

The clergy's sympathetic view of converts created the climate for indigenization. From the point of view of late nineteenth-century clergy—both local and British—the spiritual disease of lapsing back to Buddhism could be best rectified by accommodating certain cultural practices that did not contravene church law. The clergy began to rethink their approach to converting Buddhists and Hindus. They had tried maintaining the ritual format of English worship with little success. The clergy thus began to replace the former mode of parroting English worship with accepting into Ceylon Anglicanism elements that met the needs of the newly converted. In this way, the church began the process of adapting Anglican worship to the cultural setting of Ceylon.

One of the main instruments of indigenization in the late nineteenth century was music. The clergy, both local and British, argued that music was the most important vehicle for bringing Christ to the people of Ceylon.[19] The indigenization of music thus began as a strategy of conversion. Cries were heard throughout Anglican congregations to create music that would resonate with converts, especially Sinhala and Tamil speakers. Since its inception in Ceylon, the Anglican Church had offered services in four languages: Sinhala,

Tamil, Portuguese, and English. The hymns, however, were limited to English and therefore unintelligible to many. According to one priest, "It is music, good, hearty, and congregational music, which makes services attractive, especially to the young, who are first of all drawn to church for the sake of the music."[20]

Different parishes in the 1880s experimented with creating music that would bring "pleasure to converts," and sang "Sinhalese hymns to harmonized native tunes" with much success.[21] One clergyman, however, warned against "original hymns," yet invited the "Native Clergy" to translate hymns into Sinhala. He did allow, however, that English meter might be unsuited to the Sinhala language.[22] The problem to a large extent was solved by a former Buddhist, Father Senanayake, who in 1883 produced for the first time a "Singhalese Hymnal." Senanayake, however, preserved English meter.[23] The 1885 hymnal nonetheless paved the way for the full-scale indigenization of Anglican Church music.

As the church's discussion over music suggests, in the late 1800s the Anglican Church in Ceylon began to change radically. No longer an alien transplant that could be dismissed as being less authentic than other traditions in the island, the Anglican Church in Ceylon began to develop a particular Ceylonese identity.

In the 1880s, when the Anglican Church was well on its way to creating a particular Ceylonese identity and a separate religious community, Buddhists in Ceylon had already begun to affirm their Buddhist cultural heritage and hone their identity in unprecedented ways. Buddhist revivalists such as Anagarika Dharmapala, whose career has been well documented, began to stimulate lapsed Buddhists to view Buddhism anew. During the 1880s, Buddhist pride became a form of cultural resistance against the British, which gave birth to Sinhala-Buddhist fundamentalism. At that time, Dharmapala's fundamentalism helped provide Buddhists with a total worldview in which alien influence would not be tolerated. That alien influence included anything perceived to have the potential to corrupt Buddhism, including Anglicanism.

I would argue that it is not coincidental that a Ceylon Anglican identity—both Sinhala and Tamil—emerged during the period which witnessed unprecedented Buddhist revivalism and nascent fundamentalism. At that time, Buddhist revivalists argued that Ceylonese who were non-Buddhist (or non-Hindu for that matter) were less authentic Ceylonese than Buddhists (or Hindus). In this period of Ceylon history, "Otherness" was clearly determined by one's religious affiliations. Put differently, when Westernized Ceylonese in the late nineteenth century grappled with the problem of locating an identity in a colonized world, identity was coextensive with religion. In short, Buddhist revivalists cast "authentic" identity in terms of religion. Anglicans were not immune to this existing method of evaluating authenticity. While Buddhists honed an identity as one response to the perceived injustices of the British, and thus Anglican, colonial government, Sinhala Anglicans constructed their identity in response to Buddhist revivalism and fundamentalism. How to create an authentic religious identity in the face of Buddhist revivalism became the preeminent concern for the Sinhala (and Tamil) Anglicans in Ceylon in the 1880s and 1890s.

Accommodating the Other: Indigenizing the Church in Ceylon

This was as true for British Anglicans resident in Ceylon as it was for their converts. In the late 1870s one English clergyman challenged his colleagues to "find out and meet the wants" of Anglican converts in Ceylon.[24] At the same time Bishop Copleston discussed creating a "native Church"—that is, an Anglican community in Ceylon with a local episcopacy drawn from the various ethnic communities of the island.[25] In the early 1880s, the bishop remarked that this would entail taking local Anglicans "by the hand and lead[ing] them further."[26] Despite the condescending imagery, Copleston's remarks had far-reaching implications. In the past, the bishop and others had attempted to eradicate all elements of the former religion of the Other among their converts. In the 1880s and 1890s, these Anglicans no longer fought the assimilation of a few elements of Buddhism and Hinduism into Anglican worship in Ceylon. No longer would the Anglican community in Ceylon be isolated from the culture in which it had taken root. Rather, the British made overt attempts to unite "the English and the Native Church"[27]—that is, to give converts a voice. This voice was not limited to singing Christian hymns to native tunes.

In fact, in 1888 Bishop Copleston preached that Christianity might even be influenced positively by its sojourn in Ceylon:

> It is an important truth that Christianity does not involve English clothes, either literally or figuratively, and it is a noble anticipation that European Churches may have much to learn hereafter from what the national characteristics of Eastern daughter Churches may draw out from the stores of Christianity.[28]

Given prior attitudes of the British clergy to "native" traditions, the bishop's thoughts were revolutionary. He added, however, that the "natives" had not yet reached the point at which they could be "trusted" to guide the church in Ceylon.[29] His optimistic outlook on the church's response to the East nonetheless helped to redefine the church's attitudes about local culture.

At roughly the same time that Bishop Copleston highlighted positive interaction between the church and the East, a local Anglican churchman debated whether Christianity and patriotism were contradictory in the Ceylon setting. Doubtless responding to Buddhist characterizations of local Christians as unauthentic Ceylonese, this "native churchman," as he was called, refuted such claims. He argued that patriotism need not be complicit in "helping to elbow Christianity out of the way."[30] He argued for a "nationality of reflection, rather than a nationality of prejudice."[31] He claimed that while it was important to realize that Christian brotherhood transcended national or ethnic distinctions, Ceylon Christians should take pride in their "ancient dress, customs, history and the like."[32] Doubtless pressed by Buddhists to prove themselves authentic Ceylonese, Anglicans such as this local churchman responded that being Christian did not preclude loving Ceylon. It was in regard to religion, and not culture, or even nationality, that this Anglican-Sinhala churchman perceived difference between him and his Buddhist-Sinhala neighbor. It is also probable that though Sinhala Anglicans considered themselves to be different from Sinhala Buddhists, they had never been completely alienated from their "original" cultural identity. Indeed, for the local Sinhala churchman, the Buddhist was the "near Other," strange, yet familiar, the Other, yet the Self.

This idea resonates in the words of some British Anglicans in Ceylon, as well. One Britisher remarked that he looked forward to a day in which the "Anglican Native Church" in Ceylon would increase and become the "Native Anglican Church."[33] He implied that a native Anglican Church meant much more than attracting large numbers into the flock. It meant creating an Anglican community that was suited to, and a reflection of, the local cultures of Ceylon, the Self of the nation.[34]

Throughout the 1890s the question of how to accommodate converts occupied the minds of Anglican clergy, both local and British. The sources suggest that the clergy was fairly unanimous in its support of adapting Anglicanism to local culture. Some clergymen, however, issued warnings that true growth was the spontaneous worship of Christ in an Asian setting rather than change that would come from tampering with "the historic Episcopate, or the Creeds and Sacraments."[35] Moreover, as the 1890s' outrage over the British governor's listening to the *Jayamangala Gatha* indicates, British Anglicans were not willing to pay tribute to Ceylon's customs at the expense of Christianity. "Buddhist Christianity" would not be tolerated. Yet in the 1890s, clergy argued that Christianity could be adapted for, and even glorified in, the Ceylon context.

From the end of the nineteenth century to the present, the Anglican Church has continued to create an identity in Sri Lanka. In an effort to further accommodate converts, the church in the 1890s translated the Book of Common Prayer into the vernacular languages, thus incorporating a larger sector of Ceylon into the Anglican fold.[36] The rise of an urban, Sinhala middle class in the late nineteenth century also further helped to root the Anglican Church in Sinhala culture. These new entrepreneurs continued to enter the English world of "civility, refinement, and intellect" through conversion to Anglicanism.[37] In this way, the Anglican community in Ceylon became increasingly Sinhalized.

Among the emerging entrepreneurs of the late nineteenth century, perhaps the largest group was drawn from the Karava caste. The mid- to late nineteenth-century economic climate, including a burgeoning plantation economy, created a radical reduction in the primacy of the Goyigama, considered the highest caste among the Sinhala. In 1870, when the Duke of Edinburgh visited Ceylon, he was feasted by Karavas—the Jeronis de Soysa family—much to the dismay of Goyigamas.[38] The event was a great victory for the rising Karava caste and marked their formal entrance into the local Ceylon elite.

The Karava caste continued to dominate the new middle class in the latter decades of the nineteenth, and well into the twentieth, century. There is evidence to suggest that they also dominated the local Anglican elite at that time.[39] For instance, in 1883, upon the death of Samuel William Dias, a Karava church canon, the church pointed out the absence of Goyigama elite among their clergy.[40] While praising Canon Dias, an Anglican wrote that the church looked forward to seeing men of "social rank" entering the priesthood.[41] His sentiments suggest that non-Goyigamas, particularly Karavas such as Dias, dominated the Anglican Church at the turn of the twentieth century.

Aware of caste discrimination by Goyigama notables in the preceding century, Karava Anglicans in the 1910s played a major role in attempting to persuade activists to speak out against caste.[42] At the same time that Karava Christians mobilized themselves against social discrimination, Buddhists continued to critique the Anglicized and Christian population and characterize them as less than Sinhala. As is well known, Anagarika Dharmapala and others, including the novelist Piyadasa Sirisena, used Anglophile imitations and adaptations as evidence of the denationalized character of the Christianized local elite. For such Buddhists in the early decades of the twentieth century, the Anglicized were nothing but pale renditions of the truly Sinhala. In short, they were the Other. For them, the authentic were Sinhalas who were Buddhist. These Buddhists thus created a boundary—based on religion—among the local population that determined who was firmly Sinhala and who was not.

It is not surprising, therefore, to find that in the first few decades of the twentieth century the segment of the local Anglican population that pressed for indigenization was the Karava elite. In the climate of a Buddhist cultural renaissance, and Buddhist fundamentalism, more than others they had to prove their Sinhalaness: after all, they were Westernized and non-Buddhist. Given the Karava caste's newfound economic success,[43] and adoption of British ways, including Christianity, Karavas had to prove that they were just as Sinhala as the rest, that they were not "johnny-come-latelies." Moreover, their economic advances during the British period, at variance with the status accorded to them in the caste system, doubtless propelled them to exert efforts to bring their caste ranking and, I might add, their religion, into line with their economic weight.[44] Under pressure to conform to the Sinhala identity that Dharmapala and his colleagues had promoted, Karava Christians proved their Sinhalaness, and their loyalty to Ceylon, by "Sinhalizing" their religion.

In the period preceding Ceylon's independence from Britain the question of loyalty became a paramount concern among local Anglicans. One Anglican in 1919, aware of the "plea that Christianity is inconsistent with Nationalism," urged his fellow Sinhala Christians that "Christianity does not denationalize any man." Rather, it "helps him to see the true interest and welfare of his countrymen."[45] In other words, the writer argued that it was possible to be Sinhala and Christian without compromising love of country. Dharmapala and others, as we have seen, disagreed. In much the same way that Dharmapala focused upon Anglicized Sinhalas in his attack on non-patriots, Anglicized Sinhalas kept abreast of Dharmapala's vituperations. One writer even quoted from Dharmapala's musings on Christians in Ceylon to prove the Anglican success in converting the island.[46] This kind of banter was a striking feature of the presses—both religious and secular—immediately preceding Ceylon's independence. During that period, Buddhists and Christians fashioned their identities in reference to each other.

Many commentaries in the local Anglican journal addressed the role that Anglicans could play in the nationalist movement. In an example from 1920, one author argued that national aspirations could find self-expression in Anglican worship.[47] In short, he argued that the Ceylonese could express their nationalist sentiments as well in Anglicanism as they could in Buddhism.[48] Here, as in other instances, Sinhalas reconciled being Christian in an atmosphere of suspicion. They had to: among all groups of Christians, the Anglicans were perhaps the closest to the British. In urging other Anglicans to continue pursuing nationalist interests and to aim for independence from Britain, contributors to the Anglican journal heralded a new phase of Anglican history in Ceylon. One argued that Anglicanism could be a vehicle for celebrating Ceylon's "national" culture and religion:

> In the form of solemnisation of matrimony, some edifying *national* customs may be introduced and the service made more elaborate. In spite of the theory of transmigration the dead are long remembered in this

> country. Therefore the doctrine of the Communion of Saints may be emphasised and a form of commemorating the faithful departed may be added.[49]

In other words, he argued that Christians were well suited to be purveyors of Ceylon's "customs." It is striking that from his point of view these customs, and beliefs, such as transmigration, were "national" rather than religious. His view suggests a Christian colonization and transformation of Buddhism as national culture, or the culture of the Sinhalas. It is not surprising that he thus argued that Anglicans, the majority of whom were Sinhala, could also glorify "traditional" Sinhala culture.

In this preindependence atmosphere Sinhala Anglicans affirmed and asserted their Sinhalaness in unprecedented ways. From the 1920s onward, the Anglican journal of the period, the *Ceylon Churchman*, published numerous articles about indigenization. Karavas dominated the discussion on indigenization.[50] Adopting Buddhist rhetoric, they pointed out that the vast majority of Anglicans lived as foreigners in their own country.[51] Though these writers accepted it "as inevitable that Christianity should have come to [them] clothed in a Western garb,"[52] the time had come to address their alienation from traditional "culture."[53] This discussion continued well into the postindependence period since, in this period, Anglicans lost much of their colonial backing and legitimacy. Much of the discourse of the postindependence period, much like it had in the late nineteenth century, hinged on music.[54] The first Ceylonese bishop of Colombo, Lakdasa de Mel—a Karava from a powerful landowning family—argued in 1955 that in addition to music, chapels, liturgy, and art should be fashioned in "Sinhalese style."[55] In other words, he continued the preindependence transformation of Buddhism into a national, Sinhala culture. For both Buddhists and Anglicans, this culture was rooted in the "Aryan" cultures of north India.[56]

In much the same way that Buddhists such as Dharmapala attempted to recapture an "Aryan" past in their reformation of Buddhism, many Anglican priests in the postindependence period looked to the "Aryan" cultures of India as a source of indigenization. In my 1993 interviews with Sinhala Anglican priests, many of them recounted their journeys to Bengal, their stays in Christian *ashrams* there, and their reintegration into Sri Lanka as "unalienated" Sinhalas. It is significant that Sinhala-Anglican priests chose to go to Bengal as part of their training and as part of the indigenization process. At the same time and earlier, Buddhists were making claims that their ancestors, particularly Vijaya, alleged to be the first Sinhala, were Aryans from Bengal. Their view of history was based on the *Mahavamsa*, the fifth-century Pali work that chronicles the development of Buddhism in the island. Co-opting much of that myth, specifically the interpretation of the Sinhalas' connection to Bengal, these Anglican priests affirmed their Sinhalaness. In this way, they assuaged their strong sense of alienation from their own "national culture."[57] At a time that saw increasing state sponsorship of Sinhala culture, these Sinhala Anglicans reiterated their connection to the island by spending time in Bengal, rather than Tamil Nadu, where there were also opportunities for Anglican *ashram* work and study. South India, however, was Tamil country, "non-Aryan," and thus unable to legitimate the Sinhala Anglican priests' rising Sinhala consciousness. Moreover, as the distinction between Tamil/alien/Other and Sinhala/national/Self continued to be honed in the postindependence period despite centuries of mixing, Sinhala Anglicans, associated with European imperialism, glorified their Sinhalaness even though being Sinhala by that time meant being Buddhist. The rise in the number of Sinhala Anglicans involved in the JVP (Janatha Vimukti Peramuna) in the late 1980s rather tragically reveals this trend toward the "Sinhalization" of Anglicans.[58] That the JVP, a revolutionary Sinhala group with fundamentalist Buddhist roots, can attract Anglicans into the fold, suggests the extent to which Sinhala-Buddhist identity has percolated down to non-Buddhist groups.

Conclusion

In the present period, Sri Lankan Anglicans continue the process of making their community more authentically Sri Lankan. The dynamic and expansive religious system that they have built, according to the present bishop of Colombo, continues to "baptize" things "Sri Lankan" and make them Anglican.[59] In the 1890s, the *Jayamangala Gatha* symbolized the threat of Buddhism to the Ceylon-Anglican community and its converts from Buddhism. Today, the *Jayamangala Gatha* is an important feature of the Anglican liturgy in most Anglican churches in Sinhala-speaking areas of Sri Lanka. The present bishop of Colombo even weaved its traditional melody into his installation ceremony. In short, for Anglicans the *Jayamangala Gatha* and other traditionally Buddhist symbols are now Sinhala rather than Buddhist.[60] Among Sinhalas in Sri Lanka, then, it seems that identity is cast in terms of ethnicity, race, and language, rather than in terms of religion, as was the case in the nineteenth century.

Religious conversion means something different today in Sri Lanka than it did one hundred years ago. As the history of the Sinhala-Anglican community suggests, the history of this convert group is best discussed in relation to the organization of state power in Sri Lanka.[61] In short, in the present context, indigenization means Sinhalization, a movement toward empowerment. This is a welcome trend for many. As one Anglican priest commented, Sri Lankan Anglicans have "maintained their Sinhala hearts throughout history though in the nineteenth century this was not completely apparent." Like the other Sinhala Anglican priests I interviewed, he added that his main identity referent is his race rather than his religion. Echoing him, other Sinhala Anglicans in the present claim that they have the right to indigenize because they are just as Sinhala as the rest. And, because being Sinhala means being empowered, this minority group within a majority community will doubtless continue to become more Sinhalized. This means continuing to "baptize" into their worship other elements of Sinhala "culture." Already, this has entailed modeling churches, church music, and even attire along what many Anglican priests refer to as "Sinhala cultural patterns." Sinhala Anglicans are now less alienated from what they call their "Sinhala heritage." Now, more like the Other that they feared one hundred years ago, Sinhala Anglicans today are paradoxically faced with the problem of how to maintain an identity without being completely absorbed into the majority Buddhist-Sinhala identity. In much the same way that power has shifted from the Westernized to the Sinhalized, so has the identity of Sinhala Anglicans in Sri Lanka.

Notes

1. For more on this, see also R.L. Stirrat, *Power and Religiosity in a Post-Colonial Setting: Sinhala Catholics in Contemporary Sri Lanka* (Cambridge: Cambridge University Press, 1992), p. 186. For a discussion of Muslim identity markers, see de Munck in this volume.

2. See, for instance, Stanley Jeyaraja Tambiah, *Buddhism Betrayed? Religion, Politics, and Violence in Sri Lanka* (Chicago: University of Chicago Press, 1992).

3. For more on the Christian community in India, see Susan Bayly, *Saints, Goddesses and Kings* (Cambridge: Cambridge University Press, 1992).

4. It is likely, however, that there were Christians in Sri Lanka before the Portuguese period. Yet the extent of their "community" remains an open question.

5. "The Church in Ceylon," *Ceylon Diocesan Gazette* (6 May 1885): 98.

6. For instance, "A Sermon," *Ceylon Diocesan Gazette* (2 March 1878): 82–85, alleges that the church faced many difficulties surrounded by the "heathen religions" of Ceylon.

7. "Native Candidates for Holy Orders," *Ceylon Diocesan Gazette* (1 October 1884): 18–20.

8. "Church Law in Ceylon," *Ceylon Diocesan Gazette* (3 December 1879): 46–47.

9. Examples include *Ceylon Diocesan Gazette* (15 February 1887 and 15 July 1890).

10. "The Buddhist "Address" at Badulla," *Ceylon Diocesan Gazette* (3 December 1886): 67.

11. Ibid., 68.

12. Ibid.

13. "The Kalutara Burial Case," *Ceylon Diocesan Gazette* (2 March 1878): 88–89.

14. "Pastoral Letter," *Ceylon Diocesan Gazette* (2 March 1878): 89.

15. "A Sermon," *Ceylon Diocesan Gazette* (2 March 1878): 85.

16. Ibid.

17. "The Prayer for Labourers," *Ceylon Diocesan Gazette* (2 December 1876): 39.

18. Ibid., 41.

19. For instance, "Sinhalese Church Music," *Ceylon Diocesan Gazette* (19 November 1892): 132–33.

20. "S. Paul's, Kandy," *The Ceylon Diocesan Gazette* (4 May 1881): 107. One English clergyman summed up the predicament thus: "We have not yet any good music either in Tamil or Sinhalese so arranged for organ accompaniment. Will no one, whom God has blessed with musical talents, devote himself to work and give us one Sinhalese and Tamil Service with good music, so that every man "in his own tongue" shall be able to sing God's praises at the Eucharistic Feast?," *Ceylon Diocesan Gazette* (4 December 1883): 56.

21. "Buona Vista," *Ceylon Diocesan Gazette* (3 January 1883): 57.

22. "Letters to the Editor," *Ceylon Diocesan Gazette* (3 November 1880): 29.

23. "Ceylon Church News," *Ceylon Diocesan Gazette* (1 April 1885): 95.

24. "Letters to the Editor," *Ceylon Diocesan Gazette* (4 May 1878): 111.

25. "Copy of a Letter from the Bishop of Colombo to the Metropolitan," *Ceylon Diocesan Gazette* (2 June 1877): 2.

26. "Children of One Father," *Ceylon Diocesan Gazette* (5 September 1883): 3.

27. *The Ceylon Diocesan Gazette* (1 November 1882): 30.

28. "Sermon Preached by the Lord Bishop of Colombo," *Ceylon Diocesan Gazette* (14 July 1888): 127.

29. Ibid.

30. "Christianity and Patriotism,—in Ceylon," *Ceylon Diocesan Gazette* (2 June 1886): 99.

31. Ibid., 100.

32. Ibid.

33. *The Ceylon Diocesan Gazette* (4 August 1886): 132.

34. This period of questioning the proper association between Anglican Christianity and local culture also included discussions of Hinduism. In the early 1800s, as they had done among Buddhists, British Anglicans tried without success to create among converted Hindus congregations that were free from "native" influence. Things began to change, however, in the 1880s and 1890s. When Bishop Copleston learned that Tamils had introduced the *tali* or necklace, often laden with Hindu symbols, to replace the ring in wedding ceremonies, the problem of "lapsing into heathenism" again came to the fore. That such a Hindu custom could work its way into Anglican weddings symbolized the church's inability to safeguard Anglican Christianity in Ceylon. In the case of the *tali*, however, the bishop relented; he proclaimed that the *tali* was "at best a necessary evil," "The Lord Bishop's Address to the Synod," *Ceylon Diocesan Gazette* (24 October 1893): 117. For the bishop, the specter of change that the *tali* symbolized was far less threatening than the possibility of alienating converted Hindus by insulting their customs. The bishop's willingness to grant a certain degree of autonomy to converted Hindus suggests he realized that change was imminent.

35. "The Native Churches," *Ceylon Diocesan Gazette* (June 1898): 54.

36. "The Lord Bishop's Address to the Synod," *Ceylon Diocesan Gazette* (24 October 1893): 115.

37. Michael Roberts, Ismeth Raheem, and Percy Colin-Thome, *People Inbetween* (Ratmalana, Sri Lanka: Sarvodaya Book Publishing Services, 1989), p. 41.

38. Ibid., pp. 28–30.

39. However, most Karava Christians, have been, and continue to be, Catholic. For more on Karava Catholics, see Michael Roberts, *Caste Conflict and Elite Formation: The Rise of a Karava Elite in Sri Lanka, 1500–1931* (Cambridge: 1982).

40. "In Memoriam: Samuel William Dias," *Ceylon Diocesan Gazette* (6 June 1883): 115.

41. Ibid.

42. Michael Roberts et al., *People Inbetween*, p. 135.

43. For more on their economic success, see Roberts, *Caste Conflict*, pp. 98–130. According to Roberts, "In percentage terms, the Karava constituted 46 percent of the Sinhalese proprietorships in the 1927 [holdings] list, held 53 percent of the plantation property and 56.8 percent of the cultivated land."

44. Ibid., pp. 132–33.

45. "Nationalism Versus Christianity," *Ceylon Churchman* (January 1919): 4.

46. "Ceylon Practically a Christian Country," *Ceylon Churchman* (July 1921): 135.

47. "The Church in Ceylon and Her Worship," *Ceylon Churchman* (October 1920): 160.

48. Ibid., 165.

49. "The Church in Ceylon and Her Worship," *Ceylon Churchman* (December 1920): 213.

50. Among the writers are John Cooray, Lakdasa de Mel, Lakshman Pieris, and Sydney Weragoda.

51. For instance, John Cooray, "Indigenisation on the Word Made Flesh," *Ceylon Churchman.*

52. "Report of the Committee," *Ceylon Churchman* 34 (1939).

53. Lakdasa de Mel, "Experiments in Ceylon," *Ceylon Churchman* 52 (1956): 30–34.

54. For instance, "Music in Worship," *Ceylon Churchman*, 17 (October 1945).

55. Ibid., 31.

56. For more on this, see Tessa Bartholomeusz, "Dharmapala at Chicago: Sinhala Chauvinist or Mahayana Buddhist?," in *A Museum of Faiths: Histories and Legacies of the 1893 World's Parliament of Religions*, Eric Ziolkowski, ed. (Atlanta: Scholars Press, 1993).

57. I would like to thank Father Lionel Pieris, chaplain to the bishop of Colombo, for helping me develop these ideas.

58. Ten Anglican priests I interviewed in Sri Lanka in 1993 told me that they lost many young Anglican men to the JVP in the 1980s.

59. I interviewed the bishop of Colombo on several occasions in July 1993.

60. There are numerous examples. For instance, in many contemporary Anglican churches, the *sesath*, or Kandyan spear associated with Buddhism, is carried in the procession before worship services. Many clergy urge their parishioners to wear white during worship. White is the color associated with the Buddhist laity.

61. For a similar thought, see Susan Bayly, *Saints, Goddesses and Kings*, p. 9.

Chapter 8

Catholic Identity and Global Forces in Sinhala Sri Lanka

R. L. Stirrat

Introduction

This paper is concerned with some preliminary aspects of contemporary Roman Catholic identity in Sri Lanka, mainly in Sinhala-speaking parts of the island.[1] It does not claim to be comprehensive: after all, one aspect of the argument is that today it is difficult to talk of "a Catholic identity," no matter how frequently such an entity is invoked. To do so is to adopt an unwarranted essentialism, for what it means to be a Catholic now as in the past is contextual: it depends upon the circumstances in which that identity is being called upon. Furthermore, there are disagreements as to what it means to be a Catholic. It is not that Sinhala Catholics do not share some idea of a "community of Catholics," but that there is little agreement as to what that "community" might mean. Far from there being a chorus of harmony there is rather a series of alternative ideas of what "being Catholic" entails: of alternative constructs of Catholic identity. If, as we are told, the postmodern world is a world of discontinuities, fractures, and fault lines, a world of increasing cultural anarchy and disorder, then Sinhala Catholics are very much members of this new world.

The argument of this paper is that an understanding of changing Sinhala-Catholic identity has to place it within the broad processes of "globalization," which involves not just the centuries-old increasing interdependence of different parts of the world at an economic level, but also the more recent phenomenon of a growing sense of "global consciousness" in which distinctions between the universal and the particular collapse. What we see today is the result of processes working over the last four centuries in terms of a complex interplay between global and local forces. Much of what is presented as local, particular and culturally specific, is the result of this interplay. Globalization in this context does not imply growing homogeneity (the "convergence" theory associated with modernization), but rather the reproduction and generation of heterogeneity within a global context.[2]

It should perhaps be admitted at the outset that the stress on globalization in this paper may well be overplayed. After all, a focus on Catholics leads one inevitably to stress the "universal church," the actions of missionaries and colonialists, and the continuing institutional and other ties between Catholics in Sri Lanka and Catholics elsewhere in the world. Furthermore, the stress on external forces tends to downplay the agency of Sri Lankans: their active resistance to colonial rule and the ways in which global forces have been transformed by the actions of Sri Lankans. Yet even so, the rise of Sinhala-Buddhist nationalism and associated fundamentalisms, which has had a major impact on the changing forms of Catholic identity in Sri Lanka, owes much to ideas of nationalism first developed in the colonial West, and to orientalist constructions of Sinhala culture and society. Globalization does not deny agency: it only makes agency a more complex issue.

The Creation of a Colonial Identity

In 1883, there was a riot between Catholics and Buddhists in Kotahena, a suburb of northern Colombo.[3] The occasion for the riot was a Buddhist procession passing the road leading to the Catholic cathedral on Easter Sunday. The procession was attacked by a large group of Catholics who had been incensed by a series of rumors that claimed that the procession was carrying sacrilegious images. Although the violence was in the main committed by urban working-class Catholics, the priesthood came out in their support and may have been actively involved in orchestrating the Catholic role in the riots at Kotahena and elsewhere. It appears that there was general support for Catholic participants in these riots throughout the Catholic population of Sri Lanka—or at least, no criticisms are recorded. Over the next forty years there was a series of violent clashes between groups who defined themselves and each other in terms of religion: Catholic, Buddhist, Hindu, and Muslim.[4]

The participation of Catholics in violent conflicts with adherents of other religions was only the most visible aspect of a more general phenomenon: the manner in which the Catholics in Sri Lanka acted as a unified entity whose spokesmen were the senior clerics. In matters concerning education, politics, economics, or whatever, Catholics spoke, at least publicly, with one voice. Of course there must have been some discordant voices, but these are difficult to identify. The picture that emerges is one of unity and homogeneity; a particular form of nineteenth-century Catholicism that stressed faith and devotion, obedience to the priesthood, and a sense of historical destiny.

This unity of purpose, homogeneity of belief and practice, and strong sense of identity did not just happen. Rather a number of factors were at work producing the particular situation in which Sri Lankan Catholics found themselves in the late nineteenth century, including the history of Catholicism in the island.

Catholicism was introduced into Sri Lanka as part of the global expansion of the Portuguese empire in the sixteenth century. During the period of Dutch rule in the seventeenth and eighteenth centuries, Catholics suffered various degrees of persecution from the authorities, but small groups of Oratorian priests from Goa maintained some sort of presence.[5] Even so, when a new wave of European missionaries arrived from the 1830s onwards, what they found was not a unified and homogeneous group of Catholics but a series of scattered groups of people who claimed to be Catholics and who practiced what, to the missionaries, were somewhat heterodox forms of Catholicism.

Throughout the nineteenth century, the missionary "project" involved the establishment of homogeneity where once there was heterogeneity; of establishing control and discipline over the minds and bodies of Sri Lankan Catholics. It involved the imposition of their particular imagination on the Catholics of Sri Lanka: of particular forms of religious practice and religious organization. Thus an ecclesiastical hierarchy—a strong parish organization created with an internal system of discipline including fines and penances—and a church controlled system of schools and seminaries were established. Through local feasts and pilgrimage centers, Catholics were encouraged to think of themselves as a community. Through these systems the teachings of the church were instilled in the laity and a strong sense of identity inculcated in which Catholics were encouraged to see themselves first and foremost as members of the universal church, and only secondarily as Sri Lankans.[6]

How successful these efforts were is now difficult to determine in any detail. Other forms of identity such as caste and class certainly existed, but their significance was minor compared with religion. Certainly there were forms of "syncretic" belief and behavior, which continued throughout the nineteenth century, but such alternative imaginings of what being a Catholic might involve were marginal. The main institutional threat to the unity of the church, the so-called Goan schism, was put down vigorously.[7] The European missionary hierarchy educated in the seminaries of Italy, France, and Belgium appears to have been generally successful in imposing their vision of what it was to be a Catholic on the laity of Sri Lanka.

The success of the missionaries in creating this sense of identity owed much to the way in which British colonial rulers created "space" in which "religion" as an autonomous domain could develop. In contrast to previous colonial rulers who had elided political and religious power, from the early years of the nineteenth century the British allowed a large degree of religious freedom, in part a response to the Buddhist majority in the island, and in part a response to the growing separation of religion and the state in Britain. In a sense, the creation of this space can be seen as the "invention" of religion: the modernist and postenlightenment idea that religion was a matter for the individual conscience and not an area in which the state could legislate.[8] "Politics" and "religion" were increasingly defined, formally at least, as separate domains, each governed by its own logic.[9] The only area for dispute was where the boundary between the two domains lay.[10]

As far as Sri Lanka was concerned, this stood in contrast to the situation under the Portuguese or Dutch rulers where religion was in general a matter for state intervention. On the other hand it marked a contrast with, for instance, south India (and perhaps Kandyan Sri Lanka) where religious affiliation was a means by which members of different religious groups could be integrated into state structures.[11] Nineteenth-century colonial rule saw the development of a new articulation of religious identities and the state, in which rulers neither imposed a form of religion nor integrated religious identities into one totality.

If the British creation of space for religion allowed the church to develop its own institutions and encourage its own forms of loyalty and identity, it also encouraged the same process to get under way among followers of other religions, particularly the Buddhists. Whereas in precolonial Sri Lanka Buddhism had been closely connected with concepts of kingship and rule, the "disestablishment" of the *sangha* created a situation where new forms of Buddhism could develop, in particular the so-called Protestant Buddhism of the southwestern coastal zones.[12] And this ushered in a complex process involving both local and global factors.

First, the separation of state and religion allowed Buddhists in the coastal zone to develop their own institutional forms of Buddhism partly in response to the status pretensions of the preexisting *sangha*, and partly in response to missionary (particularly Protestant) pressure. Second, the form this took was in part derived from other parts of Buddhist Asia but also from the West. At one level this consisted of Western organizational forms (e.g., the YMBA) and techniques (e.g., the printing press) but it also involved linkages with Western "rationalists" and "theosophists" who, for one reason or another, were opposed to Christianity. Thirdly, it involved the development of forms of Buddhism that in part were the result of Western orientalist scholarship, in particular ideas about "pure Buddhism." And finally, at various points, as for instance just before the 1883 Kotahena riot, it gained the support of influential elements in the colonial government. So, far from being simply an endogenous or "nativistic" reaction to foreign rule, this resurgence was the result of both local and global processes. It provided groups of Sinhala Buddhists who had benefited from the economic and political results of colonial rule a means of asserting their own identity in terms of a recovery of "true Buddhism" and the beginnings of what was later to become Sinhala-Buddhist fundamentalism.

The rise of these Buddhist groups, their assertion of what they saw as their rights to hold processions and build temples, provided the most "significant Other" against which Catholic identity was defined. The riot at Kotahena was one manifestation of the way in which both Buddhist and Catholic identities fed off each other, violence being both a manifestation of, and a factor in, more and more exclusive identities. The late nineteenth century was the period when the strength of Catholic identity in Sri Lanka was at its peak. Led (or controlled) by a powerful and self-confident European missionary clergy, Catholics saw themselves as qualitatively different from the followers of other religions in Sri Lanka. "Nothing can check [the church's] progress," thundered the *Catholic Messenger* in 1909, "because she is endowed with a divine vitality and a supernatural power . . . because she is THE TRUE RELIGION [sic] and truth will always win."[13]

Nationalism and Catholic Identity

In January 1995 the pope visited Sri Lanka as part of a tour of Southeast Asia. The highpoint of this trip was an open air Mass on Galle Face Green in the center of Colombo, which was attended, so it is claimed, by over 300,000 people, equivalent to over 30 percent of the total Catholic population of Sri Lanka.[14] On the face of it, the presence of such a high proportion of the total Catholic population of the country could be interpreted as signifying the continued existence of a strong sense of identity among the country's Catholics. But I think the situation is more complex. Today, it is difficult to imagine that Sinhala Catholics as Catholics would mass on the streets of north Colombo and attack a Buddhist procession. Today, there are fewer and fewer occasions when Catholics act as a group to defend or assert what they see as specifically Catholic interests. Today, there is less and less agreement as to what it means to be Catholic. And just as in the nineteenth century the development of a strong Catholic identity was intimately linked to global processes, so the present fragmentation of Catholic identity and of what it means to be a Catholic, is in part the result of these continuing processes.

By far the most obvious of present-day fractures in Sri Lankan Catholic identity is that between Tamil and Sinhala Catholics. Since the early 1980s there has been an increasing gap between the church in the north of Sri Lanka and that in the Sinhala-dominated south of the country. The result has been in effect a split between a Tamil Church and a Sinhala Church. During the 1983 riots Catholics were involved alongside Buddhists in attacking Tamils, no matter what the latters' religious affiliation.[15] In the north, the Catholic Church is closely identified with the LTTE (Liberation Tigers of Tamil Eelam) and many individual priests and members of the laity identify themselves with what they see as a war of liberation against the Sri Lankan state. The statements of the Catholic bishops calling for peace have little impact on the generality of the laity.

This is only the most obvious manifestation of the way in which nationality or ethnicity has become the dominant way in which identity is imagined in contemporary Sri Lanka.[16] Whilst in the late nineteenth century "being Sinhala" or "being Tamil" was for many people secondary to "being Catholic" or "being Buddhist," today the situation has reversed. Thus throughout even the most uniformly Catholic areas of southern Sri Lanka, people see themselves first and foremost as Sinhala; only secondly do they identify themselves as Catholics. So as far as the war is concerned, most Sinhala Catholics are much more shocked by reported LTTE atrocities against Sinhala than they are by government military attacks on churches in the north or the deaths of Tamil Catholics. Whilst a shared religious affiliation is recognized, this does not generate any strong sense of identification with the Catholics of the north.

What has happened, of course, is that one way of imagining the world, of seeing it as divided into groups identified on grounds of religious affiliation, has been replaced by another, the "imagined community" of the nation (Anderson 1983). Indeed, much of the history of Sri Lankan Catholics in the twentieth century has been concerned with how they should and could react to the growing dominance of "the nation" as the dominant mode of defining identity.

As many writers have argued, the concept of the "nation state" developed in western Europe and in effect was exported to the rest of the world as part of the cultural baggage of colonialism.[17] Indeed, one of the ironies of colonial rule in Sri Lanka as elsewhere is that it provided much of the ideological ammunition that undermined the colonialists' claim to rule. This, of course, is not to say that there was no resistance to colonial domination prior to nationalism. Indeed, in part the Buddhist resurgence of the nineteenth century was a form of resistance to British rule and cultural domination. Rather, such resistance did not take the form of nationalism.[18] And what is also striking is the way in which during the twentieth century Sri Lankan concepts of nationalism were increasingly built upon social categories, which the colonial authorities used to organize and understand the social composition of the island's population.

In her recent book, Nira Wickremasinghe shows how the dominant mode of classifying the population of Sri Lanka used by the British stressed "racial" categories, and how these formed the basis for selection to various institutions, for instance the Legislative Council (Wickremasinghe 1995). Whilst in the early twentieth century members of the Sri Lankan elite may have thought of themselves as "Ceylonese," "ethnic" identity became increasingly important and built upon the "racial" categories utilized by the British. Appeals to ethnic identity, she argues, have dominated Sri Lankan politics ever since. Thus what appears as "local" and "indigenous" is, at least in part, a product of a form of classification that derives from nineteenth-century European modes of thought. In a sense, she argues that the present war between the LTTE and the Sinhala-dominated Sri Lankan state has its origins in nineteenth-century racism and its influence on forms of colonial government.

Yet as Van der Veer (1995) has pointed out for India, the forms of nationalism that have developed in South Asia are rather different from those that developed in Europe. He argues that whilst the latter stress secularism and distinguish between religion and nationality, the concept of a secular nation has had a much less easy passage in South Asia.[19] What is at issue here, he claims, is the Western discourse of "modernity" which opposes the religious to the secular and sees religion as associated with tradition and secular nationalism with modernity. Such an identification of religion with tradition and secularism with modernity is incorrect. In the Indian case, Van der Veer argues that "religious nationalism," where religion is a basic element of national identity, is of greater importance than secular models of Indian identity.[20]

Certainly, religion has become one of the key features in the definition of the nation and national identity in Sri Lanka, particularly amongst the Sinhala.[21] In the nineteenth century, the "Buddhist revival" was not in itself a nationalist movement. Indeed, in many temples built during this period the British royal coat of arms was prominently displayed in the image house. But by the early twentieth century writers such as Anagarika Dharmapala, making use of historical materials (particularly the *Mahavamsa*) concerning pre-modern kingdoms, were able to generate concepts of Sinhala nationalism in which race, language, and religion became the three defining elements of Sinhalaness.[22] Within this construction of "the nation," religious identity became a stressed element of national identity.

The result was that through the twentieth century, Sinhala Catholics had to face attack not just from those who identified themselves as Buddhist but increasingly from those who stressed Sinhala nationalism of which Buddhism was a major component. Catholics were attacked by Sinhala-Buddhist fundamentalists as "denationalized," controlled by foreign missionaries, owing their allegiance to a foreign pope, and as the heirs to foreign imperialism. Catholics were represented as "mongrels" and aliens, lacking in true patriotism and loyalty.[23]

As independence approached, the Catholic hierarchy began to accept that Catholics were inevitably going to be a minority in a Buddhist-dominated state. Even so, after independence they continued to attempt to exercise control over the Catholic laity and to encourage a strong sense of a separate Catholic identity in the country. However, the takeover of church-run schools and restrictions on the entry of foreign missionaries in the 1960s, were major challenges to this ideal of a separate Catholic entity. For a number of reasons, church-control of the schools was a, if not the, key symbol of Catholic identity. Not only were they the means through which Catholics had gained a relatively advantageous position in the bureaucracy and the private sector, but they were also the means through which the idea of a separate "Catholic community" was reproduced. The takeover of the schools meant that no longer was the agenda of education set primarily in terms of Catholicism: now it was set by the agenda of the newly independent state. Increasingly the curriculum was directed by Sinhala-Buddhist nationalist interests.[24]

The loss of control over the church schools was only symptomatic of the general decline of the power of the church and the clergy. The church as a whole had little choice but to adjust to the realities of Sinhala-Buddhist domination of the country. The area of competence over which the church claimed authority shrank: what was once seen as dangerously Buddhist was now accepted as part of Sri Lankan or Sinhala culture. Thus during the seventies and the eighties, the church ceased to direct the faithful as to how they should vote, in part to avoid criticism from nationalists that the church was "meddling in politics."

In the missionary church, the priest had played a pivotal role. Not only was he the channel through which flowed grace; not only did he hold a monopoly over contact between mortals and the divine, but he also acted to a large extent as lord of the parish. Priests often had a remarkable degree of control—spiritual, social, and economic—over the lives of their parishioners and also acted as mediators between the laity and the colonial government. Such a system of control could only work successfully under a colonial regime. But with the spread of electoral politics and the political decline of the church in the face of Sinhala nationalism, the position of the priest vis-à-vis the laity was severely eroded. Discipline, which was one of the key means by which homogeneity was maintained by the colonial church, could not now be exercised by the priests. No longer could they control access to the centers of power.

The result has been for the church to concentrate less on what marks out Catholics as a separate group in Sri Lanka and more on what Catholics share with others in Sri Lanka. At one level this has meant a continuation of a policy that first developed in the earlier years of the twentieth century: that nationalism was nothing to do with religion. Yet the problem continually has been to distinguish between what is the realm of "religion" and what is the realm of "the nation." And within the context of a country where ethnic or national identities have become increasingly important, the sense of "being Catholic" has become less and less salient and more restricted in its area of relevance.

Yet even if there had not been these direct responses to the growing direct political power of Sinhala Buddhists in Sri Lanka, it is doubtful whether a strong sense of a Catholic rather than a Sinhala identity could have been maintained in terms of broader cultural changes taking place in the island. Through the mass media, at first radio and newspapers and more recently television, Catholics have become more and more exposed to forms of nationalist and fundamentalist rhetoric. Similarly, the takeover of the schools by the state has ensured an education that stresses nationalist rather than sectional themes: a history that stresses the past of the nation rather than the past of the Catholics. Whilst pilgrimages to the great shrines of the church in Sri Lanka still take place, these are often combined with visits to the great centers of Sinhala civilization—Anuradhapura, Pollonaruwa, Kandy, and Kataragama—which of course are resonant with a Sinhala-Buddhist identity and history. And finally, developments in the economy have led to a greater mixing of people of different religious backgrounds.

The overall result has been to decrease the salience of a specifically Catholic identity. Increasingly what is stressed is national identity. Thus in Catholic fishing villages, in many ways the heartlands of Sri Lankan Catholicism, which I have known for the last twenty-five years, there is an increasing stress on what is shared between them and non-Catholic villages in the same area. Whilst difference is still acknowledged, identity in the face of what is seen as greater difference—for instance, between Sinhalas and Tamils and between Sri Lankans and foreigners—is what counts more and more. This is true even for those who use Tamil as their first language. Admittedly, there are still memories of a Catholic past, for instance the persecutions of the Dutch period and the takeover of Catholic schools in the 1960s, but these are not as salient as they were even twenty years ago. Today, young Catholics in these villages are more likely to know stories of the great Sinhala mythical heroes of the past than they are to know stories of missionary prowess. Increasingly, the cultural heritage that is called upon is one that stresses unity with other Sinhalas whether or not they be Catholic, rather than one which stresses the history of Catholicism. Similar processes are evident elsewhere. At a minor level, traditional Catholic names—Maria, Anthony, David, and so on—are less and less common; younger Catholics more and more are given Sinhala names. In terms of jobs, increasingly Catholics are working alongside Buddhists and there is less of a "ghetto" feeling in the coastal towns and villages.[25]

Not surprisingly there is an increasing number of marriages across religious lines.

Thus the "dominant discourse" of identity even in Catholic areas of southern Sri Lanka is one that stresses "nation" or "ethnicity," "we Sinhalas" rather than "we Catholics." As a point of difference the importance of religion is downplayed. Increasingly, the contrast is presented in terms of nature versus nurture: that "being Sinhala" is a quality that comes through birth whereas "being Catholic" is a matter of choice or even accident. So it is conceivable to change one's religion—but not one's ethnic identity.

Globalization and the Church

So far I have concentrated on the ways in which the rise of Sinhala nationalism has led to a reduced stress on a particular Catholic identity. Yet the nationalist movement was not unique to Sri Lanka. Even if Sri Lanka regained its independence before most colonial territories, this was simply an early moment in the collapse of European-dominated empires in the postwar world. Since the middle of the century the "nation-state" has become the globally dominant form of political organization. The world has changed from the empires of the late nineteenth century.

It was partly in response to this global change that the Second Vatican Council was called. Whereas the church since the mid-nineteenth century had set itself against such evils as modernism, secularism, and communism, and had in general been only too happy to ally itself with colonial and repressive regimes, by the 1960s it was clear even in the Vatican that there had to be a reevaluation of the church's role. The implementation of the decisions of the Council had a direct impact on Catholics in Sri Lanka, which both weakened and threw into question what it meant to be a Catholic in independent Sri Lanka.

Some of the changes brought in by Vatican II directly encouraged the increasing stress on nationalist identity. Changes in the liturgy, most notably the use of vernacular languages in the Mass but also new forms of prayer and worship modeled on "traditional" indigenous forms, encouraged people to consider themselves as part of local society. Similarly, the new approach to other religions, presenting them as alternative ways of approaching God, led to novel points of contact between Catholics and adherents of other religions. So whilst the decline in the salience of a specific Catholic identity was in part a result of the rise of Sinhala nationalism and Buddhist fundamentalism, this was encouraged by the actions of the universal church.

Yet of equal if not greater importance was the way in which Vatican II redefined both the role of the priest and what it meant to be a "good Catholic."

Earlier, I mentioned the pivotal role played by priests in mediating between both humanity and God and the ruled and the rulers. Vatican II questioned this definition of the priest and encouraged priests to be exemplars rather than mediators. Furthermore, priests were encouraged to become socially active. Spiritual devotion was downplayed and the role of the priest as an activist involved in assisting the poor, the dispossessed, and the marginal in seeking social justice was stressed. Similarly, the forms of religious practice encouraged by the missionaries—cults, devotions, pilgrimages, cycles of prayer, and so on—were increasingly represented by the church as of minor importance. Salvation was to be achieved through this-worldly actions rather than a narrowly-defined spiritual life or blind obedience to a set of rules defined by the hierarchy.

These changes have thrown into question the nature of Catholic identity not just in Sri Lanka but throughout the world. Much of what the church had presented as central to any claim to be a "good Catholic" is now in question. Old certainties and old dogmas are no longer unquestionable. For many Catholics in Sri Lanka as elsewhere this poses a major problem: What does it mean to be a Catholic? How is one to follow a Catholic life in a world where there is no certainty—where even the teachings of the church change? And rather than form a global monolithic entity, the Catholic world has become an arena of dispute. Various groups argue for their definition of what it means to be Catholic, each claiming to be the repository of "true Catholicism" and, to a greater or lesser extent, attempting to impose their definitions of identity on others.

The result in Sri Lanka is a flowering of difference. Within the broad category of "the Catholic community," a series of different interpretations of what it means to be a Catholic have been and are developing. All involve different "imaginings" of Catholic identity in a postindependence, post Vatican II, Sri Lanka, and all are in a sense incomplete: they are in a continual state of "becoming." With the demise of the old certainties there is a "search for identity"—or rather identities, through which "being Catholic" might become a viable option. Within the space of a short paper it is impossible to map out the range of such new forms of identity. Indeed, given the state of flux, such a project would involve a misrepresentation of the situation for there is no constancy, only a fluid search for meaning. All that can be done is to map out a few of the ways in which new identities have been and are being constructed over the last couple of decades.

One response has been for some Catholics to increasingly present their religious identity as being of purely private significance and in effect to cut themselves off from the wider flows of Catholic life. Faced with the major changes that have taken place over the last few decades, they seek a private identity as Catholics and reject what they see as a confused and confusing church. At one extreme such individuals see themselves as little more than Catholics in name, an accident of birth.

Another response which has become increasingly popular is to join one or other of the Protestant Evangelical churches that are expanding rapidly in urban Sri Lanka (not to mention Latin America and Africa) and converting what to the church are worryingly large numbers of Catholics. In part the motivation for these conversions appears to be the certainties on offer in these congregations and a sense of "belonging" lacking in the Catholic contexts from which these converts come.[26]

Within the church itself there are large numbers of both clergy and laity who reject what they see as modernizing trends in the church and identify themselves as "traditionalists." For them, true Catholicism involves forms of religious practice and belief that are more or less the same as those of the missionary church: a stress on devotion and prayer; a rejection of modernist tendencies in the church; a stress on the role of the priest as mediator between man and God, and so on. At a conscious level such traditionalists see themselves as part of a worldwide movement within the Catholic Church. They stress their linkages with other conservative elements, and stress the importance of international Catholic shrines such as Fatima and Lourdes as models for their shrines in Sri Lanka.[27] Through international pilgrimage wealthier traditionalists meet other members of a global network of traditionalist Catholics, but more mundane forms of communication, most notably various forms of literature, pamphlets, international prayer circles, statues, and other devotional objects are also important.

Yet if one axis of the identities evoked by "traditionalist" Sinhala Catholics is that of international conservative Catholicism, others stress a more local context. Legitimation of traditional Catholicism depends in part on the exorcisms and "miracles" that take place at their shrines and churches. On the one hand the "demons" that are expelled are frequently the gods of the Sinhala and thus evince a continuing strand of anti-Buddhist sentiment. On the other, the discourse of possession and miraculous powers has much in common with the broader context of Sinhala Buddhism.[28] And even if many of these traditionalists would see themselves as Catholic first and Sinhala second, they still tend to support the more militant aspects of the Sinhala-dominated state's war against Tamil separatists.

Very different configurations of what it means to be a Catholic are associated with those who would see themselves as "radical Catholics."[29] For them, the forms of Catholicism associated with the "traditionalists" are misguided and involve a failure to understand the true meaning of Christianity. Radical Catholics have taken on the message of Vatican II and in some cases have extended it beyond the ways in which it is now interpreted in Rome or by the Sri Lankan bishops. Here, the stress is on the social role of Catholics, most notably in the role of Catholics to fight poverty and oppression. Great stress is placed upon what unites Sri Lankans, no matter what their religion or ethnic identity. Thus linkages between Catholics and members of other religions are stressed and major attempts are made to produce a specifically Sri Lankan form of Catholicism.

Here again, despite the stress on a specifically "Sri Lankan" form of Catholicism, global cultural processes are important. The forms of "contextual theology" developed in Sri Lanka are local counterparts of a more general phenomenon in the Catholic world, and there are close linkages with groups of Catholics elsewhere. Much of the original impetus for the development of these radical Catholic identities was a result not just of Vatican II nor the Sri Lankan situation but from developments in Latin America and elsewhere that talked in terms of "liberation theology." Furthermore, despite the stress on developing specifically Sri Lankan forms of Catholicism, there is a sense in which this effort has failed. Admittedly, links have been created with radical elements in other religious traditions, notably with Buddhists, but because of these radicals' stress on a "Sri Lankan," rather than a more limited "Sinhala" identity, radical Catholics have been exposed to attacks as "anti-nationalists" by various Sinhala-Buddhist groups. Furthermore, they have failed to develop strong linkages with the mass of the Sinhala-Catholic laity.

One example of this is the recent dispute over the Iranawila relay station, which is about to be constructed by the Voice of America (VOA). Iranawila is a predominantly Catholic fishing village about fifty miles north of Colombo where the government of Sri Lanka has agreed to lease out over six hundred acres of land to the VOA for twenty years. Opposition to the relay station has largely been orchestrated by "radical Catholics," many of them priests. On the one hand, they have formed an alliance with non-Catholic activists including some fundamentalist Buddhist priests, an alliance that was also active in attempting to prevent the Kandalama hotel scheme on environmental grounds. On the other, they are allied with more "main stream" Catholics, for instance the bishop of Chilaw in whose diocese Iranawila lies.[30] In part the opposition is on the grounds of the impact the project is expected to have on fishing, but also it is opposed in terms of the loss of coconut land and in terms of American "neoimperialism."

Clearly, there are a number of strands that could be pursued here. For instance, the stress on environmental issues once again harps back to a global interest in the environment and a sense of common identity, which lays stress on environmental issues rather than religious issues. The opposition to American "neoimperialism" again resonates with global forms of hegemony and resistance, a theme that unites both Sinhala-Buddhist fundamentalists and leftward leaning Catholic radicals. One element in the campaign involves calling on instances of such relay stations in other parts of the world. But the opposition to the relay station is also part of a longer running attempt by both radical and more conservative elements in the church to oppose forms of commercial development, particularly tourism, along the west coast of Sri Lanka. For the radicals, opposition is justified in terms of the exploitive relationships involved in the tourist trade; for conservatives it is justified in terms of the impact tourist development has on "traditional morality and culture." And of course there is a certain irony here in that at least some of the heirs to one moment in the process of globalization—the missionary endeavor of the sixteenth to nineteenth centuries—are now opposed to a new moment—the spread of global American influence.[31]

Yet what is perhaps most striking is how limited the attraction of these appeals to resistance are to the majority of Catholics in the coastal belt. In Iranawila there is undoubted opposition to the relay station among those whose immediate interests are directly threatened, but there are also those who see the project as beneficial. A few miles away the general feeling among Catholics is one of indifference to the project. More generally, there is little sense in which Catholics as Catholics are opposed to tourism and other forms of development along the west coast. In part this is a matter of identity: for most Catholics resistance to tourism and other projects is not a matter seen as being associated with their identities as Catholics. Opposition is greatest amongst the old and among those whose material interests are threatened. Radical Catholic groups have failed to impose their definitions of what it means to be a Catholic.

Given this variety in what it means to be a Catholic in contemporary Sri Lanka, what then is the significance of the huge crowd that turned out to welcome the pope in January 1995? Of course, to some extent it was a celebration of the Catholic community in Sri Lanka, but that was in spite of, rather than because of, any strong sense of a shared common identity or a shared idea of what it means to be a Catholic today. In a sense the pope is so distant from the day-to-day aspects of what it means to be a Sinhala Catholic that he can act as a symbol of Catholic unity, a unity more dreamt of than realized. Just for a moment, Catholics who hold very different ideas of what their Catholicism involves could participate in a grand spectacle that was not a manifestation of a common identity but an occasion in which various imaginings of what that identity might mean were disguised under a semblance of unity.

Conclusion

Except at the most general level, there is little if any sense of a common Catholic identity in Sri Lanka. Rather, what it means to be a Catholic and an individual's sense of identity as a Catholic is a matter that is continually being transformed and remade. Furthermore, it is not just a matter of variety, to be seen as analogous with a series of "little traditions" encompassed by some "great tradition." Between the proponents of different styles of Catholicism, different ways of "being Catholic," there is at times a high level of resentment and even conflict. "Traditionalist" Catholics frequently deny that the "radicals" are Catholic rather than see them as "bad" or "failed" Catholics.

My "history" of Catholic identity as presented in this paper describes a process of fragmentation. From a unified homogeneous body in the late nineteenth century, cultural and political forces have worked to generate difference and confusion. Implicit in this description is the changing role of the institutional church: its ability to control Catholics in the nineteenth century and its inability to control them in the twentieth century. Yet it has to be admitted that this is a problematic argument for the sources I have used all have a vested interest in the depiction of a united "Catholic community" in the nineteenth century. From the church's point of view, relations with Rome and relations with the colonial government depended in part on the church's ability to present a picture of ecclesiastical control. Similarly, critics of the church, not just Sinhala Buddhists but also European Protestants and other anti-Catholics, were also interested in presenting the church as an all-powerful monolithic and indeed totalitarian body.

Yet there are many hints that all was not as it was presented. We know that there were practices that the church considered to be "heretical." We know that Catholics attended Buddhist and Hindu shrines. We know that there were local disputes between priests and the laity, and between different groups of Catholics. So how strong a shared sense of a "Catholic identity" was in the nineteenth century must, at the moment, remain an open question. The traditional sociological picture of a move from "community" to the "individual"; from "homogeneity" to "heterogeneity"; from "tradition" to "modernity" is only too easy to impose on a shadowy past.

This leads on to a much more important question: How useful is it to talk of a "Sinhala-Catholic identity" not just now but also in the past? Much of the recent literature on identity has focused on issues concerning identity politics as it involves gays, lesbians, feminists, and blacks both in North America and Europe. One of the common strands in this literature is that identities are always incomplete, fragmentary, and contradictory.[32] Thus black feminists have argued that to talk of "woman" as an identity is to efface the role of race. Similarly, among Catholics, to talk of a "Catholic" identity is to ignore the very real differences in the ways in which Catholicism has constructed female and male in gender terms, and how the experience and thus the identity of Catholic men and women is very different.[33] And this is not the only cleavage that has to be considered. Caste for instance has been and still is important in the internal organization of the church. Individual churches were closely associated with different castes, and where castes shared the same church, the internal organization of the congregation was often based on caste. Caste has also been important in recruitment to the priesthood and in the allocation of priests to particular parishes. Here again, to talk simply in terms of a "Catholic identity" is to ignore these differences. Occupation, class, urban versus rural, and even age are also ways in which the specificities of "being Catholic" vary.

Thus to return to the opening sentence of this chapter, this has been a preliminary attempt to investigate changing Catholic identities in Sinhala Sri Lanka. It has dealt at an extremely general level and has ignored many of the most interesting and challenging aspects of Catholic identity in Sri Lanka: the ways in which it intersects with, reinforces, negates, contradicts, other forms of identity both personal and collective. In writing this chapter what I have realized is how little I for one know about "contemporary Catholic identity" in Sri Lanka.

Notes

1. The lack of attention to Tamil-speaking parts of the island is mainly due to my lack of knowledge of these areas.

2. The literature on globalization is growing daily. Some of the more important writings include M. Featherstone, ed., *Global Culture* (London: Sage, 1990); A. Giddens, *The Consequences of Modernity* (Cambridge: Polity Press, 1990); R. Robertson, *Globalization* (London: Sage, 1992); and R. Robertson and W. Garrett, ed., *Religion and Global Order* (New York: Paragon, 1991). M. Waters, *Globalization* (London: Routledge, 1995) provides a comprehensive overview.

3. On the Kotahena riot, see G.P.V. Somaratna, *Kotahena Riot 1883: A Religious Riot in Sri Lanka* (Colombo: 1991); K.H.M. Sumathipala, "The Kotahena Riot and Their Repercussions," *Ceylon Historical Journal*, 19 (1969–70), 65–81; L.A. Wickremeratne, "Religion, Nationalism and Social Change in Ceylon, 1865–1885," *Journal of the Royal Asiatic Society (Ceylon Branch)*, 56 (1969), 123–50; J. Rogers, *Crime, Justice and Society in Colonial Sri Lanka* (London: Curzon Press, 1987); Tessa Bartholomeusz, "Catholics, Buddhists, and the Church of England: The 1883 Sri Lankan Riots," *Journal of Buddhist-Christian Studies*, vol. 15 (1995), 89–104; and R.L. Stirrat, "Constructing Identities in Nineteenth Century Colombo," in J. Campbell and A. Rew, ed., *Cultural Identity* (Reading: Harwood [forthcoming]).

4. Discussions of these clashes can be found in the voluminous publications of Michael Roberts. See, for instance, M. Roberts, "Ethnicity in Riposte at a Cricket Match: The Past for the Present," *Comparative Studies in Society and History*, 27 (1985a), 401–29; M. Roberts, "'I shall have you slippered': The General and the Par-

ticular in an Historical Conjuncture," *Social Analysis*, 17 (1985b), 17–48; and M. Roberts, "Noise as Cultural Struggle: Tom-tom Beating, the British, and Communal Disturbances in Sri Lanka," in Veena Das, ed., *Mirrors of Violence* (Delhi: Oxford University Press, 1990).

5. R. Boudens, *The Catholic Church Under Dutch Rule* (Rome: Catholic Book Agency, 1957) provides an overview of the Dutch period from a Catholic point of view. V. Perniola, *The Catholic Church in Sri Lanka: The Dutch Period* (Colombo: Tisara Prakasakayo, 1983–85) presents a collection of documents written during this period.

6. One factor in the strength of Catholic identity in coastal Sri Lanka may have been that many of the groups in this area were relatively recent immigrants to Sri Lanka and not fully integrated into Sinhala society. See M. Roberts, "From Southern India to Lanka: The Traffic in Commodities, Bodies and Myths from the Thirteenth Century Onwards," *South Asia* 4 (1980), 36–47.

7. The Goan schism was primarily an argument over ecclesiastical control between the Oratorian priests based in Goa and European priests controlled from Rome. The main focus of the dispute was the control over the shrine at Madhu, the most important Catholic shrine in the country. See R. Boudens, *Catholic Missionaries in a British Colony: Successes and Failures in Ceylon, 1796–1893* (Immensee: Nouvelle Revue de Science Missionaire, 1979).

8. For an analysis of the "invention" of Buddhism as a religion, see P.C. Almond, *The British Discovery of Buddhism* (Cambridge: Cambridge University Press, 1988).

9. Of course, this was not a smooth process. Throughout the nineteenth century there was pressure on the Sri Lankan colonial authorities from Christian groups (see K.M. de Silva, *Social Policy and Missionary Organizations in Ceylon, 1840–1855* [London: Longmans, 1965]). It was only in 1881 that the Church of England was formally disestablished in the island. And throughout colonial rule, membership of the Anglican Church appears to have been advantageous to ambitious Sri Lankans.

10. Of course, this is not to say that religious affiliation was not important to the British rulers. Anglicans in particular and Protestants in general remained favored Sri Lankans under British rule.

11. S. Bayly, *Saints, Goddesses and Kings: Muslims and Christians in South Indian Society* (Cambridge: Cambridge University Press, 1989).

12. There is a large and growing literature on the "Buddhist revival." See for instance G.D. Bond, *The Buddhist Revival in Sri Lanka* (Delhi: Motilal Banarsidass, 1992); K. Malalgoda, *Buddhism in Sinhalese Society 1750–1900* (Berkeley: University of California Press, 1976); G. Obeyesekere, "Sinhalese-Buddhist Identity in Ceylon," in G. de Vos and L. Romanucci-Ross, ed., *Ethnic Identity: Cultural Continuities and Change* (Palo Alto: Mayfield Publishing House, 1975); G. Obeyesekere, "The Vicissitudes of the Sinhala-Buddhist Identity through Time and Change," in M.

Roberts, ed., *Collective Identities, Nationalisms and Protest in Modern Sri Lanka* (Colombo: Marga, 1979); B.L. Smith, "Sinhalese Buddhism and the Dilemmas of Reinterpretation," in B.L. Smith, ed., *The Two Wheels of Dhamma: Essays on the Theravada Tradition in India and Ceylon* (Chambersburg: American Academy of Religion, 1972); D.K. Swearer, "Lay Buddhism and the Buddhist Revival in Ceylon," *Journal of the American Academy of Religion*, 38 (1970), 255–75; L.A. Wickremaratne, "Religion, Nationalism and Social Change," 1969.

13. *Catholic Messenger*, 10 September 1909.

14. There has been no census in Sri Lanka since 1981, but the population today is estimated at around eighteen million of which approximately 6 percent are Catholic, a total of just over one million.

15. R.L. Stirrat, "The Riots and the Roman Catholic Church in Historical Perspective," in J. Manor, ed., *Sri Lanka in Change and Crisis* (London: Croom Helm, 1984).

16. The use of terms such as "nationalism," "ethnicity," "race," and "communalism" courts criticism from one quarter or another, but I do not see any alternative in this context.

17. See, for instance, B. Anderson, *Imagined Communities: Reflections on the Origin and Spread of Nationalism* (London: Verso, 1983); P. Chatterjee, *Nationalist Thought and the Colonial World: A Derivative Discourse?* (London: Zed Books, 1986); and E. Hobsbawm, *Nations and Nationalism Since 1780* (Cambridge: Cambridge University Press, 1991).

18. Thus although the 1848 rebellion was directed against British rule, it is difficult to interpret it as a nationalist rising rather than a dynastic coup attempt.

19. Given the present situation in Yugoslavia and in other parts of eastern Europe, the stress on the secular nature of European nationalism may well appear to be overplayed.

20. This is not to say that there are no problems with Van der Veer's conceptualization of "nationalism." In a sense he uses the term in such a way that almost any form of collective identity, whether it be based on ideas of race, language, religion, or class, could be described as nationalism.

21. The situation appears to be different among the Sri Lankan Tamils involved in the LTTE. Here, despite the predominance of Hindus, religion does not seem to be a stressed element to the same degree as among the Sinhala. Whether this is a matter of the importance of the lower castes in the LTTE or of the numerical importance of Catholics in northern Sri Lanka is an open question.

22. Obeyesekere, G. "Sinhalese-Buddhist Identity," 1975; and "Personal Identity and Cultural Crisis: the Case of Anagarika Dharmapala of Sri Lanka," in F. Reynolds and C. Capps, ed., *The Biographical Process* (The Hague: Mouton, 1976);

see also R. Gombrich and G. Obeyesekere, *Buddhism Transformed: Religious Change in Sri Lanka* (Princeton: Princeton University Press, 1988).

23. Many of these attacks on Catholics were orchestrated by the All Ceylon Buddhist Congress led by G.P. Malalasekera.

24. S. Perera, "Teaching and Learning Hatred: The Role of Education and Socialization in the Sri Lankan Ethnic Conflict" (unpublished Ph.D. thesis: University of California, Santa Barbara, 1991).

25. One area where Catholic identity still seems to be of some importance is in migrant labor. Whilst many Catholics migrate to the same areas as other Sri Lankans, mainly the Middle East, there are separate Catholic circuits that link Sri Lanka to southern Europe, particularly Italy. In one west coast town a street of opulent houses is known as "Little Italy," the houses supposedly constructed from migrants' remittances.

26. As yet, no detailed work has been published on these Protestant Evangelical groups. This is a major gap in our knowledge of religion in Sri Lanka. They are also seen as a threat by Buddhist organizations and a number of attacks have been made in the press and elsewhere on the Evangelicals by Buddhists. The Catholic hierarchy has attempted to distance "Catholic" Christianity from the Christianity of the Evangelicals.

27. I have discussed these shrines at length elsewhere. See R.L. Stirrat, *Power and Religiosity in a Post-Colonial Setting: Sinhala Catholics in Contemporary Sri Lanka* (Cambridge: Cambridge University Press, 1992).

28. See G. Obeyesekere, "Psychocultural Exegesis of a Case of Spirit Possession from Sri Lanka," in V. Crapanzano and V. Garrison, ed., *Case Studies in Possession* (New York: John Wiley, 1977); "Social Change and the Deities: The Rise of the Kataragama Cult in Modern Sri Lanka," *Man* 12 (1977), 1–23; and B. Kapferer, *A Celebration of Demons* (Bloomington: Indiana University Press, 1983).

29. See for instance U. Dornberg, *Searching through the Crisis: Christians, Contextual Theology and Social Change in Sri Lanka in the 1970s and 1980s* (Colombo: Logos, vol. 31, nos. 3 and 4, 1992); A.J.V. Chandrakanthan, *Catholic Revival in Post-Colonial Sri Lanka: A Critique of Ecclesial Contextualization* (Colombo: Social and Economic Development Centre, 1995); and the voluminous writings of Tissa Balasuriya.

30. Details of the agreements and opposition to the project can be found in, *Iranawila—Voice of America (The Irana-gate Scandal)* produced by the Iranawila Peoples Solidarity Forum. This is published through the Centre for Society and Religion, one of the more radical Catholic organizations in Colombo, and is said to have been written and compiled by the bishop of Chilaw.

31. A further irony is almost at the moment when the church adopts modernism the world of postmodernism with its stress on variety, individuality, and indeed fundamentalism becomes increasingly dominant.

32. C. Calhoun, ed., *Social Theory and the Politics of Identity* (Oxford: Blackwell, 1994), p. 14.

33. Thus in the reports of the 1883 Kotahena riot, all the Catholic "voices" are male. What part, if any, women played in the riot except as victims of attack, and what their thoughts and opinions of the riot were, is not mentioned.

Chapter 9

Buddhist Burghers and Sinhala-Buddhist Fundamentalism[1]

Tessa J. Bartholomeusz

Introduction

> Never in one *hundred* years, never in one *thousand* years, never in one *million* years will you find a Burgher who's a Buddhist. If you do, it means he's *crazy*; it means he's off his nut. *Burghers* are *Christians* and *Catholics*.

Thus proclaimed a Burgher in Negombo[2] when I asked him if he knew any Burghers who had become Buddhist. His attitude is rather typical of Burghers, the descendants of Portuguese, Dutch, and British colonizers of Sri Lanka.[3] Like their forefathers, Burghers are aligned with Christianity.[4]

On the other hand, when I asked a Buddhist Sinhala if he knew any Burghers who were Buddhist, he exclaimed,

> Well, of course, and they are the *real* Buddhists; their Buddhism isn't diluted by rituals and other things that have nothing to do with Buddhism. Their Buddhism is rational; it is pure.[5]

Both the Burgher and the Sinhala implicitly said something about their cultural identity in their critique of Burghers who have become Buddhist, or about those I call "Buddhist Burghers." Though their numbers have been, and continue to be, negligible,[6] Buddhist Burghers have contributed in significant ways to Buddhist revivalism in Sri Lanka. In this chapter, I explore their position in Sinhala-Buddhist society, as well as Sinhala and Burgher attitudes about them. Such study affords us a glimpse into the ways that identities and "communities" in Sri Lanka are often forged in relation to Sinhala-Buddhist fundamentalism.[7]

Here I propose a reformulation of the development of "Sinhala-Buddhist" cultural nationalism, even fundamentalism, that emerged in the late nineteenth century, a nationalism that shapes current ethnic strife in Sri Lanka between Sinhalas and Tamils. The standard view is that Anagarika Dharmapala, a Sinhala-Buddhist patriot, provided the blueprint for the contemporary strife in his diatribes against Tamils. The sources suggest, however, that Dharmapala's colleague, a Buddhist Burgher—A.E. Buultjens—was as much an architect for the construction of Sinhala-Buddhist identity, nationalism, and Buddhist fundamentalism as Dharmapala. My purpose is not to judge Dharmapala's writings on Tamils; I need not review in detail here Dharmapala's life and attitudes toward ethnic groups in Sri Lanka, both of which have been studied by many scholars. Rather, in a historical and anthropological synthesis that incorporates much new research data, I describe the events and ideologies that have shaped contemporary Sinhala-Buddhist fundamentalism by tracing it to Buultjens, as well as to Dharmapala.

In addition to revising standard views on Sinhala-Buddhist cultural identity in Sri Lanka, these new data illumine the *inclusive* nature of Sinhala Buddhism, usually ignored due to the common, erroneous perception that "Sinhala civilization has preserved its religio-cultural purity"[8] throughout history. The new research data that I introduce here confirm what scholars have argued recently—namely, that Sinhala Buddhism has assimilated much that is usually perceived as dangerous to Sinhala-Buddhist identity.[9] The assimilation of Buddhist Burghers into Sinhala-Buddhist society offers another important instance of the inclusive nature of Sinhala Buddhism. Moreover, this study provides an interesting, and perhaps unique, instance of a community that has converted others, only later to find some among them converting to the very religion that they had encouraged others to denounce. This study, then, is also a study of conversion.

Burghers and the Buddhist Revival

My narrative of Burghers who have converted to Buddhism begins in the late nineteenth century when Sri Lankans witnessed the rise of nationalism and anticolonialism, and began to ask whether Burghers were Asians or Europeans. Correspondents of the local newspapers of the period often classified Burghers along with the other "native" populations of the island—that is, the Sinhala and the Tamil.[10] For instance, one writer, praising young

Burgher scholars who were "ornaments to their country," characterized Burghers as "sons of the soil."[11] As Stanley Tambiah notes, "sons of the soil" "is widely used in India and elsewhere in Southeast Asia . . . as an emotionally charged overriding claim of the "indigenous" people;[12] it is opposed to "alien." Indeed, for many writers, Sri Lanka, rather than Portugal or Holland, was the only home of the Burgher.

On the other hand, some contributors to the newspapers did not consider Burghers native Sri Lankans.[13] One writer, a Burgher cognizant that late nineteenth-century anticolonialism could render Burghers vulnerable, argued that the Burgher community stood apart from the others, and grappled with the idea of assimilation:

> Our choice is now, either to be prepared to perish as a body and be fused down by a huge "amalgamation" into the native masses, losing our names and prestige, or to join hands amongst ourselves and elevate ourselves above the level of the flood which threatens to swallow us up.[14]

The writer gave the latter as the only viable option. In the course of the appeal, he or she added that though some among the Burgher community advocated being "swallowed up," they had not clearly thought through the proposition. It would mean that the Burghers would have to "embrace the Sinhalese nationality," and that they would have to "extinguish [their] light in the vast ocean of the Sinhalese population."[15] This was inconceivable for a people who, as the writer reported, "claim[ed] to be a connecting link between Europe and Asia."[16] Yet, though Burghers in many ways had "honorary European status," in the eyes of the British their birth in Sri Lanka consigned them to subordinate status—even though in their names, manners, customs, clothing, language, religion, and even ancestry many were indistinguishable from the British.[17] It is thus no surprise that some Burghers, like many Sinhalas, criticized the British and their discriminatory policies. Those Burghers who criticized the British continued to be "connecting links" between Europe and Asia, albeit the nature of that relationship had changed. Out of these contradictions emerged a very few Burghers who chose to defend the island against the perceived destructive force of the British government—Christianity. In so doing, they helped to direct the Buddhist revival and promote Buddhist fundamentalism.

It indeed was not the trend for Burghers to become Buddhist revivalists, nor for them to criticize Christianity. In fact, when Henry Steele Olcott of the Buddhist Theosophical Society (BTS) tried to engage some Burghers to help in his struggle to resuscitate Buddhism after his arrival in Sri Lanka in 1880, he learned firsthand the attitudes of most Burghers toward Buddhism. Olcott described his experience thus:

> The aged High Priest . . . let me into a nice embarrassment. He begged me to call on a list of Europeans and to write to twenty Burghers (half-race descendants of the Dutch) inviting them to join with the Buddhists in forming a Branch of the [Buddhist] T.S. In my innocence, I did so, and the next morning could have bitten off my finger for shame, for they sent me insulting replies, saying they were Christian and wanted to have nothing to do with Theosophy or Buddhism.[18]

The sources suggest, however, that within a few years of Olcott's arrival, some Burghers not only joined the BTS; they became its most active members, as well.

The main activity of the BTS in its early years in Sri Lanka was the promotion of Buddhist schools, schools that offered an alternative to British Christian missionary education. Just as "education has been at the heart of postindependence politics,"[19] it was the major concern of many Buddhists[20] in Sri Lanka at the turn of the twentieth century. The journals and newspapers of the period are replete with BTS criticisms of the government's lack of interest in promoting Buddhist education. At an 1893 meeting of the BTS, in which the education of Buddhist children was the issue, T.B. Panabokke, a Sinhala advocate of Buddhist education, proposed that as Buddhist children are daily "running the risk of getting perverted into Christianity," Buddhists should organize more schools for their children. A Burgher, Dr. Anthonisz, seconded Panabokke's motion.[21] Their interest in education had already launched Mahinda College in Galle, the object of which was to give "sound instruction in the knowledge of Buddhism." The opening of the school drew a "reputable gathering of Sinhalese, Moors, Tamils and Burghers."[22]

The BTS also gave female children the option of a Buddhist education with the establishment of the Sanghamitta School for Girls in 1892. A Burgher, A.J. Ferdinands, served as the first principal.[23] Her ethnicity was noted in the media; she was considered to be "an accomplished Burgher lady."[24] In fact, a Burgher was actively sought for her position.[25] Ferdinands was assisted by many Burgher women, including an Anthonisz,[26] Claessen,[27] Loos, and LaBrooy.[28] As was the case with Mahinda College, Sinhalas, Tamils, Moors, and Burghers were present at the opening celebration of the Sanghamitta School.[29] Sybil LaBrooy, swept by the tide of Buddhist revivalism and nationalism, was associated with the Sanghamitta from its inception in 1892 until its demise in 1900. She even renounced her lay identity and lived as a Buddhist nun for many years, though her family, like the other Burgher families of the island, was Christian.[30]

The Burghers who became Buddhists in the late nineteenth century associated with the Sinhala revivalist, Anagarika Dharmapala who, by that time, had become a symbol of religious and national pride. Dharmapala was prejudiced against the Portuguese and the Dutch from whom the Burghers of his day descended—for him, they were the Other—that is, alien and thus threatening to Buddhist identity in Sri Lanka.[31] He nonetheless befriended Burghers who had become Buddhists, as well as those with leanings toward Buddhism, and made them "insiders." One of them, Dr. Rodrigesz, suggested that they send Buddhist missionaries to Cuba.[32] Dharmapala wrote that another Burgher, Mr. Van Rozan, had "shown [him] some sympathy."[33] He even referred to a Burgher colleague, Mr. Jansz, as a "brother."[34] He hoped that Jansz and his other colleagues could remain "united" in the "work for the consummation of [their] ideal—the elevation of [their] nation and religion."[35] Religious work was national work, and implicit in this work was a critique of Portuguese and Dutch colonial policies, Christianity, and its legacy in Sri Lanka.

A.E. Buultjens: Mediator between East and West

As we have seen, the late nineteenth-century critique of the British did not exclude descendants of Christian colonizers, or Burghers, from the wave of nationalism and Buddhist revivalism that swept the country. In fact, at that time, one of the most vociferous critics of the Portuguese, the Dutch, and the British in the island was not a Sinhala, but rather a Dutch Burgher, Alfred Ernst Buultjens. He, too, was a colleague of Dharmapala.[36]

Buultjens, as a student in the 1880s at St. Thomas' College, the prestigious Anglican school for boys near Colombo, won a scholarship to study at Cambridge.[37] While studying in England, he became increasingly interested in his own ethnicity—that is, his heritage as a Dutch Burgher. He wrote frequently to Colombo newspapers, as well as to journals, about the Dutch contribution to Sri Lankan culture.[38] It is probable that Buultjens was the victim of racism in England. His writings imply that he felt that the British knew little of his island,[39] and that they discriminated against non-Christians.[40] Disturbed by the immorality of the English—that the wealthy "exist[ed] side by side with groveling debasement, poverty and misery," and that "hopeless drunkenness" and "prostitution" were the rule rather than the exception in the seat of the Church of England—he renounced Christianity.[41] In effect, he helped to mark boundaries between Buddhists and Christians, between East and West, and thus between Sinhalas and European descendants.

When in 1888 Buultjens returned to Sri Lanka, after graduating with honors from Cambridge, he informed his mother that he was no longer a Christian. According to Buultjens, his mother could not accept his news; she was convinced that he was insane.[42] She set up sessions with the family priest, a Sinhala Anglican; not he, nor anyone, could dissuade the young Burgher from changing his mind. Buultjens summarized the aftermath of his discussions with the Anglican priest in his typical dramatic fashion:

> It became noised abroad that an infidel was let loose on Society of Matara, and I became a marked man—mad, some said. Then some Buddhist friends met me, and enquired whether I would see a Buddhist Bhikkhu [monk] on the subject of Buddhism.[43]

Knowing that "social ostracism" would follow if he declared himself a Buddhist, he nonetheless became an "avowed Buddhist" in 1888 and was "looked upon as worse than a lunatic."[44] Soon thereafter, he moved to Colombo, where he joined Dharmapala, Olcott, and others in their Buddhist educational and national work. He spent much of 1890–1894 touring the island with Olcott and Dharmapala, opening Buddhist schools[45] and giving talks on Buddhism.[46] Many Buddhists took an interest in Buultjens, the young champion of Buddhism. One reporter wrote that:

> At such a time while the Europeans are in Sri Lanka saying Christianity is the whole truth and Buddhism completely untrue, the Buddhist people gathered to hear Buultjens [were] surprised that such educated people would embrace Buddhism.[47]

One European, Dr. Daly, an associate of Olcott, wrote that the Sinhala people should emulate Buultjens' untiring commitment to the resuscitation of Buddhism. Buultjens, after all, had given up even family connections for the sake of the Sinhala people.[48] Doubtless anticipating the future of the Burgher community in Ceylon in the face of rising Buddhist fundamentalism, combined with his newfound religious convictions that he developed in England, Buultjens dedicated himself to the elevation of Buddhism under the British.

Buultjens was indeed tireless: he became the first Sri Lankan principal of the first Colombo Buddhist school for boys, which he had helped to organize.[49] He served also as the editor of the first English medium magazine for the propagation of Buddhism, *The Buddhist*. He used the magazine as a forum to defend Buddhism against misrepresentations by European writers;[50] he filled its pages with his own translations of Pali *suttas*.[51] He also contributed commentaries on the corrupt policies of the British,[52] as well as the supremacy of Buddhism over Christianity by arguing that Buddhism was a rational religion—a Western ideal—whereas Christianity was not. In addition, he led the campaign against the "Quarter Mile Clause," or the law imposed by the British that schools could not be built within a quarter of a mile of an already existing school, in effect prohibiting Buddhists from establishing rival schools to Christian missionary institutions. He wrote to the Marquis of Ripon on behalf of the Buddhists of Sri Lanka that "the entire Buddhist Community [was] roused by a sense of injustice."[53] He urged the British to change their education policies because they were "directed against the nation."[54] Buultjens was among the first Sri Lankans to articulate a connection between education and Sinhala-Buddhist nationalism, a connection that remains an important issue in the island today.

While editor of *The Buddhist* and manager of Buddhist schools, Buultjens was one of the first of his period to align Buddhism and nationalism, surmising that "the Sinhalese" of his day were "realising the truth that the Buddhist schools [were] their own national schools," and that "the [Buddhist] education [they] offered [was] in harmony with the national spirit."[55] He led the Buddhists in their resistance against the proposed erection of a church "in the proximity to the sacred and historical shrines of the Buddhists at Anuradhapura."[56] Buultjens argued that Christian education, and Christianity, would spread "Western civilization and Western ideas with all their concomitant evils of drunkenness and worldliness." They would "eventually replace . . . Eastern ideals of spirituality and asceticism" in Sri Lanka.[57]

In *The Buddhist*, Buultjens wrote that Sri Lanka was the repository of "pure" Buddhism, and that the Sinhala people are responsible for its safekeeping.[58] Doubtless Buultjens' perception of the role of the Sinhala people was shaped by his reading of the *Mahavamsa*, a fifth-century Pali work that chronicles the history of Buddhism in Sri Lanka. *The Mahavamsa* alleges that the legitimate inhabitants of the island are the descendants of the Indian Vijaya who, with his followers, began to colonize the island on the very day that the Buddha died. Before his death, the Buddha calls upon the god Vishnu to protect Vijaya and the others, for the Buddha himself predicts that it is in Lanka that his religion will be established. According to the *Mahavamsa*, Vijaya's progeny are known as the Sinhala, while their right to inhabit the island is based upon their custodianship of the Buddha's teachings. As H.L. Seneviratne has commented, this "Mahavamsa-view" of history, which was given prominence in the late nineteenth century by British colonial historians, is the "view which has lent itself to distortion by Sinhalese extremist groups seeking to legitimise violence on the minorities."[59] In other words, extremists can argue that it is their duty by any means to ensure the protection of Buddhism from threats from "alien" cultures, a feature, as we saw in the Introduction, of Buddhist fundamentalism in Sri Lanka.

It is thus a paradox that Buultjens, who argued that there is an irrefutable connection between the Sinhala people and Buddhism, set the stage for this "distortion." After all, his own people, the Burghers, as much as any other non-Buddhist group, were among those who were not perceived as real members of society because they did not ensure the prosperity of Buddhism. In this way, Buultjens began to architect Sinhala-Buddhist fundamentalist identity, an identity that has continued to take shape to the present.

As Benedict Anderson points out, a print-medium is a necessary prerequisite for the formation of a community. It unifies fellow readers who perhaps have never, and will never, meet, thus providing boundaries between those who read within a particular market and those who do not.[60] In *The Buddhist*, Westerners sympathetic to Buddhism, as well as Sri Lankans[61] such as Buultjens, wrote to each other, honing and chiseling an image of the Sinhala Buddhist, as well as an image of Sri Lanka as the repository of "true" Buddhism. In fact, *The Buddhist*, established in 1889, has continued to perpetuate through the written word the notion that Sinhala Buddhists form a discrete "community," a notion that has been divisive in the contemporary context.

In sum, Buultjens, as editor and major contributor of *The Buddhist* in its earliest years, helped to plant the seeds for Sinhala-Buddhist nationalism that others harvested.[62] In doing so, he helped to set the stage for the perceived redundancy of the Burgher community. It is thus an irony that Buultjens, a Burgher, contributed to conditions that would eventually displace Burgher hegemony in positions of power in Sri Lanka in favor of the Sinhala, conditions that would leave many Burghers with only two viable options: emigration, on the one hand, and assimilation, including conversion to Buddhism, on the other.

Twentieth-Century Buddhist Burghers

Early postcolonial Sri Lanka witnessed an emigration of Burghers that has continued unabated since the 1940s. Scholars have recently explored the reasons for the diaspora of the Burghers by setting it in the context of rapid changes brought about by related events, including Sinhala nationalism, the advent of universal suffrage, and *swabhasha*.[63] During the 1940s and 1950s, Burghers and Sinhalas wrote to Sri Lankan newspapers voicing their opinions about the future of the Burgher community. One Sinhala writer encouraged Burghers to stay in Sri Lanka and to educate their children in *swabhasha*, so that they would be able to communicate and work in languages other than English, in order to keep their top posts.[64] At the same time, while many Burghers wrote to newspapers voicing their fears, one Burgher, Bryan de Kretser, wrote editorials poking fun at Burghers, especially those who claimed pure descent on both sides.[65] At a time in which it was imperative to prove one's European lineage in order to migrate to Australia (the goal of the Burgher community), which had a "white only" policy, Burghers desiring to emigrate were not amused by de Kretser. Many of the Burghers I interviewed remember de Kretser and his editorials. At least ten members of the Dutch

Burgher Union in the course of one of my conversations with them suggested I interview de Kretser because he had converted to Buddhism. Some added that he was a "peculiar" man; had "gone native;" and was "a bit mad."

In my interview with de Kretser,[66] I learned that he was not a Buddhist at all. After the death of his first wife, a Burgher, he married a Buddhist woman—much to the dismay of his family—but had remained a Christian, though he had left the Presbyterian Church to become Catholic. He was amused that Burghers had said that he was Buddhist; he knew that for them a Burgher's conversion to Buddhism would be tantamount to madness.

The common Burgher equation of conversion to Buddhism—going "native"—with madness is a striking feature in the biographies of every Buddhist Burgher, including Buultjens', that I collected in Sri Lanka. In my conversations with Corrine Baptist,[67] the daughter of the late Egerton Baptist, a Buddhist Burgher who wrote thirty books on his adopted religion, she suggested that her father was no doubt mentally ill—his conversion to Buddhism proved it. Corrine Baptist told me that when her father converted to Buddhism—grief stricken after her grandmother's death—she became ashamed of him. She remembered the way her father would play Buddhist chants on their phonograph, loud enough for the whole neighborhood to hear. She could not understand, either then or now, why her father would become *more of a Sinhala-Buddhist than a Sinhala-Buddhist*: he completely disavowed his Burgher, Catholic heritage. Like Buultjens decades earlier, Baptist urged Sinhala people to affirm their own culture, rather than parroting the colonizers.

Eric LaBrooy,[68] an elderly Burgher and former judge, would have agreed with Baptist that Sinhalas should affirm their Buddhist heritage. He too became a Buddhist after the death of a family member, in his case, his infant daughter. Long before his conversion, however, the former Anglican became a devotee of the god Kataragama, who shows favor "even to Christians." At present he attempts monthly pilgrimages to the god's abode in southeast Sri Lanka, despite ill health. A *bhakta* of Kataragama and a Buddhist, he no longer identifies with the Burgher community.

LaBrooy and his second wife, Coralee Jansz, a Burgher, spend much of their time studying the Pali *suttas*, in addition to meditating. Mr. LaBrooy meditates up to four hours each day. Mrs. LaBrooy, too, considers herself a Buddhist. Nonetheless, she noted that there is a gulf between her and her Sinhala counterparts: she remains "culturally a Christian," preferring, for instance, Christian music and hymns to *pirit*. However, like her husband, Mrs. LaBrooy no longer feels connected to the Burgher community. In fact, the LaBrooys do not refer to themselves as Burghers; instead, they call themselves Sri Lankans which, in the present context, aligns them with Sinhala Buddhists. They have very few of the same friends they had before their conversion and have little to do with their Christian relations.

This was also the case with Barbara Lamb Gunasekera[69] and Esme Hingert Mutukumara,[70] both of whom related that they had had leanings toward Buddhism before marrying into Sinhala-Buddhist families. Like the LaBrooys, they consider themselves "officially"[71] Sri Lankans, or Buddhists, rather than Burghers, and have little or no communication with their birth families. In fact, this "bridge-burning act" is part of the process of their conversion.[72] In other words, they have both taken "the symbolically important action of cutting ties with an old way of life and [have moved] into a new one."[73] They both told me that their relations think that they are "slightly mad" for renouncing Christianity, and that their families had predicted that the converts would eventually see the error of their ways. As yet, that has not happened. In fact, Gunasekera, now in her sixties, would like to become a Buddhist nun. No doubt, such a move would confirm her natal family's suspicions about her sanity.

Conclusion

It would be simple to frame this study of Buddhist Burghers with traditional research on conversion—namely, deprivation theories that assume a passive subject.[74] In such theories, the convert is viewed as a person "forced to seek out religious or other experiences to compensate for life's shortcomings."[75] In short, the theory assumes deprivation (and) or psychological strain. Proponents of this passive subject model argue that conversion is a result, for instance, of economic and social deprivation.[76] In this model, then, conversion is not a choice; social forces make the choice for the convert. Burghers, indeed, have been forced to rethink their social and economic positions as a result of independence, the pressures of their neocolonial world, and the power of Sinhala-Buddhist fundamentalism. Yet, this model, in which the convert is a passive subject upon whom various forces work, fails to recognize the active role that converts have played in their own conversion.

Another lens through which to view the Buddhist Burgher hinges on a different conversion theory, or the traditional conversion paradigm of the "Pauline Experience,"[77] which also views the convert as passive. This experience, the paradigm of which is Saul's conversion on the road to Damascus, is "sudden, dramatic and emotional; it ha[s] a definite irrational quality to it."[78] Expanding on the Pauline experience, proponents of this view argue that this type of experience can best be attributed to powerful unconscious psychological influences, such as madness[79] (or, in the traditional Christian view, God). In fact, when I discussed Buddhist Burghers with Christian Burghers, most responded that the Buddhist Burgher was psychologically unbalanced. They tended to discredit the Buddhist Burgher by implying that conversion to Buddhism was one manifestation of the person's obvious emotional illness. In other words, some Christian Burghers, much like traditional scholars of conversion might, view Burgher converts to Buddhism as passive actors in a drama (that is inexplicable to the Christian Burgher). I argue, however, that both passive paradigms explored here fail to address adequately Burgher conversion to Buddhism. Following new conversion research,[80] I argue instead that study of the conversion of Burghers to Buddhism must allow for an "acting and conscious human agent,"[81] who views Buddhism as fulfilling. In short, such study must pay attention to meaning.[82] As other essays in this volume suggest, being Sinhala and Buddhist in Sri Lanka means being empowered; this force might push a non-Buddhist toward conversion. Yet, for the convert, Buddhism is part and parcel of a creative and active transformation of life.

Though the majority of the Christian Burghers I interviewed argued that the Buddhist converts were insane, some avoided altogether the discussion of conversion by claiming that the person in question was not a "real" Burgher. They then suggested instead that the convert was "really a Eurasian," thereby disassociating themselves and their community from such Buddhists.[83] In other words, they have moved renegade Burghers from the center of the Burgher community to its periphery. In this way, Buddhist Burghers have thus become the "Other's Other"—that is, strange, alien, and threatening even to those who have been considered strange, alien, and threatening, as Dharmapala's writings suggest.

Sinhala Buddhists, however, generally critical of colonial culture, nonetheless affirm Buddhists Burghers and are eager to Sinhalize them. This is most apparent in the writings of a powerful Sinhala-Buddhist monk, the Venerable Madihee Pannaseeha,[84] whose name is often associated with Sinhala chauvinism. In fact, he has argued repeatedly that Sinhalas have declined so much so that they are now an endangered species.[85] Nonetheless, in one writing, he calls Buultjens a "Sinhala Burgher"—a term that I have never seen used anywhere before or since—thus completing Buultjens' transformation.[86] In other words, he has moved Buultjens from the periphery of Sinhala-Buddhist society to its center. He has thus empowered him and, by extension, other Burghers who have become Buddhist. This Sinhalization—whether a conscious decision made by Burghers themselves, or whether imputed, supports John Holt's thesis that Sinhala Buddhism is inclusive rather than exclusive, inasmuch as "ideas, expressions, and fashions" and, I might add, "alien" peoples "are welcome if they seem to be efficacious on the level of practical everyday life and they are responsive to the contemporary social experience."[87]

In much the same way that Buddhists have Sinhalized the Tamil king, Kirti Sri Rajasinghe, and consider him the greatest patron of Buddhism during the Kandyan period,[88] Sinhala people I interviewed consider a few Burghers among the greatest Buddhist revivalists of the modern period. Many, for instance, said that Alec Robertson, a Burgher convert to Buddhism who has been at the forefront of lay Buddhist meditation in Sri Lanka for the past thirty years, is one of the most influential Buddhists in Sinhala-Buddhist society.[89] Robertson, echoing other Buddhist Burghers I interviewed, told me that he identifies more with the Sinhala than the Burgher, and that for all intents and purposes, though a Burgher, he is a Sinhala Buddhist.[90] Robertson's reflections upon his identity in many ways affirm former President J.R. Jayewardene's contention that "just as one does not have to be Roman to be a Roman Catholic, one does not have to be Sinhala to be a Sinhala Buddhist."[91]

Buddhist Burghers' significant contribution to the formation of Sinhala-Buddhist national identity and associated fundamentalisms, and their transformation into Sinhala Buddhists, both suggest that Jayewardene just may be right. We are dealing with a remarkably small number of converts to a majority religious tradition. Still, the contribution of these Buddhist Burghers has been enormous to the formulation of the role of Buddhism as a focus for national, Sinhala identity. More importantly, their conversion to Buddhism dramatically highlights the power of Sinhala-Buddhist fundamentalism to shape identity in Sri Lanka.

Notes

1. Research was funded by an Indiana University Faculty Development Grant. I would like to thank Professors William Harman and Chandra de Silva for their comments on this paper. I read a version of this paper at the South Asia Conference, Madison, Wisconsin, November 1992.

2. I interviewed Mr. David Thomasz, a hotel manager, on June 13, 1992. The emphasis is his.

3. Although the Dutch Burgher Union (DBU) does not recognize descendants of the Portuguese and the British as Burghers, the term "Burgher" is used by Sinhalas and Tamils to refer to all descendants of European colonizers. It is a common practice among Burghers to distinguish between "Dutch Burghers" and "Portuguese Burghers," though few of the Sinhala people I interviewed make this distinction.

4. For instance, in an article about marriage in Sri Lanka, Maureen Seneviratne finds three customs: Sinhala/Buddhist, Tamil/Hindu, and Burgher/Christian; see *Explore Sri Lanka*, vol. 6, no. 2 (June 1992): 62.

5. Mr. Gunawardena of the Young Men's Buddhist Association, Borella, August 10, 1992. In many ways, Gunawardena's estimation of Buddhist Burghers accords with reality: all the Buddhist Burghers I interviewed eschew worship and alms-giving in favor of meditation and textual study. Like many Europeans who have either studied Buddhism, or become Buddhists, Buddhist Burghers' interpretation of Buddhism tends to be more toward its rational and ethical sides.

6. While it was relatively simple to locate male Buddhist Burghers, it is difficult to locate Burgher women who have become Buddhist. As in most cultures, once a Sri Lankan woman marries, she usually assumes her husband's name. Thus, if a Burgher woman marries a Sinhala man, her history as a Burgher is often lost. Moreover, children of such couples refer to themselves as Sinhalas, rather than Burghers. I interviewed four Buddhist-Burgher women and collected data on fifteen Buddhist-Burgher men. Space does not allow me to provide biographical data for all the Buddhist Burghers I discovered while exploring the topic. Some of the more notable Burghers not included in this study are: George Keyt, whose artistic contribution to the Buddhist renaissance has been fully documented elsewhere [H.A.I. Goonetileke, *George Keyt: A Life in Art* (Colombo: The George Keyt Foundation, 1989)]; and Carl (Ananda) Cooke, whose translations of *Jataka* tales appeared in the *Ceylon Observer* from 1 January 1955 through 18 May 1956. Burghers (both Christian and Buddhist) have never comprised more than one percent of the population of Sri Lanka (Dennis McGilvray, "Dutch Burghers and Portuguese Mechanics: Eurasian Ethnicity in Sri Lanka," *Comparative Studies in Society and History*, 24 (1982): 236).

7. Following Benedict Anderson, by "communities" I mean ethnolinguistic nationalism in which fellowships are imagined. See *Imagined Communities: Reflection on the Origin and Spread of Nationalism* (New York: Verso, 1991), passim.

8. Reggie Siriwardena, "Cultural Conformity vs. Cultural Diversity," *The Island* (Colombo), 11 November 1984, quoted in John Clifford Holt, *The Buddha in the Crown* (New York: Oxford University Press, 1991), p. 18. Siriwardena does not hold that Sinhala civilization has remained unadulterated.

9. See especially Gananath Obeyesekere and Richard Gombrich, *Buddhism Transformed: Religious Change in Sri Lanka* (Princeton: Princeton University Press, 1988).

10. For instance, an 1881 letter to the editor about legislative representation includes Burghers along with the other major "native" ethnic groups of the island ("To the Editor of the Ceylon Catholic Messenger: The Ferguson Testimonial," *Ceylon Catholic Messenger*, 26 August 1881). In the committee, there was "only one Tamil, two Singhalese (sic), and three Burghers." Covering the 1877 controversy over a statue in Governor Gregory's honor, someone wrote that "not a single native, be he Singhalese (sic), Tamil, or Burgher . . . ," had shown interest in the memorial ("Native Independence," *Ceylon Catholic Messenger*, 20 July 1877).

11. "Sons of the Soil," *Ceylon Catholic Messenger*, 10 October 1876. A similar article, "Provincial: Kandy, praising Ceylon's sons," appeared prior to this on 8 February 1876.

12. Stanley Jeyaraja Tambiah, *Buddhism Betrayed? Religion, Politics, and Violence in Sri Lanka* (Chicago: Chicago University Press, 1992), p. 86.

13. Writing on the volunteer army, a correspondent remarked that it "did not receive the co-operation it deserved at the commencement, at the hand of the natives

and even of the Burghers" ("The Ceylon Light Infantry Volunteers," *Ceylon Catholic Messenger*, 22 July 1881).

14. "Correspondence: Burghers Unite," *Ceylon Catholic Messenger*, 24 November 1876.

15. Ibid.

16. Ibid.

17. For instance, the British did not permit Burghers, or other Sri Lankans, to enter their exclusive clubs and discouraged marriage to them. Thus, in many ways, the British treated Burghers like another section of the "colored" population of the island. Anderson makes a similar point in his study of Spaniards and Creoles in the early nineteenth century (*Imagined Communities*, p. 58).

18. Henry Steele Olcott, *Old Diary Leaves* (Edinburgh: Hill and Co., Limited, 1900), p. 160. The parenthetical remark about the Dutch is Olcott's.

19. Stanley Tambiah, *Buddhism Betrayed?*, p. 64.

20. And, I might add, Hindus.

21. "The Work in Ceylon," *The Buddhist*, vol. v, no. 1, January 6, 1893, 2.

22. "Mahinda College, Galle," *The Buddhist*, vol, iv, no. 11, March 11, 1892, 84.

23. *The Buddhist*, vol. vi, no. 2, 14; vol. vi, no. 47, 371.

24. *The Buddhist*, vol. vi, no. 4, 1894.

25. "Sanghamitta Girls' School Colombo," *The Buddhist*, vol. vi, no. 1, January 12, 1894, 12: "Term began on Monday, the 8th instant, with good attendance. A European or Burgher Lady Principal is required." According to a letter from Donald Ferguson, co-editor of the *Ceylon Observer*, the school had to be "staffed by Christians" because Buddhists had neglected to educate women. For him, this proved the debased condition of Buddhism in the island. *The Monthly Literary Register*, vol. iii-iv, no. 1, contains more of his unsympathetic attitudes toward Buddhism.

26. *The Buddhist*, vol. vi, no. 25, July 6, 1894, 200. I cannot ascertain from the data whether she was related to Mr. Anthonisz mentioned above.

27. "The Buddhist Girl's School," *Ceylon Independent*, 9 October 1894.

28. Ibid., 246.

29. M. de S. Canavarro, *Insight into the Far East* (Hollywood, CA, 1925), p. 73.

30. For more on LaBrooy, see Tessa Bartholomeusz, *Women under the Bo Tree: Buddhist Nuns in Sri Lanka* (Cambridge: Cambridge University Press, 1994; reprinted, 1996). The sources are silent about LaBrooy's family's feelings concerning her renunciation.

31. For instance, Dharmapala's diary entry for December 4, 1891: "Are the Sinhalese so degenerated as not to think of their glorious ancestors? Will they choose to have Dutch sailors and ragamuffins as their ancestors or will they have Aryans as their forefathers?" In other words, "why do the Sinhala mimic past colonizers?"

32. Dharmapala's diary entry for October 16, 1898.

33. Dharmapala's diary entry for September 4, 1894.

34. Dharmapala's diary entry for May 23, 1891; his entries from August 1, 1891, until September 21, 1891, are replete with references to Jansz.

35. Dharmapala's diary entry for May 23, 1891.

36. Issues of *The Buddhist* from 1890 until 1894, as well as Dharmapala's diaries, are filled with references to their work together.

37. "*Why I Became a Buddhist?*" A Lecture Delivered by the Late Mr. A.E. Buultjens, BA (Cantab.) in 1899. Compiled, printed and published by C.A. Wijesekera, Colombo, 1984.

38. "On Some Dutch Words commonly Used by the Sinhalese," reprinted in *The Journal of the Dutch Burgher Union*, vol. xix, no. 2 (October 1929): 96–101. The article is signed, "A.E. Buultjens, St. John's College, Cambridge." Buultjens wrote that a study of loan words in Sinhala "will illustrate what we call the *negative* side of Sinhalese civilization—the progress which they had *not* made" (96; emphasis Buultjens').

39. "*Why I Became a Buddhist?*" Buultjens wrote that "just as a misunderstanding prevails in the East as to the vileness of man in 'heathen' lands alone, and his virtue in Christian countries of the West, so is there a misunderstanding in the West as to the trials and troubles of missionaries sent to the 'heathens.' I had frequently to assure educated and intelligent people in England that it was not considered a delicacy here [in Ceylon] when a roast missionary was served at dinner! There were people still who believed that Ceylon was a cannibal island" (9).

40. After granting leave to Buultjens from compulsory chapel attendance at Cambridge upon Buultjens' crisis of faith, Buultjens' dean tried to persuade him that Christian morality was supreme. Buultjens responded that he "came from a Buddhist country, where the Buddhist Home would be just as happy, if the moral precepts were observed" "*Why I Became A Buddhist?*," 6.

41. Ibid., 8. According to Buultjens, his renunciation of Christianity was painful: "Only those who have experienced in their hearts the throes of agony, which must be endured, alone and in silence, when they are compelled upon sincere conviction to give up beliefs . . . know the pain when it becomes necessary to wrench those beliefs from heart and mind" (4).

42. Ibid., 9. "I was looked upon as peculiar and strange. . . ." Also, see below.

43. Ibid., 10.

44. Ibid.

45. Buultjens' trips to school-openings are well documented in the *Sarasavisandaresa*: e.g., 25 April 1890, describes Buultjens participation at a prize-giving at a Buddhist school with Dharmapala in Panadura; 12 April 1890 notes Buultjens' and Olcott's presence as keynote speakers at the opening of the Horona English Buddhist Girls Institution; 11 November 1890 relates that Buultjens and Olcott were among the notables at the opening of the Nugegoda Buddhist Institution; 9 January 1891 describes Buultjens' tour through the Matara district Buddhist schools; 31 August 1894 mentions the lectures that Buultjens gave in six villages on how to organize schools. All but one of the articles describe the enthusiasm of his listeners; it relates that while in Horana, it "was clearly evident that these villagers weren't very enthusiastic about Buultjens and Dharmapala's talks. So they decided to have a series of talks in several adjoining villages"(6 May 1890).

46. E.g., *Sarasavisandaresa*, 20 June 1890.

47. *Sarasavisandaresa*, 18 July 1890. This is reported of Buultjens and Daly, an Irishman who was also involved in the BTS.

48. Upon Daly's retirement as manager of Buddhist schools, he wrote to *The Buddhist* that his successor, A.E. Buultjens, was a "man who has disregarded the decided prospects of an unusually brilliant academic training, sacrificing even family connection, to throw his lot in an unpopular cause," the elevation of Sri Lankan Buddhists and thus the "Sinhala nation." ("Retirement of the Manager," *The Buddhist*, vol. iv. no. 36, 9 September 1892, 283).

49. "The Colombo Buddhist Fancy Bazaar, *The Buddhist*, vol. iv, no. 45, November 11, 1892, 356.

50. For instance, "An Interesting Episode," *The Buddhist*, vol. v, no. 44, November 17, 1893. In this article, Buultjens describes tongue in cheek his critique of Bishop Copleston's book on Buddhism, as well as Copleston's reaction to the critique.

51. For instance, vol. vi, no. 7, February 23, 1894, 49–51; vol. vi, no. 9, March 9, 1894, 68–69; vol. vi, no. 15, April 27, 1894, 116–20; vol. vi, no. 16, May 4, 1894, 123–27; vol. vi, no. 16, May 11, 1894, 129–30, 132–36; vol. vi, no. 18, May 18, 1894, 137–43.

52. "The Ceylon Government and the Buddhists, *The Buddhist*, vol. iv, no. 33, August 19, 1892, 260–61.

53. "Quarter Mile Clause," *The Buddhist*, vol. vi, no. 26, July 13, 1894, 207.

54. *The Buddhist*, vol. iv, no. 49, December 9, 1892, 387.

55. "The Work in Ceylon," *The Buddhist*, vol. v, no. 1, January 6, 1893, 1–4.

56. "Anuradhapura Church Site," *The Buddhist*, vol. iii, no. 6, February 16, 1894.

57. "The Ceylon Government and the Buddhists," *The Buddhist*, vol. iv, no. 36, September 9, 1892, 284.

58. "The Early Religion of Ceylon," *The Buddhist*, vol. iv, no. 29, July 22, 1892, 228–29.

59. H.L. Seneviratne, "Identity and the Conflation of Past and Present," in *Identity, Consciousness and the Past*, H.L. Seneviratne, ed. (Adelaide: University of Adelaide Press, 1989), p. 6.

60. Benedict Anderson, *Imagined Communities*, pp. 37–46.

61. The Buddhists who were involved in the Buddhist revivalism of the late nineteenth century were, for the most part, Western educated and English-speaking.

62 In the early 1890s while Buultjens was defending Buddhism against the British, Dharmapala was spending much of his time traveling to America, Japan, and India as a Buddhist missionary.

63. Michael Roberts, Ismeth Raheem, and Percy Colin-Thome, *People Inbetween* (Ratmalana, Sri Lanka: Sarvodaya Book Publishing Services, 1989).

64. "Why Go?," *Ceylon Observer*, 29 March 1956.

65. One of the goals of the DBU, founded in 1908, was to provide genealogies for Dutch Burghers in Sri Lanka. The DBU published, and continues to publish, genealogies for their members. It is striking how few of them contain Sinhala or Tamil names, in spite of manifest Sinhala and Tamil bloodlines within the Burgher community. For more on the DBU, see Michael Roberts et al., *People Inbetween.*

66. I interviewed de Kretser on July 1, 1992, at Pritipura Children's Home, a refuge for abandoned and retarded children that he and his wife established and continued to manage until his death in 1997.

67. I interviewed Corrine Baptist on July 1, 1992.

68. LaBrooy is related to Sybil LaBrooy who became a Buddhist nun in the late nineteenth century. See above. I interviewed the LaBrooys on June 8, 1992, and August 17, 1992.

69. I interviewed Barbara Lamb Gunasekera on July 9, 1992.

70. I interviewed Esme Hingert Mutukumara on August 15, 1992.

71. That is, on census forms.

72. For more on "bridge-burning acts" in the conversion process, see James T. Richardson, "Paradigm Conflict in Conversion Research," *Journal for the Scientific Study of Religion*, vol. 24, no. 2 (June 1985): 170.

73. Ibid.

74. For more on conversion theories, see Brock Kilbourne and James T. Richardson, "Paradigm Conflict, Types of Conversion, and Conversion Theories," *Sociological Analysis: A Journal in the Sociology of Religion*, vol. 50, no. 1 (spring 1989): 1–21.

75. James Richardson, "Paradigm Conflict in Conversion Research," 166.

76. See C. Glock, "On the Origin and Evolution of Religious Groups," in *Religion in Sociological Perspective*, C. Glock, ed. (New York: Wadsworth, 1973).

77. James Richardson, "Paradigm Conflict in Conversion Research," 164.

78. Ibid., 165.

79. In mind are the 1970s discussions of Americans who had converted to the Hare Krishna movement.

80. See, in particular, Lorne Dawson, "Self-affirmation, Freedom, and Rationality: Theoretically Elaborating 'Active' Conversions," *Journal for the Scientific Study of Religion*, vol. 29, no. 2 (June 1990): 141–63.

81. James Richardson, "Paradigm Conflict in Conversion Research," 167.

82. For more on the role of meaning in conversion, see Ibid., 167–69. See also Clifford L. Staples and Armand L. Mauss, "Conversion or Commitment?, "*Journal for the Scientific Study of Religion*," vol. 26, no. 2 (June 1987): 133–47.

83. One of the goals of the DBU was to decide who could really be called a "Burgher."

84. He is the leader of the powerful Amarapura Nikaya (monastic fraternity).

85. Stanley Tambiah, *Buddhism Betrayed?*, p. 124.

86. The Venerable Madihee Pannaseeha, "A.E. Buultjens: The First Ceylonese Buddhist who Worked for the Elevation of Ananda College," in *Shasanika ha Jatika Viravarayoo* (Maharagama: Sasana Seevaka Samitiya, 1987), p. 27. See also the Venerable Balangoda Ananda Maitreya's laudatory remarks about Egerton Baptist in the Forward to Baptist's *In the Footsteps of Sakyamuni* (Colombo, 1962) for another example of the process of "Sinhalization."

87. John Holt, *Buddha in the Crown*, p. 19.

88. The *Culavamsa*, the continuation of the *Mahavamsa*, alleges that "when a king is Buddhist he automatically becomes Sinhalese" (Seneviratne, "Identity and the Conflation of Past and Present," 7). According to Seneviratne, the chronicles as late as the eighteenth century refer "to Kirti Sri Rajasingha" (sic), a king of the South Indian Nayakkar dynasty, who was an enthusiastic supporter of Buddhism, as "our Sinhalese king"." Kirti Sri Rajasinghe ruled in the mid-eighteenth century.

89. Among those I interviewed were members of the Maha Bodhi Society, the Sinhala Arakshana Samagama (the Society for the Protection of Sinhala Culture), the

Young Men's Buddhist Association, and the All Ceylon Buddhist Congress, all of which, it can be argued, are responsible to one degree or another for perpetuating Sinhala-Buddhist fundamentalism. Implicit in Robertson's lectures is an anti-Western message.

90. I interviewed Robertson on August 3, 1992, in Colombo, and had several informal conversations with him throughout June, July, and August 1992.

91. I interviewed President Jayewardene on July 19, 1992, in Colombo.

Chapter 10

The Persistence of Political Buddhism

John Clifford Holt

In the final paragraph of the Introduction to this volume, Tessa Bartholomeusz and Chandra de Silva have promised that this conclusion will contain some ideas regarding the future of Sinhala-Buddhist fundamentalist politics in Sri Lanka and how, perhaps, other visions of unity might fare in comparison. Prognostications about the political future of Sri Lanka tread on very slippery turf indeed, and conjecturing about what is in store would be somewhat antithetical to the ethos of Sri Lanka's infamous political unpredictability, an unpredictability that has not been always serendipitous. From a careful reading of the essays in our volume, however, it is possible to highlight some of the many salient issues that have been raised with the expectation that many of these will persist in one form or another during the years ahead. In what follows, then, I want to revisit and comment upon some of the important issues and patterns raised by our contributors. These are issues and patterns that I suspect will continue to be forces well into Sri Lanka's future. I will then further comment on the manner in which some of these are bound to be sustained.

One of the basic questions raised in the Introduction asks: Who are the Sinhala-Buddhist fundamentalists? On the surface, the question seems innocent enough and readily answerable: my own response would be militant and politically motivated Buddhists of the more urbanized sections of the populace who are heirs to the type of puritanical religiosity fostered by an early twentieth-century reformer, the Anagarika Dharmapala. But the question becomes exceedingly more difficult to answer when one tries to specify who those followers are in more precise fashion. First, as Bartholomeusz and de Silva point out in the Introduction, there really is no one identifiable Buddhist group in Sri Lanka that is institutionalized as such. Nor, I would add, is there any corresponding group who might actually want to lay claim self-consciously to the label of "fundamentalism." "Fundamentalism," in fact, is a term that is usually deployed by those who are quite "other" to the "fundamentalists" they seek to identify, analyze, oppose, or expose. It is clearly an outsider's term that carries somewhat negative overtones. Nobody wants to own it. So, in invoking fundamentalism as a category for analysis, one must accept that there will be a certain faceless quality to its referent(s) in Buddhist Sri Lanka. Moreover, there is a an inherent danger risked in deploying the abstract noun "fundamentalism" as a descriptive way of designating the religiosity of a given people: the phenomena and processes under consideration can be easily essentialized in reductionistic fashion. In their provocative essays, Pradeep Jeganathan and Oddvar Hollup have warned against the similar danger of essentializing "Tamilness" or the apparent cultural differences that exist between various ethnic communities in Sri Lanka. Further, it is also clear, especially from a reading of de Silva's essay in which he ascertains an array of religio-political views from a broad cross-section of Buddhist monks, that a wide and representative spectrum of religio-political perspectives prevails within the pluralistic *sangha*, so that pinning the fundamentalism tag on the monkhood in general is as difficult as pinning it on an identifiable section of the laity.

My sense, from personal experiences in Sri Lanka, is that those we would characterize as Buddhist fundamentalists are something of a minority, albeit a powerful minority that continues to influence Sri Lankan political dynamics with a force far exceeding what one might expect given their actual numbers. Finally, it is also quite clear, especially from George Bond's chapter on the acrimonious relations that obtained between President Premadasa and Sarvodaya's A.T. Ariyaratne, that different types of fundamentalist orientations seem to exist within the Buddhist community as a whole: Bond sees the former as stressing Buddhist identity for purposes of political empowerment, while the latter as stressing Buddhist values as a means to develop a prosperous and morally conscious society. There are, no doubt, other types of fundamentalism afoot in Sinhala Buddhist society that could be identified as well.

If it is so difficult to identify precisely who, how many, and what types constitute the Sinhala-Buddhist "fundamentalists" of Sri Lanka, it is just as difficult to define in a satisfying way exactly what Sinhala-Buddhist fundamentalism is. My suggestion, in this regard, is one that seems implicit in the Introduction and in most of the proceeding essays: by shifting questions about fundamentalists slightly from the who question to the what, and by further shifting the what question from a consideration of the abstract noun "fundamentalism" to the descriptive adjective "fundamentalist," our inquiries will then seek not so much to identify specific social institutions, individual people, or a specific system of thought and practice, but rather focus upon the designation of a religious trait or propensity, a trait or propensity often articulated through exclusive and uncompromising claims to truth made on the basis of literalistic readings of sacred, authoritative texts containing powerful and idealistic mythic visions of the past. For the fundamentalistically inclined, this vision of the past is what also serves as a blueprint for the future and, as H.L. Seneviratne has noted in another place,[1] has sometimes functioned as a rationalization for the perpetration of violence against or the political marginalization of others in the present. Being fundamentalistic, then, denotes a particular way in which some people claim their religiousness. But this is a type of religiousness that seems also subservient to militant and often intolerant political machinations. It tends to breed, for instance, fear (the "shadow" hanging over Jeganathan's Colombo Tamils), alienation (in Hollup's Plantation Tamils), an acquiescent assmilation (in Bartholomeusz's Anglicans and Burghers or Stirrat's Roman Catholics) or a countering and correspondent fundamentalistic antipathy (in de Munck's Sinhala Muslims) in other Sri Lankan communities.

From the essays comprising this volume, we have also learned that being fundamentalistic is also a particular way in which some people who are religious in the aforementioned regard are simultaneously political. This does not mean that, in Sri Lanka, being religious necessarily means being political. I would argue that this is not necessarily always the case on the basis that some *religieux* quite consciously eschew politics. De Silva's résumé of monastic views on the politics of the Sri Lankan current ethnic conflict indicates that some monks, following an ancient Theravada tradition that delineates between forest dwelling/meditating and village/social service orientations of the monkhood, do not see the religious path to *nibbana* as an inherently political enterprise. Nevertheless, de Silva's and Bartholomeusz's more measured opinion that Sinhala-Buddhist fundamentalism is inherently political seems to qualify the issue more exactly and gives us a cue with regard to the type of religiosity under consideration here in this volume.

While it can be argued that not all ways of being religious, or more specifically not all ways of being Buddhist, are inherently political in nature, we can entertain the assertion that the quest for gaining or maintaining political power is intrinsic to Sinhala-Buddhist fundamentalist religiosity. Taking this one step further, I tend to conclude, on the basis of reviewing the previous essays of this volume, that political power is usually the primary aim for Sinhala Buddhists with the fundamentalist trait. In fact, it seems to be their hallmark.

Laying claim to this conclusion, however, does not mean that the dynamics of the current ethno-political conflict in Sri Lanka can be understood strictly along the lines of religious divides. While both Stirrat in his essay and Bartholomeusz and de Silva in the Introduction emphasize how religious and national identities were conflated in the colonial context of the late nineteenth century, virtually all the contributors to this volume recognize that language, race, and ethnicity are now just as important factors in generating social identity and alienation between communities in the present. Jeganathan has also rightly indicated how class remains an important factor for collective identity. Morover, no one familiar with the causes and dynamics of the Janatha Vimukti Peramuna (JVP)/government strife between 1988 and 1990 would dispute the importance of class differences, perceived or real, in generating identity and conflict between various communities within the Sri Lankan context either. That is, communal identity, let alone ethnic or national identity, is no longer necessarily coextensive with religion. In fact, being Sinhala or being Tamil is precisely what now divides virtually all Christian communities in Sri Lanka, especially the Roman Catholic.

What is primarily significant, then, about contemporary fundamentalistic Buddhists is that, like their late nineteenth-century predecessors for whom religion and ethnicity were largely conflated, their Buddhism is intimately linked to political ideology. The difference between the nineteenth-century context and the present, however, is this: in the nineteenth century the revival of Buddhism (with its anti-Christian stance) implied the beginnings of a much wider anticolonial political agitation against the British waiting to gain fruition across almost all sections of Ceylonese peoples. In the present, Buddhism is consciously invoked by politically motivated Sinhalas to advance their own empowerment (usually to the exclusion of other communities) or to rationalize their agendas for actions taken against other communities in *post hoc* fashion. In the former nineteenth-century instance, the revival of Buddhism contributed to the formation of a new national political consciousness; in the latter instance of the present, Buddhism becomes a powerful trope for expressing a matured political ideology that may be more appropiately identified as communal (since it is not inclusive enough to be truly national for a multiethnic society). Not only is this political ideology that invokes Buddhism as a trope not really broad enough in conception to be truly national in scope, I would suspect, quite frankly, that it is not *primarily* religious either, especially since its avowed aims are not ultimately soteriological in nature.

The traditional Sinhala adage that "the country exists for the sake of the religion," a statement that formerly characterized the rationale for Buddhist kingship in Sri Lanka and other Theravada countries, would no longer seem to hold in relation to the aims of these political Buddhists. Rather, it may be more accurate to say that for fundamentalistic Sinhala Buddhists of the present, the religion exists for the sake of those aspiring to control the state. Buddhism is a trope of continuing powerful appeal in a world of political expediencies.

Having said that, it also needs to be emphasized that since the 1950s, politics among the Sinhala constitutency has been dominated by just such appeals to Buddhism for the sake of legitimation and in the service of expediency. Since that time, Buddhism has been afforded a special place in the nation's series of constitutions with each new government stopping just short of declaring it, de facto, the official religion of the state. In practice, or de jure, it has functioned as such, at least publicly, for the Buddhists in power.

For instance, on the Vesak holiday of May 1997, the most sacred of days for Buddhists in Sri Lanka, when the birth, enlightenment, and *parinibbana* of the Buddha is celebrated, President Chandrika Bandaranaike Kumaratunga issued the following message:

> I am happy to issue this message on the occasion of the Vesak Full Moon Day of the year 2541 in the Buddhist Era. My joy is all the greater in view of the fact that this is a time that a vigorous revival of Buddhism takes place in its land of birth, India, and in other Asian countries, and also in the West.
>
> At the present time the great truths taught by Buddhism are being substantiated even by the discoveries of modern science. The Vesak Full Moon Day which is connected with the greatest events of the Lord Buddha's Life, has great significance to the Buddhists of Sri Lanka due to several reasons. Our national chronicles disclose that the landing of Prince Vijaya, the founder of the Sinhala Nation and his followers and the laying of the foundation of the great Ruwanweli Dagoba in Anuradhapura, also took place on the Vesak Full Moon Day. In view of these events Vesak Day becomes the greatest day of religious and national significance to the Buddhists of Sri Lanka.
>
> Buddhism is, basically, a philosophy which provides guidance for the success of our present life and life hereafter. Lord Buddha's sermons such as the Mangala Sutra, the Parabhawa Sutra and the Singlaowada Sutra, also the great collection of His sayings, the celebrated Dhammapada, can be referred to in this regard. Here is a relevant stanza from the Dhammapada:
>
> *Punnan ce puriso kayira,*
> *Kayirath'etam punappunam*
> *Tamhi chandam kayiratha,*
> *Sukho punnassa uccayo.*
>
> This means, "if a man does what is good, let him do it again and again. Let him find pleasure therein. Blissful is the accumulation of good."

Thus, Dhammapada contains many sayings of the Buddha which unfailingly ensure the happiness of human beings in this life and life after death.

Also for the resolution of the grave national problems we face today, the teachings of the Lord Buddha could provide invaluable guidance. He has pointed out how defilements of mind such as suspicion, anger, jealousy and hatred can be overcome by genuine practice of compassion and Maitree or Loving-kindness.

If we think on the lines recommended by Buddhism, ugly situations like communal or ethnic conflicts will never arise in this world. We recently had a time when the image that Sri Lanka had traditionally as "Dharmadeepa" or land of righteousness, was greatly tarnished as a result of undesireable happenings. But our Government has now launched on an effective program of spreading Buddhism infusing in the process the spirit of the noble teachings of Buddhism in the lives of the people, and also, bringing about the welfare and promotion of the Buddha Sasana. This program will not fail to deliver its valuable results in the very near future.

This program contains many practical measures which ensure the development of the Buddha Sasana, such as the issue of Dhamma School books to children, giving teacher appointments to persons who have passed the Dharmacharya Examination, extending recognition to Dhamma School Teachers by appointing them as Justices of the Peace, taking the valuable teachings of Buddhism through appropriate programs, developing the environs of the Sri Dalada Maligawa of Kandy and the Jaya Sri Maha Bodhi of Anuradhapura and assisting many thousands of Buddhist Temples to effect necessary improvements to them.

Since my government came into power financial assistance totalling over Rs. 23 million has been granted from the President's Fund for the development of Buddhist Viharas and Dhamma Schools.

Arrangements are under way for the holding of a conference of representatives of the Maha Sanga of Theravada Buddhist countries in Sri Lanka shortly. The main objective of this conference is to improve relations between Buddhist countries and bringing about consensus and agreement regarding matters relating to the faith.

We Buddhists perform many meritorious acts of piety to mark the Vesak Festival. Even the humblest home displays its veneration of the Lord Buddha by lighting a coconut lamp. We must remind ourselves on the Vesak Day that Lord Gautama Buddha's teachings contain values and

> virtues helpful not only for the edification of our personal lives but also for advancement as a nation and a country on sound principles. Let us therefore, resolve on this year's Vesak Day to strive to usher in an era which will bring peace and prosperity to all, shedding all thoughts of enmity, jealousy and hatred towards each other! Let thus, thereby, win back our fair name as "Dharmadeepa" in all its glory![2]

Before unpacking the significance of this passage in terms of its substance, it needs to be pointed out that this is exactly the type of message that Buddhists in Sri Lanka have expected to hear from their presidents on Vesak *poya*, a message that clearly states how the government is going about providing its support to Buddhism. This was an especially important point to get across this year, because during the past few months, the *mahanayaka*s of the two leading Buddhist monastic systems in Kandy, widely regarded as the leading representatives of the traditional *sangha* in Sri Lanka, had resigned their positions on a Buddhist advisory council to President Kumaratunga in protest against her government's position regarding the devolution of power, a position viewed by fundamentalistic Buddhists as weakening their hegemony. Hence, the President, now projected by some fundamentalists (such as the *mahanayaka*s) as having capitulated to interests inimical to the Buddhist *Mahavamsa* view regarding the island's sovereignty, would want to emphasize how her government continues to act not only in the interest of promoting Buddhism, but how it also subscribes to the *dhammadipa* vision of Sri Lanka.

From a reading of this passage, it is evident that President Kumaratunga's Vesak message contains many of the themes touched on by our volume's contributors. The basic theme of the message is concerned with recovering and realizing the *Mahavamsa*'s image of Sri Lanka as the "Dharmadeepa," here translated as the "land of righteousness." It is significant to note that by "Dharmadeepa," President Kumaratunga is not directly invoking Sinhala-Buddhist territorial claims on the island (the issue at stake with the disgruntled *mahanayaka*s), but is, instead, appealing to various Buddhist inspired virtues which, when observed, lead to the cultivation of a morally conscious society. Her fundamentalistic take on the *Mahavamsa*, if we are right in applying the term fundamentalistic here, seems to be based on a literalistic ("text-critical free") reading of this sacred, authoritative text. Yet, it is a reading that is more in harmony with the value orientation of Sarvodaya's A.T. Ariyaratne than with the politically focused orientation of former President Premadasa. It stresses the recovery of certain values and virtues not only for personal spiritual advancement, but for the resolution of the country's "grave national problems," specifically "ugly situations like communal or ethnic conflicts." It is a message that is, in part, sincerely religious yet, in part, sincerely political, a religio-political blend that mirrors the tight rope walk she has chosen as her path. It is fundamentalistic not only by virtue of its appropriation of a literal reading of the *Mahavamsa*, but also in its idealization of the past, a past reconstructed in such a way as to be a blueprint for the nation's future. It is exclusionary in the sense that Buddhist monastic chronicles are identified as "our national chronicles." Yet, it understands the *Mahavamsa* not as a political charter legitimating Buddhist hegemony, but rather as an inspirational source for the inculcation of moral "righteousness."

The remainder of President Kumaratunga's Vesak text then consists of underscoring a litany of efforts now being made by her government to promote Buddhism throughout the country in order "to win back our fair name as 'Dharmadeepa' in all its glory." Here, the cosmogony of Sri Lanka is directly linked to its eschatology. In essence, then, this is a message in which Buddhism is invoked as a trope for the means to establish a social and religious condition modelled on an idealized image derived from the *Mahavamsa.* It remains a fundamentalistic exercise in the historicization of myth (how the mythic past functions as a blueprint for the present and future), which, in turn, builds upon a historically previous process of mythologizing history (the text of the *Mahavamsa* itself). It is a message of political significance, but one that has been tempered.

President Kumaratunga's Vesak message is not dramatically revolutionary in its substance and tone. Indeed, it is almost liturgical, exactly what one would expect from a moderate Buddhist politician, given the nature of this ritual occasion. Indeed, it is precisely because of this ritual occasion, and the calendrical annual celebrations of other *poya* (full moon) holidays such as Poson in June and Asala in July/August, that the image of the *dhammadipa* is routinely perpetuated in public discourse. That is, the historicization of mythic images embedded in the *Mahavamsa* is continuously facilitated by the institutionalization or ritualization of national holidays celebrating landmark moments in the mythologized history of Sri Lanka's Buddhism. As long as governments in Sri Lanka ritualistically promote Buddhist holidays as celebrations of *national* importance, pledge their resources and energies to the propagation of Buddhist ideals, and invoke Buddhist images of what constitutes a moral and just society, then we can continue to expect the idealization of the Buddhist past to be articulated as the blueprint for the nation's present and future. That is, we can expect that that ritualistic invocation of mythic imagery will continue to serve and inform Sinhala-Buddhist political consciousness. In this regard, it is highly relevant to recall Donald Swearer's observation (noted by de Silva) that "the primary 'fundamentalism' extracted from the sacred 'source texts' of Sri Lanka (the myths and legends) is properly speaking more reflective of, and at the service of, the nationalist rather than the Buddhist worldview."[3]

Swearer's observation is an important one, for it signals what is, in some ways, the basic dilemma faced by what de Silva has referred to as the more "benign" orientation of the Sinhala-Buddhist community and perhaps by President Kumaratunga herself. It is a dilemma faced by Sri Lanka's more secularized liberals as well. The dilemma is this: How to construct an inclusive nationalist discourse which recognizes the importance of a Buddhist *historical* past yet transcends its fundamentalistic myth-and-ritual function as a blueprint for the present and future. That is, How is it possible to transcend the sacred canopy of Buddhist nationalist discourse so that a new more inclusive discourse can recognize the diversity of Sri Lanka's various communities? What's at stake is the discovery of a new political vision for Sri Lanka's future, one that is not simply dependent upon a pandering to ethnicity, language, and religion. This new vision may not be, as the editors of this volume seem to suggest is taking shape now, one that can "homogenize Sri Lanka." Rather, it might be one that celebrates the recognition of difference and the history of Sri Lanka's ethnic and religious diversity. For centuries, as I have argued elsewhere,[4] the genius of Sinhala-Buddhist culture was expressed through its remarkable inclusivity and assimilations, a theme taken up by Bartholomeusz's study of Burghers. What seems to be required now is a resurrection of that same spirit of inclusivity, but one that does not privilege solely a *Mahavamsa* Buddhist mythic vision of the past. What might be privileged instead is the history of an island which not only is home to the oldest continuing Buddhist civilization in the world, but also an island which has served as a vital crossroads for a variety of religious traditions and ethnic communities. In fact, Sri Lanka's religious demography, with a significant percentage of Buddhists (65%), Hindus (18%), Muslims (8%), and Christians (8%) of both Protestant and Roman Catholic persuasions, may be as variegated as any in the world. An inclusive discourse that celebrates recognition of difference has the potential power to marginalize fundamentalistic and totalistic persuasions on the one hand, and militant separatists on the other. An apparent obstacle to unity (i.e., religious diversity) could become, potentially, a powerful *raison d'être* for an inclusive political dynamic. What Sri Lanka might recover is not so much its image as the *dhammadipa*, but its lost and more recent "image" as a model multiethnic and multireligious society.

In the end, however, this may prove to be an overly idealistic sentiment, much too much to expect in a South Asian political climate which continues to be fragmented or totalized by appeals to religion and ethnicity. Sri Lanka is certainly not alone in this struggle. Pakistan, Bangladesh, and the Maldives are essentially Islamic states, while India is witnessing a surging wave of Hindu fundamentalist politics. Whatever the future portends, more totalizing or fragmenting politics or not, religion, fundamentalistic or not, is certain to remain an important player in the dynamic.

Notes

1. H.L. Seneviratne, "Identity and the Conflation of Past and Present," in H.L. Seneviratne, ed., *Identity, Consciousness and the Past* (Adelaide: University of Adelaide Press, 1989), p. 6; cited by the editors in the Introduction to this volume.

2. "Let us win back our fair name as Dharmadeepa—*President*," *Daily News* (May 21, 1997), p. 1. Grammar and spellings are faithfully reproduced.

3. Donald K. Swearer, "Fundamentalistic Movements in Theravada Buddhism," in Martin Marty and R. Scott Appleby, eds., *Fundamentalisms Observed* (Chicago: University of Chicago Press, 1991), p. 650.

4. See my *Buddha in the Crown: Avalokitesvara in the Buddhist Traditions of Sri Lanka* (London and New York: Oxford University Press, 1991).

Select Bibliography

Abayakoon, C. D. F. "The Ceylon Moors Can Be Proud of Their History," in *Glimpses from the Past of the Moors of Sri Lanka*, A.I.L. Marikar, A.L.M. Lafir, and A.H. Macan Markar, eds. (Colombo: Moors' Islamic Home Publication, 1976), 89–96.

Ahmed, Akbar. *Discovering Islam: Making Sense of Muslim History and Society.* (New York: Routledge & Kegan Paul, 1988).

Almond, P. C. *The British Discovery of Buddhism.* (Cambridge: Cambridge University Press, 1988).

Anderson, Benedict. *Imagined Communities: Reflections on the Origin and Spread of Nationalism.* (New York: Verso, 1993).

Arasaratnam, S. *Ceylon.* (New Jersey: Prentice Hall, 1964).

Ariyaratne, A. T. *The Power Pyramid and the Dharmic Cycle.* (Ratmalana, Sri Lanka: Sarvodaya Vishva Lekha, 1988).

Bandarage, A. *Colonialism in Sri Lanka: Political Economy of the Kandyan Highlands 1833–1886.* (Berlin: Mouton, 1983).

Bartholomeusz, Tessa. "Buddhist Woman as Self and Other," in *Daughters of the Soil*, Kumari Jayawardena, ed. (Colombo: Social Scientists' Association, forthcoming).

———. "Catholics, Buddhists, and the Church of England: The 1883 Sri Lankan Riots," *Buddhist-Christian Studies*, vol. 15 (1995), 89–104.

———. "Dharmapala at Chicago: Sinhala Chauvinist or Mahayana Buddhist?," in *A Museum of Faiths: Histories and Legacies of the 1893 World's Parliament of Religions*, Eric Ziolkowski, ed. (Atlanta: Scholars Press, 1993), 235–50.

———. *Women under the Bo Tree: Buddhist Nuns in Sri Lanka.* (Cambridge: Cambridge University Press, 1994; reprinted 1996).

Bayly, Susan. *Saints, Goddesses and Kings: Muslims and Christians in South Indian Society 1700–1900.* (Cambridge: Cambridge University Press, 1992).

The Betrayal of Buddhism: Report of the Unofficial Buddhist Committee of Inquiry. (Balangoda: Dharmavijaya Press, 1956).

Bond, George D. *The Buddhist Revival in Sri Lanka: Religious Tradition, Reinterpretation and Response.* (Columbia: University of South Carolina Press, 1988; republished by Delhi: Motilal Banarsidass, 1992).

Boudens, R. *The Catholic Church Under Dutch Rule.* (Rome: Catholic Book Agency, 1957).

Boudens, R. *Catholic Missionaries in a British Colony: Successes and Failures in Ceylon, 1796–1893.* (Immensee: Nouvelle Revue de Science Missionaire, 1979).

Brow, J. "In Pursuit of Hegemony: Representations of Authority and Justice in a Sri Lankan Village," *American Ethnologist*, 15 (1988), 322–27.

———. "Notes on Community, Hegemony and the Uses of the Past," *Anthropological Quarterly*, 63 (1990), 1–6.

Calhoun, C., ed. *Social Theory and the Politics of Identity.* (Oxford: Blackwell, 1994).

Carrithers, Michael. *The Forest Monks of Sri Lanka: An Anthropological and Historical Study.* (Delhi: Oxford University Press, 1983).

Cartman, James. *Hinduism in Ceylon.* (Colombo: Gunasena, 1957).

Chandrakanthan, A. J. V. *Catholic Revival in Post-Colonial Sri Lanka: A Critique of Ecclesial Contextualization.* (Colombo: Social and Economic Development Centre, 1995).

Chandraperuma, C. A. *Sri Lanka: The JVP Insurrection, 1987–1989.* (Colombo: Lake House, 1991).

Chatterjee, Partha, and Pradeep Jeganathan, eds. *Community/Gender/Violence: Essays on the Subaltern Condition.* (Oxford: Oxford University Press, forthcoming).

Chatterjee, Partha. *Nationalist Thought and the Colonial World: A Derivative Discourse?* (London: Zed Books, 1986).

Chattopadhyaya, H. P. *Indians in Sri Lanka.* (Calcutta: O.P.S. Publisher, 1979).

Dale, S. F. *The Mappilas of Malabar, 1498–1922: Islamic Society on the South Asian Frontier.* (Oxford: Clarendon Press, 1980).

Daniel, E. Valentine. *Charred Lullabies: Chapters in an Anthropography of Violence.* (Princeton: Princeton University Press, 1996).

———. "The Nation in Sri Lankan Tamil Gatherings in Britain," *Pravada*, 2, no. 6 (1992), 12–17.

———. "Three Dispositions towards the Past: One Sinhala Two Tamil," *Social Analysis*, no. 25 (1989), 22–41.

———. "Tea Talk: Violent Measures in the Discursive Practices of Sri Lanka's Estate Tamils," *Comparative Studies in Society and History*, 35, no. 3 (July 1993), 568–600.

Das, Veena, ed. *Mirrors of Violence: Communities, Riots and Survivors in South Asia*. (Delhi: Oxford University Press, 1990).

———. *Critical Events: An Anthropological Perspective on Contemporary India*. (Delhi: Oxford University Press, 1995).

Dawson, Lorne. "Self-affirmation, Freedom, and Rationality: Theoretically Elaborating 'Active' Conversions," *Journal for the Scientific Study of Religion*, 29, no. 2 (June 1990), 141–63.

de Alwis, Malathi. "Motherhood as a Space of Protest," in *Appropriating Gender: Women, the State and Politicized Religion in South Asia*, Amrita Basu and Patricia Jeffreys, eds. (New York: Routledge, 1997).

de Munck, Victor. "Sufi, Reformist and National Models of Identity: The History of a Muslim Village Festival in Sri Lanka," *Contributions to Indian Sociology*, 28 (1994), 273–93.

Denham, E. B. *Ceylon at the Census of 1911*. (Colombo: Government Printer, 1912).

de Silva, Chandra Richard. *Sri Lanka: A History*. (Delhi: Vikas Publishing House, 1987; reprinted 1992 and 1997).

de Silva, K. M. *Managing Ethnic Tensions in Multi-Ethnic Societies: Sri Lanka, 1880–1985*. (Lanham, Maryland: University Press of America, 1986).

———. "Religion and the State," in *Sri Lanka: Problems of Governance*, K. M. de Silva, ed. (Kandy: International Centre for Ethnic Studies, 1993), 306–44.

———. *Social Policy and Missionary Organizations in Ceylon, 1840–1855*. (London: Longmans, 1965).

de Silva, K. M., and Howard Wriggins. *J. R. Jayewardene of Sri Lanka: A Political Biography*. (Honolulu: University of Hawaii Press, 1994).

Dornberg, U. "Searching Through the Crisis: Christians, Contextual Theology and Social Change in Sri Lanka in the 1970s and 1980s," *Logos*, 31, nos. 3 and 4 (1992).

Douglas, Mary. *Purity and Danger: An Analysis of Concepts of Pollution and Taboo*. (London: Ark Paperbacks, 1966).

Durrany, K. S. *The Impact of Islamic Fundamentalism.* (Delhi: Indian Society for Promoting Christian Knowledge, 1993).

Featherstone, M., ed. *Global Culture.* (London: Sage, 1990).

Garnett, R. "The Study of War," *The American Sociologist* (Fall 1988), 270–82.

Gatewood, J. B. "Loose Talk: Linguistic Competence and Recognition Ability," *American Anthropologist*, 85 (1983), 378–87.

Giddens, A. *The Consequences of Modernity.* (Cambridge: Polity Press, 1990).

Gilsenan, M. *Recognizing Islam: Religion and Society in the Modern Arab World.* (New York: Pantheon Books, 1973).

Glock, C. "On the Origin and Evolution of Religious Groups," in *Religion in Sociological Perspective*, C. Glock, ed. (New York: Wadsworth, 1973).

Goffman, E. *Asylum.* (Garden City, N.Y.: Anchor Books, 1961).

Gombrich, Richard, and Gananath Obeyesekere. *Buddhism Transformed: Religious Change in Sri Lanka.* (Princeton: Princeton University Press, 1988).

Goonetileke, H. A. I. *George Keyt: A Life in Art.* (Colombo: The George Keyt Foundation, 1989).

Granovetter, M. "The Strength of Weak Ties," *American Journal of Sociology*, 78 (1973), 1360–80.

Gunasinghe, Newton. *Changing Social Relations in the Kandyan Countryside.* (Colombo: Social Scientists' Association, 1990).

———. "The Open Economy and its Impact on Ethnic Relations in Sri Lanka," in *Sri Lanka's Ethnic Conflict: Myths, Realties and Perspectives.* (Delhi: Navrang, 1984), 97–214.

Goonewardena, K. W. "Moors in the Portuguese Period," in *Glimpses from the Past of the Moors of Sri Lanka*, in A. I .L. Marikar, A. L. M. Lafir, and A. H. Macan Markar, eds. (Colombo: Moors' Islamic Cultural Home Publications, 1976).

Gunesekera, Tamara. *Hierarchy and Egalitarianism: Caste, Class and Power in Sinhalese Peasant Society.* (London: Athlone Press, 1994).

Guruge, Ananda, ed. *Anagarika Dharmapala: Return to Righteousness.* (Colombo: Department of Cultural Affairs, 1967).

Handelman, Don. "On the Desuetude of Kataragama," *Man* (n.s.), 20, no. 1 (1985), 156–59.

Herring, R. J. *Land to the Tiller.* (New Haven: Yale University Press, 1983).

Hobsbawm, E. *Nations and Nationalism Since 1780.* (Cambridge: Cambridge University Press, 1991).

Holdrege, Barbara A. *Veda and Torah* (Albany, New York: State University of New York Press, 1996).

Hollup, O. *Bonded Labor-Caste and Cultural Identity among Tamil Plantation Workers in Sri Lanka.* (New Delhi: Sterling Publishers Private Ltd., 1994).

———. "Ethnic Identity, Violence and the Estate Tamil Minority in Sri Lanka," *The Round Table*, no. 323 (1992), 315–38.

———. "Trade Unions and Leadership Among Tamil Estate Workers in Sri Lanka," *Journal of Contemporary Asia*, 21, no. 2 (1991), 195–211.

Holt, John C. *Buddha in the Crown: Avalokitesvara in the Buddhist Traditions of Sri Lanka.* (New York: Oxford University Press, 1991).

Humbel, R. "Decreasing Extent of Tea Plantations. Chance for Agricultural Diversification or Ecological Threat?," Master's Thesis, Department of Geography, University of Zurich-Insel, 1989.

Ismail, Qadri, and Pradeep Jeganathan, eds. *Unmaking the Nation: The Politics of Identity and History in Modern Sri.* (Colombo: Social Scientists' Association, 1995).

Jayaraman, R. *Caste Continuities in Ceylon.* (Bombay: Popular Prakashan, 1975).

Jayawardena, Kumari. *Ethnic and Class Conflicts in Sri Lanka.* (Colombo: Center for Social Analysis, 1986).

Kapferer, B. *A Celebration of Demons.* (Bloomington: Indiana University Press, 1983).

———. *Legends of People: Myths of State.* (Washington D.C.: Smithsonian Institution, 1988).

———. "Nationalist Ideology and a Comparative Anthropology," *Ethnos*, 54 (1989), 161–99.

Karunaratne, S. *Olcott's Contribution to the Buddhist Renaissance* (abridged version of Olcott's diary, *Old Diary Leaves*). (Colombo: Ministry of Cultural Affairs, n.d.).

Kemper, Steven. "The Nation Consumed: Buying and Believing in Sri Lanka," *Public Culture*, 5 (1993), 377–93.

———. *The Presence of the Past: Chronicles, Politics and Culture in Sinhala Life.* (Ithaca: Cornell University Press, 1992).

Kilbourne, Brock, and James T. Richardson. "Paradigm Conflict, Types of Conversion, and Conversion Theories," *Sociological Analysis: A Journal in the Sociology of Religion*, 50, no. 1 (Spring 1989), 1–21.

King, Anthony D. *The Bungalow: The Production of Global Culture*. (London: Routledge & Kegan Paul, 1989).

———. *Colonial Urban Development: Culture, Social Power and Environment*. (London: Routledge & Kegan Paul, 1976).

Kodikara, Shelton U., ed. *Indo-Lanka Agreement of July 1987*. (Colombo: University of Colombo, 1989).

Little, David. *Sri Lanka: The Invention of Enmity*. (Washington, D.C.: United States Institute of Peace Press, 1994).

McGilvray, Dennis. "Dutch Burghers and Portuguese Mechanics: Eurasian Ethnicity in Sri Lanka," *Comparative Studies in Society and History*, 24, no.2 (April 1982), 253–63.

Mahroof, M. M. M. "Some Aspects of Social Organization and Hierarchical Structure Among the Muslims of Ceylon (Sri Lanka): 1901–1912," *Islamic Culture*, 41, no. 2 (1979), 99–109.

Malalgoda, K. *Buddhism in Sinhalese Society 1750–1900*. (Berkeley: University of California Press, 1976).

Manogaran, Chelvadurai and Bryan Pfaffenberger, eds. *The Sri Lankan Tamils: Ethnicity and Identity*. (Boulder: Westview Press, 1994).

Manor, James. "Self-Inflicted Wound: Inter-Communal Violence in Ceylon, 1958," *The Collected Seminar Papers of the Institute of Commonwealth Studies*. (University of London), 30 (1982), 15–26.

———. "Organizational Weakness and the Rise of Sinhalese Buddhist Extremism," in *Accounting for Fundamentalisms: The Dynamic Character of Movements*, Martin E. Marty and R. Scott Appleby, eds. (Chicago: University of Chicago Press, 1994), 770–84.

Manor, James, ed. *Sri Lanka in Change and Crisis*. (London: Croom Helm, 1984).

Marty, Martin E. and R. Scott Appleby, eds. *Accounting for Fundamentalisms*. (Chicago: University of Chicago Press, 1994).

———. *Fundamentalisms Comprehended*. (Chicago: University of Chicago Press, 1995).

———. *Fundamentalisms Observed*. (Chicago: University of Chicago Press, 1991).

Meyer, E. "Enclave Plantations, Hemmed-in Villages and Dualistic Representations in Colonial Ceylon," *Journal of Peasant Studies*, 19 (1992), 199–228.

———. "From Landgrabbing to Landhunger: High Land Appropriation in the Plantation Areas of Sri Lanka During the British Period," *Modern Asian Studies*, 26 (1992b), 321–61.

Mohan, V. R. *Identity Crisis of Sri Lankan Muslims*. (Delhi: Mittal Publications, 1987).

Moore, M. *The State and Peasant Politics in Sri Lanka*. (Cambridge: Cambridge University Press, 1985).

Nissan, E., and R. L. Stirrat. "State, Nation and the Representation of Evil: The Case of Sri Lanka," *Sussex Research Papers in Social Anthropology*, no. 1, 1987.

Oberoi, Harjot. *The Construction of Religious Identity Boundaries*. (Chicago: University of Chicago Press, 1994).

Obeyesekere, Gananath. "Duttagamini and the Buddhist Conscience," in *Religion and Political Conflict in South Asia: India, Pakistan and Sri Lanka*, Douglas Allen, ed. (Delhi: Oxford University Press, 1993), 135–60.

———. "The Fire Walkers of Kataragama: The Rise of Bhakti Religiosity in Buddhist Sri Lanka," *Journal of Asian Studies*, 37, no. 3 (1978), 457–76.

———. "Personal Identity and Cultural Crisis: The Case of Anagarika Dharmapala of Sri Lanka," in *The Biographical Process*, F. Reynolds and C. Capps, eds. (The Hague: Mouton, 1976).

———. "Psychocultural Exegesis of a Case of Spirit Possession from Sri Lanka," in *Case Studies in Possession*, V. Crapanzano and V. Garrison, eds. (New York: John Wiley, 1977).

———. "Sinhalese-Buddhist Identity in Ceylon," in *Ethnic Identity: Cultural Continuities and Change*, George de Vos and Lola Romanucci-Ross, eds. (Palo Alto: Mayfield Publishing Company, 1975).

———. "Social Change and the Deities: The Rise of the Kataragama Cult in Modern Sri Lanka," *Man*, 12 (1977), 1–23.

Olcott, Henry Steele. *Old Diary Leaves*. (Edinburgh: Hill and Col Limited, 1900).

Olsen, B. "Human Rights in Sri Lanka," in *Human Rights in Developing Countries*, P. Baehr, H. Hey, et al., eds. (Yearbook 1994, Oslo: Nordic Human Rights Publications, 1994).

Pandey, Gyanendra. "In Defense of the Fragment: Writing about Hindu-Muslim Riots in India Today," in *Representations*, 37 (Winter 1992), 48–60.

———. "The Prose of Otherness," *Essays in Honour of Ranajit Guha: Subaltern Studies 8*, David Arnold and David Hardiman, eds. (Delhi: Oxford University Press, 1994), pp. 188–221.

Perera, S. "Teaching and Learning Hatred: The Role of Education and Socialization in the Sri Lankan Ethnic Conflict," Ph.D. Thesis, University of California, Santa Barbara, 1991.

Perniola, V. *The Catholic Church in Sri Lanka: The Dutch Period.* (Colombo: Tisara Prakasakayo, 1983–85).

Pfaffenberger, Bryan. "The Kataragama Pilgrimage: Hindu-Buddhist Interaction and Significance in Sri Lanka's Polyethnic Social System," *Journal of Asian Studies*, 36, no. 2 (1977), 253–70.

Rajanayagam, Dagmar-Hellmann. "Tamils and the Meaning of History," in *The Sri Lankan Tamils: Ethnicity and Identity*, Chelvadurai Manogaran and Bryan Pfaffenberger, eds. (Boulder: Westview Press, 1994).

Ramanathan, P. "The Ethnology of the Moors of Ceylon," *Journal of the Royal Asiatic Society* (Ceylon Branch), 10 (1888), 234–62.

Richardson, James T. "Paradigm Conflict in Conversion Research," *Journal for the Scientific Study of Religion*, 24, no. 2. (June 1985), 163–79.

Roberts, Michael. *Caste Conflict and Élite Formation: The Rise of the Karava Elite in Sri Lanka, 1500–1931*. (Cambridge: Cambridge University Press, 1982).

———. "Ethnicity in Riposte at a Cricket Match: The Past for the Present," *Comparative Studies in Society and History*, 27 (1985a), 401–29.

———. "From Southern India to Lanka: The Traffic in Commodities, Bodies and Myths From the Thirteenth Century Onwards," *South Asia*, 4 (1980), 36–47.

———. "'I Shall Have You Slippered': The General and the Particular in an Historical Conjuncture," *Social Analysis*, 17 (1985b), 17–48.

———. "The Two Faces of the Port of Colombo," in *Brides of the Sea: Port Cities of Asia from the 16th–20th Centuries*, Frank Broeze, ed. (Honolulu: University of Hawaii Press, 1989), 173–87.

Roberts, Michael, ed. *Collective Identities, Nationalisms and Protest in Sri Lanka.* (Colombo: Marga Institute [2d edition, volume 2], forthcoming).

Roberts, Michael, Ismeth Raheem, and Percy Colin-Thome. *People Inbetween.* (Ratmalana, Sri Lanka: Sarvodaya Book Publishing Services, 1989).

Robertson, R. *Globalization.* (London: Sage, 1992).

Robertson, R., and W. Garrett, eds. *Religion and Global Order.* (New York: Paragon, 1991).

Rogers, John D. *Crime, Justice and Society in Colonial Sri Lanka.* (London: Curzon Press, 1987).

Rogers, John D. "Post Orientalism and the Interpretation of Premodern and Modern Political Identities: The Case of Sri Lanka," *Journal of Asian Studies*, 53, no. 1 (February 1994), 10–23.

Samarasinghe, S. W. R., and F. Dawood. "The Muslim Minority of Sri Lanka: A Business Community in Transition," in *Muslims of Sri Lanka: Avenues to Antiquity*, M. A. M. Shukri, ed. (Beruwela: Naleemiah Institute, 1986), 253–78.

Sayer, Derek. *Capitalism and Modernity: An Excursus on Marx and Weber*. (London: Routledge, 1991).

Schalk, Peter. "Articles 9 and 18 of the Constitution as Obstacles to Peace," *Lanka*, 5 (1990), 280–92.

Scott, David. "Conversion and Demonism: Colonial Christian Discourse and Religion in Sri Lanka," *Comparative Studies in Society and History*, 34, no. 2 (1992), 331–65.

———. *Formations of Ritual: Colonial and Anthropological Discourses on the Sinhala Yaktovil*. (Minneapolis: University of Minnesota Press, 1994).

———. "Religion in Colonial Civil Society: Buddhism and Modernity in Nineteenth Century Sri Lanka," *The Thatched Patio*, 7 no. 4 (1994), 1–16.

Seneviratne, H. L. "Identity and the Conflation of Past and Present," *Social Analysis*, vol. 25 (1989), 3–17.

Shastri, A. "The Material Basis of Separatism: The Tamil Eelam Movement in Sri Lanka," *Journal of Asian Studies*, 49 (1990), 56–77.

Sivaraksa, Sulak. *Seeds of Peace*. (Berkeley: Parallax Press, 1992).

Smith, B. L. "Sinhalese Buddhism and the Dilemmas of Reinterpretation," in *The Two Wheels of Dhamma: Essays on the Theravada Tradition in India and Ceylon*, B. L. Smith, ed. (Chambersburg: American Academy of Religion, 1972).

Smith, Jonathan Z. "Differential Equations: On Constructing the 'Other,'" Thirteenth Annual University Lecture in Religion, Arizona State University, March 5, 1992.

Snodgrass, Donald R. *Ceylon; An Export Economy in Transition*. (Homewood, Ill.: R.D. Irwin, 1966).

Somaratna, G. P. V. *Kotahena Riot 1883: A Religious Riot in Sri Lanka*. (Colombo: Deepanee, 1991).

Spencer, Jonathan. "Collective Violence and Everyday Practice in Sri Lanka," *Modern Asian Studies*, 24, no. 3 (1990), 603–23.

———. *A Sinhala Village in a Time of Trouble: Politics and Change in Rural Sri Lanka*. (Delhi: Oxford University Press, 1990).

Spencer, Jonathan, ed. *Sri Lanka: History and the Roots of Conflict*. (London: Routledge and Kegan Paul, 1990).

Staples, Clifford L. and Armand L. Mauss. "Conversion or Commitment?," *Journal of the Scientific Study of Religion*, 26, no. 2 (June 1987), 133–47.

Stirrat, R. L. *Power and Religiosity in a Post-Colonial Setting: Sinhala Catholics in Contemporary Sri Lanka.* (Cambridge: Cambridge University Press, 1992).

Tambiah, Stanley Jeyaraja. *Buddhism Betrayed?: Religion, Politics and Violence in Sri Lanka.* (Chicago: University of Chicago Press, 1992).

———. "Sangha and Polity in Modern Thailand," in *Religion and Legitimation of Power in Thailand, Laos and Burma*, Bardwell L. Smith, ed. (Chambersburg: Anima Books, 1978), 111–33.

———. *Sri Lanka: Ethnic Fratricide and the Dismantling of Democracy.* (London: IB Tauris, 1986).

Tennekoon, N. S. "Rituals of Development: The Accelerated Mahavali Development Program of Sri Lanka," *American Ethnologist*, 15 (1988), 294–310.

Tilly, C. *State-Inspired Violence, 1900–1990.* (New York: New School for Social Research, "The Working Paper Series," no. 177, 1993).

van der Horst, Josine. *Who is He, What is He Doing?: Religious Rhetoric and Performances in Sri Lanka during R. Premadasa's Presidency, 1989–1993.* (Amsterdam: VU University Press, 1995).

van der Veer, P. "Playing or Praying. A Sufi Saint's Day in Surat," *Journal of Asian Studies*, 51 (1992), 545–64.

van Creveld, M. *The Transformation of War.* (New York: Free Press, 1991).

Vittachi, Tarzi. *Emergency '58: The Story of the Ceylon Race Riots.* (London: Andre Deutsch, 1959).

Wiberg, H. "States and Nations as Challenges to Peace Research," *Journal of Peace Research*, 28, no. 4 (1991), 337–43.

Wikremaratne, L.A. "Religion, Nationalism and Social Change in Ceylon, 1865–1885," *Journal of the Royal Asiatic Society* (Ceylon Branch), 56 (1969), 123–50.

Wikramasinghe, Nira. *Ethnic Politics in Colonial Sri Lanka.* (Delhi: Vikas Publishing House PVT, 1995).

Contributors

Tessa J. Bartholomeusz is associate professor of religion at Florida State University. A graduate of the Buddhist Studies Program (Department of Religious Studies) at the University of Virginia, she is the author of *Women under the Bo Tree: Buddhist Nuns in Sri Lanka* (Cambridge 1994; 1996) and many articles and book chapters on Buddhism, gender and religion, and religion and identity. Her recent work focuses on Buddhism and Just-War Thinking, for which she has been funded by the American Institute of Sri Lankan Studies.

George D. Bond is professor and chair of the department of religion at Northwestern University. In addition to his many articles that deal with a variety of issues, his publications include *The Word of the Buddha: The Tipitaka and its Interpretation in Theravada Buddhism* (Colombo: M.D. Gunasena, 1982), and *The Buddhist Revival in Sri Lanka: Religious Tradition, Reinterpretation and Response* (Columbia, South Carolina: University of South Carolina Press, 1988). He is also co-author of *Sainthood: Its Manifestations in World Religions* (Berkeley: University of California Press, 1988).

Oddvar Hollup has contributed many articles on Tamil identity to a variety of journals, including the *Journal of Contemporary Asia* and *The Round Table*. A fellow of the Nordland Research Institute, Norway, he is author of *Bonded Labor-Caste and Cultural Identity among Tamil Plantation Workers in Sri Lanka* (New Delhi: Sterling Publishers Private Ltd., 1994).

John Clifford Holt is professor of religion and chair of the Asian Studies Program at Bowdoin College in Brunswick, Maine. He is the author of several scholarly articles and books on Buddhism, including *The Religious World of Kirti Sri: Buddhism, Art and Politics in Late Medieval Sri Lanka* (Oxford: Oxford University Press, 1996), *Buddha in the Crown: Avalokites-*

vara in the Buddhist Traditions of Sri Lanka (Oxford: Oxford University Press, 1991), and *Discipline: The Canonical Buddhism of the Vinayapitaka* (Delhi: Motilal Banarsidass, 1981).

Pradeep Jeganathan was educated at the Massachusetts Institute of Technology, Harvard University, and the University of Chicago. He is co-editor, with Qadri Ismail, of *Unmaking the Nation: The Politics of Identity and History in Modern Sri Lanka* (Colombo: Social Scientists' Association, 1995). He is currently Earl S. Johnson Postdoctoral fellow in Anthropology and the Social Sciences and assistant director of the master of arts program in the Social Sciences at the University of Chicago.

Victor de Munck received his Ph.D. in anthropology from the University of California at Riverside and is an assistant professor of anthropology at SUNY, New Paltz. He is the author of numerous articles and of *Seasonal Cycles: A Study of Change and Continuity in a Sri Lankan Village* (Delhi: Asian Educational Services, 1993) and of *Romantic Love and Sexual Practices: Persepectives from the Social Sciences* (Westport: Praeger, forthcoming).

Chandra R. de Silva, chair and professor of history at Old Dominion University, has held numerous fellowships including the Calouste Gulbenkian Fellowship, Lisbon (1971 and 1976), and the Hallsworth Fellowship at the University of Manchester. He is the author, editor, and co-editor of over a dozen books, including *Portuguese Rule in Ceylon* (Colombo: H.W. Cave and Co., 1972), *The American Impact on Sri Lanka* (Colombo: American Studies Association, 1980), *Sri Lanka: A History* (New Delhi: Vikas, 1987), *Education in Sri Lanka* (1988), and *Sri Lanka Since Independence* (New Delhi: Navrang, 1992).

R. L. Stirrat is lecturer in social anthropology at the School of African and Asian Studies, University of Sussex. He is the author of many articles on Sri Lanka, and of *On the Beach: Fishermen, fishwives and fishtraders in post-colonial Lanka* (Delhi: Hindustan Publishing Corporation, 1988), and *Power and Religiosity in a Post-Colonial Setting: Sinhala Catholics in Sri Lanka* (Cambridge: Cambridge University Press, 1992).

Index

D

E

F

G

H

I

J

K

L

M